Schumann's Late Style

Schumann's Late Style is the first study in English devoted to Robert Schumann's little-known music from the 1850s. The reason most often given for these works having been considered lesser achievements than the earlier song and piano cycles is that Schumann's mental illness had a detrimental effect on his compositions. However, this study demonstrates that there were several other, still more complex, reasons why the music from the 1850s sounded different. Schumann had started to compose 'in a new manner', depending more on preliminary sketches; he also began to write for larger forces (orchestra and chorus), which required a more 'public' style of music, as is also apparent in his works on nationalist themes, and in his more commercial pieces for children. This book thus attempts to disentangle assumptions about Schumann's late style from biographical interpretations, and to consider it in broader artistic, social and cultural contexts.

LAURA TUNBRIDGE is Lecturer in Music Analysis and Critical Theory at the University of Manchester.

Schumann's Late Style

LAURA TUNBRIDGE

CAMBRIDGE
UNIVERSITY PRESS

CAMBRIDGE UNIVERSITY PRESS
Cambridge, New York, Melbourne, Madrid, Cape Town, Singapore, São Paulo

Cambridge University Press
The Edinburgh Building, Cambridge CB2 8RU, UK

Published in the United States of America by Cambridge University Press, New York

www.cambridge.org
Information on this title: www.cambridge.org/9780521871686

© Laura Tunbridge 2007

First published 2007

Printed in the United Kingdom at the University Press, Cambridge

A catalogue record for this publication is available from the British Library

ISBN 978-0-521-87168-6 hardback

For my parents

Contents

Acknowledgements

Thanks first to staff and students from the music department at Manchester, for creating such a stimulating environment in which to complete this book. David Fallows, David Fanning and James Garratt have been especially helpful. A Small Research Grant from the Faculty of Humanities allowed me teaching relief in the autumn semester of 2005, and the School of Arts, Histories and Cultures funded the preparation of music examples, ably executed by Nina Whiteman. I have also been grateful for the advice of Vicki Cooper, Becky Jones, Jodie Barnes and Clive Unger-Hamilton at Cambridge University Press.

Roger Parker has long been a guiding voice and I cannot thank him enough for his time and encouragement. I am also deeply indebted to Robert Pascall: a more careful and generous reader would be hard to find. Further thanks are due to Carolyn Abbate, for suggesting that I start with séances, and to Scott Burnham for his continued interest in my work. This book has also been shaped by conversations with David Bretherton, Suzie Clark, Andy Fry, Wayne Heisler Jr., Roe-Min Kok, Gundula Kreuzer, Scott Paulin and Emanuele Senici. Nikolaus Bacht, James Davies, Jonathan Dunsby, Deniz Ertan, Ryan Minor, Roger Moseley, Oliver Neighbour, Beate Perrey, Michael Struck and Alastair Williams have shared papers with me, offered valuable information and recommended reading. Some of this material has been presented at music department colloquia at the universities of Cambridge, Liverpool, Nottingham, Oxford, Southampton, Stanford, and Surrey, and at conferences hosted by the Lawrence Durrell School of Corfu, Cardiff University, University College Dublin and McGill University. I have been very grateful for the invitations to speak and the feedback received.

My family have asked after the book's progress and helped in many ways, not least by reminding me to keep a sense of perspective and humour. While several friends have offered support and welcome distraction, three in Manchester deserve special mention: my brother Alec, Ian Cull, and Nick Tatnall who, in their inimitable way, have cajoled me along.

List of illustrations

Introduction: raising Schumann

In May 1853, Robert Schumann's concertmaster and future biographer, Wilhelm Josef von Wasielewski, visited the composer and found him reading a book about his latest obsession, 'Tischrücken' or table-tipping. Wasielewski reported:

To my enquiry as to the subject of his book, he replied in an elevated tone, 'Oh! Don't you know anything about table-tipping?' 'Of course!' I said jokingly. Upon this, his eyes, generally half-shut and in-turned, opened wide, his pupils dilated convulsively, and with a peculiar, ghost-like look, he said, eerily and slowly, 'The tables know all'. When I saw that he was in earnest, rather than confuse him I fell into his humour, and he soon grew calm. He then called his second daughter, and began to experiment with her aid and a small table, which accented the beginning of Beethoven's C-minor symphony.[1]

The previous month, Schumann had written to Ferdinand Hiller:

We tipped the table yesterday for the first time. Wonderful power! Just think! It delayed longer than usual with the answer: at last it began – ♪ ♪ ♪ | ♩ – but rather slowly at first. When I said, 'But the tempo is faster, dear table', it hastened to beat the true time. When I asked if it could tell me the number I was thinking of, it gave it correctly as three. We were all filled with wonder.[2]

Schumann's enthusiasm was such that he wrote an essay on the topic, now lost. He conducted séances with his friends, his children and guests, including visitors from out of town (one of which, later in the year, was Johannes Brahms). Clara was pleased that her often depressed husband became more 'jovial [and] quite pleasantly excited' at this time, writing in her diary, 'Robert is quite enchanted by these marvellous powers and promised [the table] a new dress (i.e. a new tablecloth).'[3]

Schumann's sudden interest in table-tipping poses some invigorating problems for commentators. Part of the challenge is the age-old conflict between those who believe in the supernatural and those who put their faith in more rational explanations.[4] Many of Schumann's contemporaries were sceptical about séances, crediting their messages to well-timed kicks on the table legs rather than to forces from the other side. Some even considered credulity to indicate psychological instability, a judgement particularly critical for Schumann. Wasielewski and Clara's biographer Berthold Litzmann pronounced the composer's interest in the 'wonders' of the séance the first manifestation of his mental decline. More recently Peter Ostwald has explained Schumann's fascination with the occult as a means to explain his psychosis to himself. Whether we decide to take a benign view towards Schumann's involvement with séances or treat it as something more sinister, it parallels out the difficulties and ambiguities that confront one when attempting to engage with his last works.

As with the table's messages, not everybody is convinced by the late music. Some hear its repetitions, thematic allusions and fractured forms as clumsy, even impotent. Others describe the scores as being like piano reductions or organ transcriptions, encoding music to be played elsewhere. Much as Schumann listened for Beethoven's spirit in the tapped rhythm of the Fifth Symphony, we tend to filter the late music through knowledge of the composer's biography, especially our awareness of his illness – however vague and unscientific our understanding of it may be. Thus Schumann's late music is discussed in terms of mental and creative failure and exhaustion, of an inability to communicate with the outside world.

Biography's grip on Schumann reception and scholarship has been so tight that to reject it outright would be to deny its huge influence on our historical and musical understanding. It is worth stressing, though, that this is not a straightforward biography or life-and-works study of late Schumann.[5] Some biographical and historical context is given where appropriate, and there is a chronology of Schumann's last years in the Appendix. However, I do not follow the composer's life in strict chronological order or attempt to cover every aspect of it. Instead I have grouped the late pieces according to genre, with the intention that it will aid understanding of his musical style. Nor do I intend to uncritically redeem Schumann's last works. My main concern is with discussing the late pieces in a way that helps explain the music, while also interrogating the values behind its reception in the concert hall and in scholarly literature. In so doing, I hope to make clear the extent to which the negative stance towards this music results less from something inherent in the works themselves than from listeners' changing aesthetic values, particularly those to do with musical representation and form.

The division of an artist's career into periods is always contentious. On the surface Schumann's creative life seems easier to divide than most; there is the change from solo piano pieces to song in 1840, the year of his marriage to Clara; then his declaration of a 'new way' of composing in 1845; and, finally, the move from Dresden to Düsseldorf to take up the post of Municipal

Music Director at the beginning of September 1850, now generally agreed to mark the beginning of his late period.[6] Over the next three years he wrote some fifty works, many of which received critical acclaim. As Richard Pohl pointed out long ago, Schumann would have had little inkling in 1850 that his life would end six years later, and many of the works produced around the time of his move to Düsseldorf suggest a renewed creativity.[7]

In the aftermath of the 1848–9 revolutions Schumann had been claimed as a 'democratic' composer and the rightful heir to Beethoven by his former journal, *Neue Zeitschrift für Musik*.[8] His status as a national institution – taking Mendelssohn's place as Germany's leading composer – seemed confirmed by the simultaneous performance of the closing scene from *Faust* in Weimar, Dresden and Leipzig as part of the Goethe centenary celebrations in 1849. There was a series of concerts devoted to Schumann's music in Leipzig in March 1852 (which included performances of *Der Rose Pilgerfahrt*, the *Manfred* Overture, the Third Symphony, the A minor Violin Sonata and the G minor Piano Trio); at the Lower Rhine Festival in 1853; and reasonably successful tours with Clara around Europe. Famous friends and colleagues such as Ferdinand Hiller, Joseph Joachim, Jenny Lind, Anton Rubinstein, and Julius Stockhausen also performed his works on tour. Throughout the 1850s there appeared articles considering his biography and reputation, including monographs on *Das Paradies und die Peri* and the *Szenen aus Goethes Faust*. As a result of his spreading reputation and the commercial success of his *Hausmusik* and works for children, such as the *Album für die Jugend*, Schumann's income from publications of his music increased. The arrival of the twenty-one-year-old Johannes Brahms at the Schumanns' home in September 1853 even provided an heir apparent.

Little of this positive biographical context is remembered on considering the late period. Instead, as mentioned, critics focus on Schumann's final illness. He suffered from depression and what might be described as manic episodes throughout his career, and was concerned from an early age that he might succumb to mental illness. The deterioration of his health in the early 1850s was probably exacerbated by stress from work. His relationship with the Düsseldorf authorities soured during his second season as he criticized the Gesangverein's commitment and the Allgemeiner Musikverein's choice of programmes. They, in turn, began to question the quality of his conducting, leading to his resignation at the end of November 1853. During a subsequent tour of the Netherlands, Schumann suffered a recurrence of the aural disturbances that had worried him during a depressive period in the autumn of the previous year. It was not only his conducting duties that were proving stressful. While he was virtually guaranteed good reviews from his immediate circle, the *Neue Zeitschrift für Musik* was rapidly becoming a mouthpiece for Wagnerites who were increasingly anti-Schumann. At the beginning of February 1854 Schumann discovered that 'Hoplit', author of a rebuttal of his 'Neue Bahnen' article heralding Brahms as the saviour of German music, was none other than his friend and librettist Richard Pohl.[9] News that an essay by Friedrich Hinrich that claimed Schumann's best days were over ('When we speak of Schumann, we mean the composer of the older works, approximately up until *Peri*. Since then, as can unfortunately no longer be disguised, he has declined, becoming mannered in the most melancholy sense of the word')[10] was about to be published as a separate pamphlet prompted Schumann to complain: 'Does he think that he can kill off all my post-*Peri* compositions with this pinprick? *Manfred*, the *Spanisches Liederspiel*, the three Trios, the Second Sonata for violin and piano, and the Second and Third Symphonies?'[11] A pinprick it might only have been, but that evening, 10 February 1854, Schumann's aural hallucinations returned in worsened form, over the next few days changing from sustained pitches to imagined music, including the chorale *Ein' feste Burg ist unser Gott* for distant wind band. On 17 February he wrote down a theme he later claimed was dictated to him by the spirit of Schubert, on which he wrote a set of variations (*Thema mit Variationen für das Pianoforte*). Although he seemed to recover from this episode, ten days later he suffered a relapse and asked, for Clara's protection, to be taken to an asylum. On the afternoon of 27 February, at the height of Carnival season, Schumann slipped out of the house and leapt from a bridge into the Rhine. Fishermen who had noticed his odd behaviour (he was wearing his dressing-gown and had offered his handkerchief as payment at the toll booth) immediately saved him and prevented him from jumping from their boat back into the water. The bedraggled composer was led back home through the Carnival crowds.

Again, Schumann demanded to be institutionalized, and at the beginning of March he was admitted to a private sanatorium in Endenich, a suburb of Bonn, run by Dr Franz Richarz. Although some of the treatments he received there now seem barbaric, Richarz's establishment was regarded as one of the more progressive and humane available. Schumann was allowed to take walks in the area, and had access to a piano and manuscript paper; he also received visitors. The one person he was not allowed to see was Clara. There has long been a tendency to vilify Clara's response to Schumann's incarceration.[12] It seems a little unfair to criticize Clara for following the doctor's recommendations and for her busy schedule; after all, she had to support her family and protect their reputation. Her decision to suppress certain works, such as the Violin Concerto, the Third Violin Sonata and the accompaniments to Bach's Cello Suites, and later to destroy the Five Romances for Cello was taken with the guidance of Joachim and Brahms, and was doubtless driven by a belief that they did not do her husband's talent justice.

Certainly Clara's suppression of these pieces has been taken as confirmation that Schumann's creative powers waned, the cause of which invariably is taken to be his mental illness. Schumann's 'madness' was never considered to have increased his music's profundity or inventiveness, as was often claimed to be the case with Romantic artists, but to have resulted in a 'darkening' of mood and ultimately creative failure. Félix Clément declared the Third Symphony, Overtures and Choral Ballades as having been 'clearly conceived and created under the influence of his diseased mind' and August Reissmann attributed the formlessness and chaos he perceived in Schumann's later compositions to his illness.[13] Yet these are not the works Schumann refused to have published, but ones that had enjoyed some success when the composer was still alive. As the nature of Schumann's illness became more widely known – most obviously through the publication of biographies such as Wasielewski's – symptoms began to be heard throughout his oeuvre. The *alter egos* of Florestan and Eusebius in his criticism and piano cycles have been diagnosed as manifestations of bipolar or even multiple personality disorder; the 'inner voices' or 'voices from the distance' of the *Humoreske* and *Novelletten* are thought to portray the composer's aural disturbances; the obsessive repetitions of rhythms and motives to represent the depressive's constant rocking motion. The pattern of intense creative episodes followed by unproductive periods is considered indicative of manic depression or bipolar disorder.[14] Whether or not these diagnoses are correct, they indicate how strongly we filter our appreciation of the composer's music through knowledge of his illness: discussing *Papillons* or the *Gesänge der Frühe*, we always seem to be talking about late Schumann.

Late works themselves are often explained as untimely meditations, according to which view history had yet to catch up with the artist's achievements. The models for a late period, as Edward Said wrote, often are based on reconciliation (Shakespeare's *The Tempest* and *The Winter's Tale*; Sophocles's *Oedipus at Colonus*, Verdi's *Falstaff*) or on apotheosis (Rembrandt, Matisse, Bach, Wagner).[15] Some, such as Ibsen or Beethoven, produced more intransigent late works not appreciated by their contemporaries but now considered to be their most profound and technically far-reaching. Even Schubert's last compositions today are described as bathed in the glow of the 'golden months' before his death.[16] Schumann's late music, however, remains on the fringes. This has to do with the nature of his illness and with his musical style.

When Joachim received from Schumann, then at the asylum in Endenich, a package of the Romances for cello, the *Gesänge der Frühe* and the Third Violin Sonata, what would he have made of this music, the first of which was subsequently destroyed by Clara and the last not published until 1956? We can only guess about the Romances, of course, while the *Gesänge der Frühe* and Third Violin Sonata are very different in their approach to musical structure and expression; the former favouring simplicity and unorthodox forms, the latter using sonata form for its first and last movements and including a great deal of virtuosic writing for the violinist. There is little sense of there being a consistent late style. Indeed, John Daverio, the most influential recent American scholar of Schumann, describes the composer's later music as recapitulating, 'in microcosm, the achievements of an entire creative life'.[17] Thus 'it embraces a broad diversity of styles'; the products, according to Daverio, 'of a varied array of personas', that range from the lyricism of lieder and the public style of symphonic works to Schumann as storyteller (oratorios, choral-orchestral ballades, and declamation ballads), ecclesiastic (Mass and Requiem, and the final song of the Lenau cycle, op. 90), collector (arrangements and collections), pedagogue (contrapuntal works and *Hausmusik* for children and adults), and Davidsbündler (esoteric style – late chamber and piano music). In fact, these 'personae' are genres or types rather than anything to do with musical style *per se*. I am not arguing here for some kind of musical style that exists only as a configuration of notes – as already mentioned, it would be impossible to disentangle attitudes to the music from knowledge of Schumann's life or, indeed, the world around him ('Just as the pearl is the oyster's affliction, so style is perhaps the discharge from a deeper wound', suggested Flaubert in a letter of 1852). Instead, I want to ask a slightly different question about the music from the 1850s; namely, beyond their chronological appearance, why do we hear one piece as late and another as early, or even mature?

To talk about a composer's late style these days inevitably raises the spectre of the philosopher Theodor W. Adorno, whose writings on Beethoven's late style are fast becoming the model for an artist's final period.[18] Adorno's thoughts will surface throughout this book, but never unproblematically, for Schumann's late style seems to have been conceived in almost entirely different terms. According to Said's interpretation of Adorno, in his third period Beethoven 'abandons communication with the established social order of which he is part and achieves a contradictory, alienated relationship with it', expressed through 'a peculiar amalgam of subjectivity and convention'.[19] Beethoven's late music is like a fractured landscape, torn apart in time: 'In the history of art', Adorno concludes, 'late works are the catastrophes'.[20] On the surface, Schumann's late works have a contradictory, alienated relationship with society; the composer is often described as having 'withdrawn' from the world, and his music is accused of expressive emptiness. As will be discussed in greater detail in later chapters, conceptions of subjectivity and the relationship to convention in the late music are key. However, Schumann's late works seem not to be catastrophes in Adorno's sense. They do not convey such a drastic sense of ending, of the artist as commentator on the disastrous present. Rather, Schumann's untimeliness is generally thought to result from an inability to engage with the present sufficiently to critique it. That lack of engagement results not in a meaningful fragmentation of musical discourse, as Adorno finds in Beethoven, but in creative failure.

But perhaps we can turn this around and say that it is not Schumann who fails, but that the modernist model for late style that Adorno proposes through the example of Beethoven fails him. While many elements of late Schumann can be compared to his more 'progressive' contemporaries (such as Wagner) and some harmonic and thematic traits prefigure the musical language of later generations (most obviously that of Brahms and Hugo Wolf, but also French composers at the *fin de siècle*), the challenge of late Schumann is in many ways its simplicity and, at times, its sentimentality. These are not aspects that are easily theorized. They also defy attempts to align narratives of historical progress with increasing artistic complexity. However, by sometimes writing 'simple' music in the 1850s, Schumann was not being untimely but rather participating in the culture around him; a world of choral societies, music festivals, and nationalist *Volkstümlichkeit*. In part this book hopes to show that examining the late works as products of their time and as they were judged by their time is as useful as the application of any redemptive post-Adornian theory. It might make the music's evaluation more problematic, by taking away the safety net of posthumous apologies, but also helps explain not only something about Schumann but also about the people – performers, composers, critics and audiences – around him.

* * *

As mentioned, this book considers Schumann's music from the 1850s primarily by genre; thus the first chapter discusses the songs and the second choral ballades. The third chapter is concerned with the composer's collecting habits, as they are manifest in the editions and collections he prepared of his own works and that of other composers and writers. The final three chapters concentrate on instrumental works: number four examines the orchestral music (including concertos), number five chamber music, and number six pieces for piano. There are cross-references between chapters, but they are not necessarily to be read in order or all together.

A brief overview of the chapters' topics and themes beyond their grouping by genre, though, might be helpful here. Inevitably Schumann's works from the 1850s recall and continue his earlier interests. Just prior to leaving Dresden for Düsseldorf in the summer of 1850, Schumann composed a number of lieder, a flurry of composition that resembles that of the famous 'year of song' in 1840. The later lieder may not enjoy the popularity of *Dichterliebe*, *Frauenliebe und Leben* and the *Eichendorff Liederkreis*, but they do revisit some of their poetic themes, and provide a useful starting point for consideration of how we might formulate the difference between Schumann early and late. In the settings of Nikolaus Lenau, the emotional darkness of the poems is matched by a declamatory style of vocal writing and some startling harmonic and expressive moments. The slightly later treatments of poems by Elisabeth Kulmann and Maria Stuart are more contained; the cycles explore a much smaller harmonic range, and the piano's motivic vocabulary is more limited, almost as if accompanying recitative.

The Kulmann and Maria Stuart lieder bring to the fore questions about Schumann's choice of poets; their texts are far more sentimental than those he had once chosen from Heine or Eichendorff. They are closer in spirit to Chamisso or Kerner and, in a similar manner to recent discussions of *Frauenliebe und Leben*, are perhaps best served by being considered in the context of contemporary social relations and the fashion for sentimental literature. It also seems necessary to explain Schumann's choral music in historical context; the reason for the relative obscurity of pieces such as the oratorio *Der Rose Pilgerfahrt* or the four choral ballades is partly because local choral societies tend to perform a different repertoire. In many ways, Schumann's choral works from the 1850s were written specifically for the community he served as Music Director in Düsseldorf. This was a time of nation building, particularly in the Rhineland, and while the composer's personal commitment to the ideals of the 1848–9 uprisings has sometimes been questioned (unlike Wagner, he did not fight on the barricades but retreated to the country), recent scholars such as Reinhard Kapp have argued that revolutionary political sympathies can be detected in the music and in his decision to set text by poets such as Ludwig Uhland.[21] While Kapp claims that Schumann was a 'political author' whose later works provide a running commentary on the 1848–9 revolutions, Daverio warns against the 'blanket politicization' of Schumann's compositional output between 1848–53, saying that it 'only clouds what ideally should stand out in bold relief.'[22] It is fair to say, however, that Schumann was deeply invested in creating specifically German art, as is apparent from his interest in literature to the *volkstümlich* aspects of pieces as diverse as the Third Symphony and the projected Luther oratorio to the chamber music, and even, arguably, to the theme of redemption that recurs in his choral works, from the *Szenen aus Goethes Faust* to, of course, the Mass and Requiem.[23]

National historical consciousness is an issue that also is crucial to consideration of Schumann's collecting habits. Around 1850 Schumann began to put his library and compositions in order, and edited some of his earlier works, a process that reveals much about his evolving style and also about his historical and educational concerns. Further projects from around this time include the continuation of the *Dichtergarten* project, a collection of passages on music by his favourite authors: Goethe, Jean Paul, and Shakespeare. Schumann also completed piano accompaniments for Bach's Sonatas and Partitas and Cello Suites, and continued his engagement with Baroque harmony and counterpoint through various fugal exercises. Finally, he brought together some of his earlier piano works to create the *Albumblätter* and *Bunte Blätter*, *Hausmusik* complemented by a series of piano works for children.

The music for children was pedagogical in intent, which goes some way to explain its simplicity. Yet aspects of its form and content are shared with pieces for more high-minded aesthetic consumption, making an intriguing connection between late style and the naïveté of youth. A further, more complex evocation of childish realms is found in the chamber music based on ideas of fairy-tales, the *Märchenerzählungen* and *Märchenbilder*.

Not all of the late music is simple, of course – and that which is cannot always easily be understood. Throughout this book mention is made of the different historical ideologies behind the interpretation of Schumann's final works; in other words, whether they are thought Romantic, classical, or even – guided by late Beethoven – modernist. As discussed further in Chapter 4, Schumann declared that he changed his compositional method in the mid-1840s; he began to sketch and plan, rather than letting music pour out from poetic inspiration. This 'new manner', together with his turn to large-scale symphonic forms, has been characterized as a more 'objective' and classical approach, in contrast to the 'subjective' and Romantic attitude of before.

Whether or not these binaries hold true, it is striking that in comparison to the earlier music, for which many experimental Romantic literary models have been suggested – from E. T. A. Hoffmann to Friedrich Schlegel and, of course, Jean Paul – few have been offered for the late works. At various points in the book I speculate why this might be, in part by experimenting with some possible candidates, such as Friedrich Hölderlin in the discussion of the chamber music, and Adalbert Stifter with regard to Schumann's collecting habits. I also consider whether we need to use different musical models in order to comprehend late Schumann, elements of which seem close to the oeuvre of composers such as Niels Gade. A further influence might have been one surprisingly overlooked: that of Brahms. Schumann's encouragement and influence over the younger composer has long been acknowledged, but rarely in terms of the late works and not often as a reciprocal process. While I argue in the following pages that Daverio's tendency to focus on the integrity of motivic working in, say, the Third Symphony, is primarily a means by which he tries to 'redeem' the late style through its implicit association with Brahmsian developing variation, there is something to be said for the approach, for it highlights aspects of Schumann's music that we do not find so much in his earlier works.

However dismissive Brahms might have been about Schumann's influence over him, it is apparent that his music made an impact on him artistically and personally. The E flat major piano theme with variations completed just before Schumann's suicide attempt was the source for a set of variations for Brahms (for piano duet, op. 23), who also reworked the first of the *Gesänge der Frühe* for unaccompanied choir. The music for Byron's *Manfred* – which was written in 1848 but that in many ways was strongly associated with the composer's illness – was recalled in Brahms's First Symphony. The way in which Schumann's music haunts Brahms's suggests that his spirit could be raised, much as he had tried to do with Beethoven at the séance. The question of Schumann's spirit is primary for the understanding of his late works for both listeners and performers – behind most reviews of performances of the late works lies the question whether they have accessed or raised the spirit of Schumann. A few days after his suicide attempt, on 6 March 1854, Clara and Joachim performed the Third Violin Sonata at a friend's house in Düsseldorf. Clara commented:

We played Robert's Third Sonata in A-minor, and today we both played it just with the spirit it requires. I had already made it a part of me but Joachim could not really get into its spirit last time in Hanover. Today he was enthusiastic and I too. – This is the only thing that can soothe me – his music!

We might not all find consolation in the Third Violin Sonata and, actually, Clara later decided the work should not be published, suggesting that, if she could still access her husband's spirit she did not want to through that particular piece. There is a tendency in writings on German Romanticism to find transcendence in an artwork's fractures. In the case of Schumann, such moments are often detected in the works from the early 1840s – witness the enthusiasm with which scholars have tackled the concept of the Romantic fragment as a means to explain the song and piano cycles. In the works from the 1850s, however, fractures are thought instead to indicate signs of breakdown, of the composer no longer being able to express himself not because of some kind of privileging of the ineffable but because he simply could not. I cannot claim to have access to Schumann's spirit. In pointing out some of the gaps in our understanding of his music, though, we might – like Joachim – begin to sense where it may reside.

Notes

1. Wilhelm Josef von Wasielewski, *Robert Schumann: Eine Biographie*, ed. Waldemar von Wasielewski (Leipzig: Breitkopf und Härtel, 1972), p. 486.
2. Letters to Ferdinand Hiller, 25 and 29 April 1853, *Briefe, Neue Folge*, ed. F. Gustav Jansen (Leipzig: Breitkopf und Härtel, 1904), pp. 370–1.
3. Peter Ostwald, *Schumann: The Inner Voices of a Musical Genius* (Boston: Northeastern University Press, 1985), p. 256.
4. On the spread of table-tipping in Germany see Timo Heimerdinger, *Tischlein rück' dich. Das Tischrücken in Deutschland um 1850. Eine Mode zwischen Spiritualismus, Wissenschaft und Geselligkeit* (Münster: Waxmann, 2001).
5. Those looking for a biography will find John Daverio's or Arnfried Edler's volumes the most rewarding; see Edler, *Robert Schumann und seine Zeit* (Laaber: Laaber Verlag, 1982); and Daverio, *Robert Schumann: Herald of a 'New Poetic Age'* (Oxford: Oxford University Press, 1997). The 150th anniversary of Schumann's death has seen a number of biographies appear, including Theo R. Payk, *Robert Schumanns Lebenslust und Leidenszeit* (Bonn: Bouvier, 2006); and Martin Demmler, *Robert Schumann: Eine Biographie. Ich hab' im Traum geweinet* (Leipzig: Reclam, 2006). John Worthen's revisionist account, *The Life and Death of Robert Schumann*, will appear from Yale University Press in 2007.
6. There are some disagreements over where Schumann's middle period begins – 1840 or 1842 – but almost all commentators concur that 1850 marks the end of his prime.
7. Richard Pohl, 'Reminiscences of Robert Schumann (1878)', in R. Larry Todd, ed., *Schumann and his World* (Princeton: Princeton University Press, 1994), pp. 233–67, here p. 234.
8. See Sanna Pederson, 'Romantic music under siege in 1848', *Music Theory in the Age of Romanticism*, ed. Ian Bent (Cambridge: Cambridge University Press, 1996), pp. 57–75.

9. As outlined in later chapters, Pohl's friendship with Schumann faltered when the composer rejected some of his scripts, including the planned oratorio based on the life of Luther, and an adaptation of Schiller's *Die Braut von Messina*, for which Schumann produced an overture. His turn against Schumann also resulted from his entrancement by Liszt.

10. Friedrich Hinrich, 'Zur Würdigung Richard Wagners', *Neue Zeitschrift für Musik* 39:19 (1854), 200. The editors commented: 'until now it has not occurred to us or anybody else to condemn his entire recent output in such a manner. To utter such a general verdict on a creative talent that is still most energetically active can only be described as hasty and premature.'

11. Letter to Hinrich's brother-in-law Robert Franz, 10 February 1854, cited in Joachim Draheim, 'Robert Franz und Robert Schumann – Aspekte einer schwierigen Beziehung', *Robert Franz (1815–1892). Bericht über die wissenschaftliche Konferenz anläßlich seines 100. Todestages am 23 und 24 Oktober in Halle (Salle)* (Halle: Händel-Haus, 1993), p. 185.

12. Brahms noted the 'malicious rumours' that circulated about Clara after Schumann's death and thought that some of these were spread by Bettina von Arnim, who had visited the composer at Endenich and criticized his treatment there; see Brahms's letter to Julius Otto Grimm, September 1856, *Johannes Brahms im Briefwechsel mit J. O. Grimm*, ed. Richard Barth (Tutzing: Schneider, 1974), p. 45.

13. Félix Clément, *Les musiciens célèbres* (Paris: L. Hachette, 1887), p. 545; and August Reissmann, *Robert Schumann: Sein Leben und seine Werke* (Berlin: J. Guttentag, 1865), p. 174; cited in Eric Frederick Jensen, *Schumann* (Oxford: Oxford University Press, 2001), p. 282.

14. For discussion of this diagnosis see Kay Redfield Jamison, *Touched by Fire: Manic-Depressive Illness and the Artistic Temperament* (New York: Free Press, 1993).

15. Edward Said, 'Thoughts on late style', *London Review of Books* 26:15 (5 August 2004), 3–7.

16. Jonathan Dunsby, *Making Words Sing* (Cambridge: Cambridge University Press, 2004), p. 2. Kristina Muxfeldt cautions against the tendency of recent Schubert criticism to 'discern in his music a trace of the composer's own experience' in her contribution to *The Schubert Companion*, ed. Christopher H. Gibbs (Cambridge: Cambridge University Press, 1997), p. 137.

17. Daverio, *Robert Schumann*, p. 462.

18. See, for example, Edward Said, *On Late Style* (London: Bloomsbury, 2006); and Michael Spitzer, *Music as Philosophy: Adorno and Beethoven's Late Style* (Bloomington: Indiana University Press, 2006). On Adorno's conception of late Beethoven see Rose Rosengard Subotnik, 'Adorno's diagnosis of Beethoven's late style: early symptom of a fatal condition', *Journal of the American Musicological Society* 29:2 (1976), 242–75.

19. Said, *On Late Style*, pp. 8–9. Adorno's writings on late Beethoven include the fragment, 'Spätstil Beethovens' (1937), recently translated by Susan H. Gillespie as 'Late style in Beethoven', in Theodor W. Adorno, *Essays on Music*, ed. Richard Leppert (Berkeley: University of California Press, 2002); and the collection *Beethoven: The Philosophy of Music*, trans. Edmund Jephcott (Cambridge: Polity Press, 1998).

20. Adorno, 'Late style in Beethoven', p. 567.

21. See John Daverio, 'Sounds without the gate: Schumann and the Dresden revolution', *Il Saggiatore Musicale* 4 (1997), 87–112; and Reinhard Kapp, 'Schumann nach der Revolution: Vorüberlegungen, Statements, Hinweise, Materialien, Fragen', *Schumann in Düsseldorf: Werke – Texte – Interpretationen*, ed. Bernhard Appel (Mainz: Schott, 1993), pp. 315–416.

22. John Daverio, '*Einheit – Freiheit – Vaterland*: intimations of utopia in Robert Schumann's late choral music', *Music and German National Identity*, ed. Celia Applegate and Pamela Potter (Chicago: University of Chicago Press, 2002), pp. 59–77.

23. Two recent studies have examined a similar connection between nationalism and religion in Beethoven and Brahms; see Stephen Rumph, *Beethoven after Napoleon: Political Romanticism in the Late Works* (Berkeley: University of California Press, 2004); and Daniel Beller-McKenna, *Brahms and the German Spirit* (Cambridge, Mass.: Harvard University Press, 2004).

1 | Songs of farewell

To speak of Schumann is to speak of song. The wealth of material on the lieder, and the tendency to hear traces of song forms and singing voices in the piano, instrumental and, less surprisingly, choral and operatic music, proves that Schumann's fame as a composer is largely derived from his solo vocal music. The songs of which we usually speak, though, come mainly from the famous outpouring of 1840 that produced *Dichterliebe*, op. 48, *Frauenliebe und Leben*, op. 42, the Heine and Eichendorff *Liederkreise*, opp. 24 and 39, *Myrthen*, op. 25, and so on. Yet Schumann's lieder composition did not end there. While he did not produce many lieder immediately after 1840, towards the end of the decade he had what some call his second 'year of song', composing the *Lieder-Album für die Jugend*, op. 79, the *Lieder und Gesänge aus Wilhelm Meister*, op. 98a, the *Gesänge aus Lord Byrons "Hebräischen Gesänge"*, op. 95, the *Sechs Gedichte von Nikolaus Lenau und Requiem*, op. 90, and many more. He also completed a number of solo and two- or three-part songs over the next three years. These included the *Lieder von Elisabeth Kulmann*, opp. 103 and 104, the *Drei Gedichte aus den Waldliedern von Pfarrius*, op. 119, and the *Gedichte der Königin Maria Stuart*, op. 135.

The relative obscurity of these songs today can be explained in part by their having been written on the cusp of and into his late period. Lieder tend to be conceived as vehicles for personal expression, and particularly in the case of Schumann are heard as reflections of the composer's psyche. Thus 1840's year of song said farewell to frustrated love affairs and conveyed his joy on finally marrying Clara. The songs of the late 1840s show Schumann as Biedermeier family man (the *Lieder-Album für die Jugend*) and reacting to the 1848–9 revolutions.[1] Those of the 1850s fall into his late style, and the composer's voice is interpreted accordingly: the poems chosen are full of melancholy and foreboding; the music's expression falters; rhythms and motives are pursued to the point of obsession. They thus provide a useful starting point for thinking about how 'late Schumann' is understood, especially in terms of the poetic, musical and biographical subject. Although beginning with song suggests a continuation of the traditional view that these small-scale, intimate forms were central to Schumann's compositional output and outlook, it will become apparent that the role of the subject – and the notion of subjective expression – changed substantially during his last years.

In this chapter I will use a few examples to discuss the songs' relationship to ideas about Schumann's late style.[2] As a brief aside, it should be remembered that consideration of the late lieder is slightly complicated by their publication history. Schumann devoted much time in his last years to collecting and ordering his compositions (also discussed in Chapter 3). Settings that had not yet found their way into print were thus published alongside newly composed songs. For example, 'Dein Angesicht' and 'Es leuchtet meine Liebe' originally written for *Dichterliebe* appeared as songs 2 and 3 of the *Lieder und Gesänge*, op. 127, published in 1854; 'Lehn deine Wang' and 'Mein Wagen rollet langsam', also from *Dichterliebe*, were published posthumously as op. 142 ii and iv in 1858. The higher opus numbers are not therefore necessarily 'late', which explains their absence from the present discussion. My first examples are taken from the *Lenaulieder*; I will then go on to consider the *Sechs Gesänge*, op. 107, the op. 104 Kulmann lieder and the Maria Stuart lieder. Certain themes emerge in each group: their points of contact and comparison with the earlier songs; the construction of their poetic personae and biographical interpretation; their treatment of harmonic and motivic relationships and their significance for understanding the collections as cycles; and recurring poetic images and themes. Almost all of the songs are imbued with a sense – musical and poetic – of bidding farewell. While 'that farewell voice of love is never heard again', Schumann's final lieder also express hope of salvation in the future, continuing the theme of redemption that runs through most of the vocal music from the late period.[3]

* * *

The *Sechs Gedichte von Nikolaus Lenau und Requiem* were written over three consecutive days in the summer of 1850, just before the Schumanns moved from Dresden to Düsseldorf. On their first performance, at Eduard Bendemann's house on 25 August, news came that Lenau had just died. Schumann was surprised, not least because he thought the poet already dead (the likely impulse behind the inclusion of the Requiem). The news probably increased the sense of melancholy Clara noted in her diary afterwards. Schumann tried to publish the songs straightaway, with a title page of mourning including black drapes and a shining star. He explained that he wanted to create 'a modest monument to the sad but ever so marvellous poet'.[4]

Schumann's monument to Lenau can seem like a premonition. The lieder might slightly predate the move to Düsseldorf, which is generally agreed to mark the beginning of the late period, but their poetic themes and musical treatment seem to belong with the late works. The songs are frequently characterized as being the product of a 'dark and diseased' mind, one on the cusp of insanity; a notion that in part stems from the poetry set. Lenau's poetry is often that of the solitary, lovelorn wanderer whose sorrow is echoed by nature; a familiar figure of Romantic *Weltschmerz*, perhaps, but one whose tone is darker than that of Eichendorff or Kerner, or even Mörike or Heine. The melancholy dreams of *Dichterliebe* are recast in the *Lenaulieder* as nightmares; flowers no longer cajole and console but are withered and lifeless, the hills and the birds are grey, the shepherd who wished summer a fond farewell in the *Lieder-Album für die Jugend* can no longer hear the songs of the shepherdess and assumes her dead.

Schumann had been familiar with Lenau's poetry since his youth. The diary from his year in Vienna (1838) notes sightings of the poet in cafés and downcast evenings spent reading him. Schumann wanted to include some of the poems in the *Neue Zeitschrift für Musik* but did not set any until 1850. In fact, composers did not favour Lenau at this time (the exception being Liszt and his disciple Raff), suggesting that his poetry might have been thought too extreme (indeed he was eventually taken up by Wolf, Mahler and Berg).[5] Attitudes towards him also might have been altered by his admittance to an asylum in 1844, which was where he died. Most of the poems chosen by Schumann for op. 90 are taken from the earlier collections ('Lied eines Schmiedes' is from Lenau's *Faust*, published in 1836; 'Die Sennin' is from the early *Reiseblätter*).[6] What effect Lenau's incarceration might have had on Schumann's understanding of the poetry is unknown, although knowledge of it might have roused his curiosity and sympathy. Certainly his contemporaries were quick – particularly a few years later, when Schumann was in the asylum – to draw a parallel between composer and poet.

The 'dark' quality of the *Lenaulieder* also has to do with certain musical features, not least among them their connection to earlier works. John Daverio described the *Lenaulieder* as a 'pendant' to *Dichterliebe* (he suggests that the Kulmann and Maria Stuart lieder are similarly attached to *Frauenliebe und Leben*, of which more later).[7] On the surface, the comparison seems quite straightforward; both works are concerned with the end of a poet's love affair. Thinking about what *Dichterliebe* 'means' in terms of Schumann's music and scholarship on it, however, makes the comparison much more problematic – and interesting. *Dichterliebe* is probably one of the most analyzed pieces in the nineteenth-century repertoire. It has provoked debates about musical unity and organicism, about the aesthetic of the Romantic fragment, and about the construction of poetic identity; whole books have been devoted to it, ones that must not sidetrack me here.[8] Instead, I will

consider how the *Lenaulieder* reflect on those debates. This will help in turn
to begin to unpick assumptions about Schumann's late style, its relationship
to his earlier music and its biographical resonances.

While the *Lenaulieder* share with *Dichterliebe* the topic of lost love, they
do not have the same narrative trajectory. *Dichterliebe* might not follow a
story as such, but there is a sense that by the end of the cycle the protagonist
has reconciled himself to the end of the affair, at least in order that he
may love again. The *Lenaulieder* are more final: these are farewells to love,
acknowledgements that it has passed forever. The first song, 'Lied eines
Schmiedes' ('Blacksmith's Song'), might seem like the odd one out, but if the
piano dynamic instruction for the final strophe is followed in performance
it can imply the riders are departing for heaven. In 'Meine Rose', water is as
unlikely to resuscitate the cut rose as his lover is to return; in 'Kommen und
Scheiden' the woman leaves with his dream of youth; the cowgirl's songs in
'Die Sennin' are nothing but echoes; and in 'Einsamkeit' a bird in the forest
sings his heart's sorrow. At the end of 'Der schwere Abend' he wishes he and
his lover were dead. That wish seems to have been granted by the inclusion
of the Requiem, whose words are not by Lenau but from August Heinrich
Theodor Sievers's German translation of an anonymous Latin text, Heloïse's
lament for Abelard: now an abbess, she remembers her love as a thing of the
past.[9]

The *Lenaulieder*'s preoccupation with the theme of farewell and their
rapid rate of composition (three songs were composed in one day) encourages consideration of them as a coherent group.[10] Many of the individual
songs are harmonically adventurous and, more so than in *Dichterliebe*, there
seems to be a deliberate effort on the part of the composer to make smooth
and explicit harmonic progressions between songs. This is most obvious in
Schumann's use of enharmonic relationships:

1. Lied eines Schmiedes   Eb major
2. Meine Rose   Bb major
3. Kommen und Scheiden   Gb major – F♯ major
4. Die Sennin   B major – D♯ major
5. Einsamkeit   Eb minor – major
6. Der schwere Abend   Eb minor
7. Requiem   Eb major

Although the third song ends in the enharmonic equivalent of the tonic
and the fourth song has a progressive tonality, these are not fragments in
the sense of the first two songs of *Dichterliebe*. There is not the same level
of ambiguity about how the songs might work together as a cycle, at least
in harmonic terms.[11] The *Lenaulieder* create a context for each other. For

example, at the end of the first verse of 'Meine Rose', as the protagonist brings water to the drooping rose, there is a magical modulation to the flat submediant, G flat, predicting the key of the next song.

The motivation behind the arrangement of keys in the *Lenaulieder* is not entirely abstract: it also responds to the texts set. The winsome quaver figure that seems to prompt the memories of the lovers' meetings in 'Kommen und Scheiden' is transformed for the final verse:

Und als Lebwohl sie winkte mit der Hand,
War's, ob der letzte Jugendtraum mir schwand
(When she waved goodbye it was as though
The last dream of my youth was taking leave of me).

The harmonies shift from Db flat 7 to E major flat 7; her farewell impinges on the fantasy, the piano's quaver figure no longer acting as prompt for fond memories but sinking into the bass line, becoming more accompanimental. Youth's dream is disappearing: the voice's final cadence suggests a cadence from B minor to F sharp minor, but this is subverted by the postlude immediately switching to F sharp major, the enharmonic equivalent of the original tonic, G flat; the piano even revises and reinterprets the vocal phrase from bars 28–31 (Example 1:1). The end thus prepares for the next song, 'Die Sennin', in B major. The enharmonic shift thereby serves both a poetic and a structural purpose, suggesting that the connection between songs was on Schumann's mind. This possibility is given support by 'Die Sennin', the final verse of which, having just arrived on G sharp minor, introduces an open fifth pedal on D sharp and A sharp as a vestigial pastoral drone, as the deserted hills remember the shepherdess's sad songs. The piano postlude continues their train of thought: it recalls the opening descending triplet and ascending fifth of the vocal line in G sharp minor before dying away on its dominant, a D sharp major triad (Example 1:2). Its final harmony can be explained as a reflection of the poem; like the hills the piano is waiting for her song to return.

Beyond the deserted hills and lovers there is also a sense in which the *Lenaulieder* say farewell to Schumann's earlier style of lieder composition. In part this has to do with the relationship between voice and piano that might, as Jensen suggests, indicate the lied's transition from the chamber to the concert hall.[12] 'Meine Rose' enjoys an operatic – even a Bellinian – lyricism with occasional climaxes and flourishes not often on show in Schumann but that might be the result of his recent foray into opera with *Genoveva*. The vocal writing in other songs is more declamatory; a trend

Example 1:1 'Kommen und scheiden', bb. 16–31

forecast in the *Sechs Gesänge von Wielfried von der Neun* (op. 89). 'Röselein, Röselein' from that collection combines lyrical phrases with declamatory statements, the former associated with fantasy, the latter with reality (associations continued, to an extent, in 'Meine Rose'). The voice begins in A minor without accompaniment (Example 1:3): 'little rose, why must you bear thorns?' Her subsequent dream of a rose without thorns is evoked by A major flourishes in the piano; when she wakes and the brook laughs at her for such a fantasy the declamatory style returns, along with A minor. The vocal line in both sections is not dissimilar – eschewing stepwise motion for leaps or, it could be said, melodic continuity for dramatic effect – but the contrast in character is clearly defined by the piano accompaniment.

Example 1:2 'Die Sennin', bb. 37–45

That the piano should have an important interpretative role in Schumann's lieder comes as no surprise; it has often been described as another – even the composer's – voice, sometimes telling alternative stories to those relayed by the text. In the *Zwölf Gedichte von Justinus Kerner* (op. 35), for example, the young girl of 'Stirb, Lieb' und Freud' is unaware of her beatification but it is conveyed by the piano, which transforms the music of her prayer into her halo of lilies. The piano also provides the silent music of 'Stille Liebe' and 'Stille Tränen'. Its function changes in the late songs, however; it tends less to be a locus of meaning, as in the *Kernerlieder* or 'Röselein, Röselein', to become more abstract. Significant piano postludes are shorter than those in *Dichterliebe* or *Frauenliebe und Leben*. In subsequent songs, particularly the Kulmann and Maria Stuart lieder, the piano tends to focus on more concentrated motives or figures that last at most a bar, and they appear more as punctuation and accompaniment than as independent voices. Perhaps the model for such accompanimental writing comes from recitative, or more precisely the arioso recitative (*rezitativischer Gesang*) Schumann developed in *Das Paradies und die Peri*.[13] A more extreme version (but one that makes more prominent use of the accompaniment) might have been melodrama, found in 1849's incidental music for

Example 1:3 'Röselein', bb. 1–11

Byron's *Manfred* and the declamation ballads (op. 122) discussed further in Chapter 2. This would match the rhythmically more flexible, declamatory vocal writing.

Schumann had experimented with recitative styles within lieder in his earlier cycles, most notably in 'Ich hab' im Traum geweinet' from *Dichterliebe*. It was this song that seems to have haunted him as he composed the sixth of the *Lenaulieder*, 'Der schwere Abend' (Examples 1:4 and 1:5). The two songs share the key of E flat minor, an unusual but significant tonality for Schumann. The beginning of 'Einsamkeit' from the *Lenaulieder* is the only other example of its use in his lieder. The piano more closely links 'Ich hab' im Traum geweinet' and 'Der schwere Abend' by returning to the distinctive rhythmic figure of the former (bar 3) in the latter. 'Der schwere Abend'

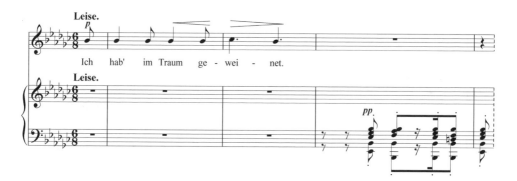

Example 1:4 'Ich hab' im Traum geweinet', bb. 1–4

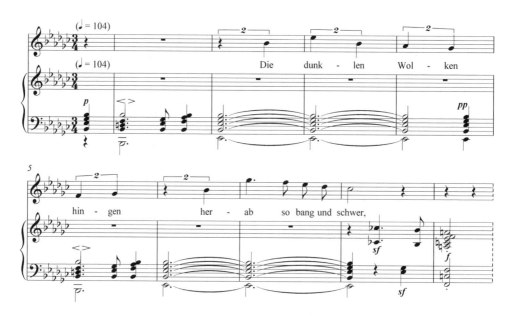

Example 1:5 'Der schwere Abend', bb. 1–9

begins with the piano alone, playing an augmented version of the earlier
song's rhythmic figure, but now legato rather than staccato, and clouded
by a swelling B♭ pedal reminiscent of the repeated B♭s in the first song's
opening vocal line.

   This reversal of vocal and piano entries in the second song signals the main
difference between Lenau's and Heine's poems, a difference fundamental to
defining the poetic choices Schumann made in 1850 in contrast to those a
decade earlier. The emphasis in the *Dichterliebe* song is on the first person;
every other line begins with 'Ich'; 'Der schwere Abend' describes the couple

walking through the sultry, starless night. The contrast in narrative positions is reflected in the songs' musical structures. While, as Beate Perrey points out, they share a similar tripartite form, their emotional trajectory – and the way in which it feeds into the dynamic between voice and piano – contrasts.[14] Within its first six bars the disjunct vocal line of 'Der schwere Abend' covers a greater range of pitches than the first twenty-eight bars of the *Dichterliebe* song, but having opened up at the beginning, the range contracts in the final verse, increasing the sense of claustrophobia and foreboding ('Ich hab' im Traum geweinet', on the other hand, expands its range in its final verse, as the dreamer wakes with renewed – if weepy – optimism). The duple rhythm of the vocal line of 'Der schwere Abend' against the $\frac{3}{4}$ time signature emphasizes the temporal dislocation between the events and their narration. The strangely distended rhythms of the accompaniment, which is kept hanging for an extra bar before the voice enters in the second verse, becomes still more protracted with the plummeting chords at the end of the postlude, whose syncopation is bloated almost beyond recognition.[15]

Perrey argues that the 'restating of musical material [from *Dichterliebe*] in different poetic contexts is a *critical* act on Schumann's part'.[16] The continuation, amplification and enhancement of 'Ich hab' im Traum geweinet' in 'Der schwere Abend' indicates that on reading the Lenau, Schumann was reminded of 'the sentiment, the "mood" or "state of mind" Heine's poem had generated years earlier'.[17] For Perrey, Schumann's return to the emotional world of *Dichterliebe* was a return to the biographical context of 1840, to the relative stability brought about by his marriage and the 'frantic production' of the 'year of song' that followed. The move from Dresden – the scene of his opera *Genoveva*'s failure and an unfriendly, conservative environment – to the seemingly more congenial Düsseldorf promised a similarly productive period. But Perrey sees Schumann also as realizing in 1850 that he had not gained the acclaim for which he had once hoped. 'Put sympathetically, op. 90 carries the tone of nostalgia', she writes: 'Put drastically, the Lenau lieder demonstrate a sense of panic.'[18]

Perrey's reading of Schumann's biography into his music is difficult to resist, particularly given the intertextual references between 'Ich hab' im Traum geweinet' and 'Der schwere Abend'. Yet aside from the bigger issue of musicology's malingering anxiety about the connection between a composer's life and works (an issue that will resurface throughout this book) there is the problem that often, once such a biographical interpretation has been made, the availability of other versions is forgotten. For example, the question of whether the *Lenaulieder* convey nostalgia or panic can be answered differently – less drastically – by recourse to psychoanalytical writings. My reason for invoking psychoanalysis here is not entirely arbitrary; nineteenth-century lieder, with their focus on individual emotional expression and its meaning, arguably shared and maybe even prophesied some of its preoccupations. Certain images return in the poetry chosen by Schumann and other lieder composers, the interpretation of which may vary according to context but which nonetheless are marked by their recurrence.

For instance, protagonists often cry.[19] In Freud's *The Interpretation of Dreams*, crying has differing meanings depending on whether the dreamer is still weeping when he wakes. If not, he is over the loss he has suffered. If so, then he does not want to rid himself of his sense of loss. The protagonist of 'Ich hab' im Traum geweinet', who wakes from each dream with tears still flowing, is indulging himself; or, to put it another way, still desires.[20] His yearning is embodied in the inverted temporal order of the verses, which recede from the future (her death), to the present (her leaving), to the past (her love). The piano's sudden animation in the final verse indicates: 'the awareness that, in the present, all this is lost imposes itself again'.[21] Having to revisit this emotional world might be thought cause for panic in itself. There is another Freudian model for dealing with loss, though, that offers relief. The young poet finds that loving what ultimately disappears is a torment to himself.[22] In order to continue living, in order to love life, Freud advises, he needs to learn how to love transience, because it is impermanence that lends experience value. 'Love at its strongest', Adam Phillips glosses, 'is an acknowledgement of transience, not a wilful denial of it. Deaths make life lovable; it is the passing of things that is the source of our happiness.'[23] In other words, the young poet needs to learn how to mourn, to break out of the cycle of loss. 'Der schwere Abend' might show Schumann had learnt to do just that, a decade after *Dichterliebe*. The borrowed rhythmic motive from 'Ich hab' im Traum geweinet' is a reminder of happier days – of love's young dream. In the final verse of 'Der schwere Abend', the poet wills their love to die, allowing himself to mourn by bidding it – and his lover – farewell. This is not nostalgia; the song is not imbued, as Perrey suggests, 'with sounds of a better past which Schumann tried to re-evoke'. Nor is it panicked. The brief turn to the relative major in the final verse of 'Der schwere Abend', as he wishes her goodnight, and wishes for their deaths, allows their loves to sink to the bottom of the Rhine as the protagonist claims to do at the end of *Dichterliebe* – a claim famously belied by the piano postlude remembering 'Am leuchtenden Sommermorgen'.

There is a difference between the tears of a song's protagonist and those of its composer; or, indeed, of its listener.[24] Knowing that Schumann cried while reading Byron's *Manfred*, or that Beethoven wept while composing the Cavatina of op. 130, indicates something other than the poetic symbolism of the *Lenaulieder*. It signals – lest we forget – that the music might seem to be intimate, because of its solo voice and piano, and its confessional text, but that it is much less so than the tears glistening in the composer's eye. The song's tears could be ours. It is much harder to say that they would have expressed Schumann's nostalgia or panic. For a famously untheatrical composer, Schumann has with surprising consistency been credited with an ability to assume different characters: most obviously those of Florestan, Eusebius and the rest of the Davidsbündler; more problematically with the female protagonist of *Frauenliebe und Leben*, as will be discussed later with regard to the feminine voices of the Kulmann and Maria Stuart lieder.[25] Amongst them can be found a Schumann persona – withdrawn and melancholic – glimpsed most frequently, it seems, in the lieder because as mentioned we assume a correlation between the composer and the solo voice. Thus Perrey decides that 'Schumann is the subject of *Dichterliebe*' and that in the dark mood of the 'Der schwere Abend' we hear the 'aphasic Schumann of 1850'.[26] But that is not to say that within 'subject-Schumann' there are not other characters – even after the watershed of 1850 when, as mentioned in the Introduction, the composer's prospects in Düsseldorf seemed promising.

One striking counter-argument against dark and gloomy, aphasic late Schumann can be found in his later settings of Lenau, the *Vier Husarenlieder von Nikolaus Lenau*, op. 117, composed in between the *Märchenbilder*, op. 113 and *Der Rose Pilgerfahrt* in the spring of 1851.[27] These are playfully strident settings that prefigure the phantom soldiers of Mahler's *Des Knaben Wunderhorn*. The real danger for the Hussar of the first song is not battle but his weakness for the age-old temptations of wine, women and song. In the middle of the third song, 'Den grünen Zeigern', there is brief reference to the rumble of cannons but that is soon forgotten with the distraction of rosy cheeks and fiddle music.

While the *Husarenlieder* offer an alternative persona for Schumann, another voice should be taken into account when considering questions of musical style: that of the performer. A dedication to a particular singer did not necessarily mean that they sang the collection, but it could sometimes indicate the type of voice Schumann had in mind. Thus the *Husarenlieder* were dedicated to the singer and actor Heinrich Behr, whom Schumann had known in Leipzig in the 1830s. The op. 89 lieder were dedicated to Jenny Lind, whom he met in early 1847 and whose interpretations – including those of his own works – he greatly admired. Two concerts with Lind in Hamburg in March 1850 were not only financial successes for Schumann but may well have encouraged his return to song composition (which began with the *Drei Gesänge* op. 83 at the end of that month). Indeed the high notes required in many of the late lieder might have been imagined for her famously clear top register. The op. 107 lieder were dedicated to the alto Sophie Schloss, an acquaintance of the Schumanns from Leipzig who also moved to Düsseldorf in 1850. That dedication and the preponderance of female characters in the collection – Ophelia, the servant girl of 'Die Fenster-scheibe', the spinning girl of 'Die Spinnerin' – might explain why the cycle has been sung almost exclusively by women. Almost all of Schumann's late songs, in fact, were written for female voices or at least female protagonists. Beyond questions of practicality and preference we might ask whether the appeal of such a gendered perspective was also that it allowed particular poetic themes to be explored, among them two of Schumann's favourites in his last years: childhood and redemption.

The *Sechs Gesänge*, op. 107 were composed in two stages. The first three songs and the last, as they appeared in print, were composed in January 1851, between Schumann's overtures to Schiller's *Braut von Messina*, op. 100, and to Shakespeare's *Julius Caesar*, op. 128 (in this time he also completed the third of the *Fünf heitere Gesänge*, op. 125). The fourth and fifth songs, settings of Paul Heyse's 'Die Spinnerin' and Wolfgang Müller's 'Im Wald', were composed a few months later, around August, after the *Märchenbilder*, the piano version of *Der Rose Pilgerfahrt, Der Königssohn*, op. 116, and the *Lieder von Elisabeth Kulmann*. Schumann's return to op. 107 throws up some interesting questions about considering the published version as a cycle.

1. Herzeleid (T. Ullrich)	E minor
2. Die Fensterscheibe (T. Ullrich)	B minor
3. Der Gärtner (E. Mörike)	D major
4. Die Spinnerin (P. Heyse)	B minor
5. Im Wald (W. Müller)	A minor
6. Abendlied (G. Kinkel)	C major

As can be seen from the list of numbers, this is one of his most disparate collections, in terms of the poets chosen and the relationship between keys. The added songs do not provide a strong harmonic link, as might have been felt necessary between the D major of 'Der Gärtner' and the C major of 'Abendlied' (assuming this was the order in which they would have been presented). Instead, they produce another stepwise move between distant keys, from B minor to A minor, separating the paired relative major-minor relationships of the final four songs (D major to B minor; A minor to C major). Other late song collections by Schumann include a number of different poets, but op. 107 is notable for including some of his rarest choices.

He set only two poems by Paul Heyse (excepting the translations from his and Emanuel Geibel's *Spanisches Liederbuch* in the two song cycles, opp. 74 and 138), and only one by Wolfgang Müller, or 'Müller von Königswater'. 'Abendlied' was taken from the 1850 edition of Gottfried Kinkel's *Gedichte*; writing being one of the many occupations of Kinkel's very varied career – again, this is the only poem by him Schumann set. As were the two poems by Titus Ullrich, taken from Gruppe's *Deutscher Musenalmanach für das Jahr 1851*. The most famous poet in op. 107, Eduard Mörike, had five poems set by Schumann, of which this is the last.[28] In some ways this is one of Schumann's most eclectic and personal collections: for the most part he knew the poets set in op. 107 personally, as demonstrated by the fact that at the time neither Heyse's nor Müller's poems were published. Schumann praised Ullrich as 'a dear man, full of lucidity and shrewdness' ('ein lieber Mensch, voller Klarheit und Schärfe').[29] He had known Müller as a contributor to the *Neue Zeitschrift für Musik*; they became close friends when Schumann moved to Düsseldorf, where Müller was his doctor. Müller and Kinkel were friends, but Schumann never met the latter; probably because of his exile from Germany after the 1848 revolutions.

In musical terms what is most striking about these songs is the folk-like simplicity of their surface, reflected back through some of Schumann's most chromatically adventurous music. These are perhaps the most obvious forerunners of Hugo Wolf. 'Herzeleid' (Example 1:6) is a gloss on Gertrude's Act IV speech on the death of Ophelia: 'There is a willow grows aslant a brook, That shows his hoar leaves in the glassy stream.' We are not told of Ophelia chanting 'snatches of old tunes'; instead, the waves whisper her name in warning. The piano accompaniment of Schumann's setting seems caught in their flow. Above semiquavers trailing down, like the willow's branches into the water, emerge gentle melodic fragments that rise and fall, perhaps lapping at her 'clothes spread wide', as Shakespeare has it. The harmony and phrasing add to the sense of Ophelia being pulled away; the first four bars are marked by a dominant pedal before moving towards the submediant, C. Bars 10–13 move back to B, meaning that the first stanza ends – as it began – on the dominant and shortly afterwards we hear a (modified) return of the material with which the song opened. This irregular harmonic pattern is itself cut across by the vocal line, which begins with a three-bar phrase that appropriately ends on the new submediant harmony with the word 'hangen' (bar 5). The third and fourth lines (bars 10–18), as the pale-cheeked, dreamy girl stares down at her reflection, are made still more uncertain and unreal as the harmonies move through the flat IV (F) on 'starr' to A minor, a passing chord of E minor being diverted

Example 1:6 'Herzeleid'

Example 1:6 (*cont.*)

to the secondary dominant of B, the dominant of the key of her unhappy reverie. It is almost as if piano and voice float by each other, sometimes coming together, othertimes drifting apart. At the end of bar 4, for instance, the piano follows the voice's semiquaver G with a demisemiquaver G, a strange dislocation of the two lines that adds piquancy to the semitone clash between bass and treble (F♯ and G). Only as it prepares for the second stanza does the piano take up the voice's opening melody instead of its original contour. Otherwise the music is repeated exactly, until the moment the waves finally speak her name aloud: 'Ophelia'. Using the familiar dotted rhythm and just rising by a tone, as if it were the first half of one of the piano's melodic fragments, Schumann sets the final words very simply, and the song is all the more haunting for it.[30]

As at the end of 'Herzeleid' there is something uncomfortable beneath the simple surfaces of the op.107 songs, derived in part from their use of rhythm and harmony. Often voice and piano work in different metres and the meaning of text and music do not always coincide. In 'Der Gärtner' the piano's opening two bars seem like a dim memory of the beginning of the previous song, 'Die Fensterscheibe', but transformed into triplets, perhaps in imitation of the princess's prancing horse. The vocal line mostly keeps to duple time, with some strange stresses that further distance it from the piano, such as the emphasis on the first syllable of 'Leibrösslein' in bar 4 and the emphasis on the second syllable of 'dafür' at the very end. The final two lines of the poem, which are repeated by Schumann, intensify these rhythmic tensions, the triplet quavers of the princess's horse – if you will – seeming to pass by the gardener regardless, only halting on the unprecedentedly extended minim high note on the first syllable of 'alle'. 'Abendlied' is breathtakingly beautiful, but again distances the vocal and piano parts through the latter maintaining a near constant triplet crotchet motion (marked 'Verschiebung' or delayed) against the duple time of the voice. The effect is less disturbing than in 'Der schwere Abend' but then the triplets probably represent the footfalls of passing angels ('Nun hört man aller Orten / Der Engel Füsse geh'n'). They only stop as the persona commands her heart to cast away its sickness (Example 1:7): 'wirf ab, Herz, was dich kränket / Und was dir bange macht!' Each stanza ends on a tonic 6/4 chord (e.g. bar 18). Despite not having reached the tonic and trailing to nothingness on the third beat of the bar, rather than reaching a stronger conclusion on the first beat as happens more often in lieder, there is a sense of serenity to the song's conclusion; in the brief postlude the piano simply pulls its triplet figure down to the tonic, C major.

Further songs from op. 107 similarly use harmony to console where others might express torment. In 'Die Fensterscheibe', the girl who cuts herself on a smashed windowpane as her beloved walks by describes the blood running over her hand. She admits that it hurt, but there is little acknowledgement of that in the music beyond the subtle shading of the first verse's shift from major in bar 7 to minor in bars 17–19 (Example 1:8). Otherwise the stanza repeats almost exactly as before, emphasis instead being put on her joy at his momentarily noticing her, at which point the strophic repetition is broken (bar 26). The wanderer of 'Im Wald' ends every verse with a repetition of 'Und ich bin so allein, voll Pein!' ('And I am so alone, full of suffering').

Example 1:7 'Abendlied', bb. 15–20

With both phrases the music cadences onto the dominant, whose major mode rings out with a strange brightness in its melancholy, minor-key surrounds (Example 1:9). But perhaps it is wrong to describe the effect of such contrary settings as uncomfortable; maybe they are better understood as consoling.

Somewhere between the folksiness of the scenes and the disavowal of the characters' suffering lies the issue of gender. This is not to say that men could not bear pain without complaint but, as becomes clearer in the Kulmann and Maria Stuart lieder, there is a sense that these young women are somehow able to redeem themselves through their suffering. As will be discussed further in later chapters, the idea of redemption recurs in many of Schumann's works, from *Das Paradies und die Peri* and – it has been argued – the Second Symphony to the late choral music, not least Faust's redemption by the eternal feminine or 'Das Ewig-Weibliche'.[31] Against these ambitious large-scale pieces the late songs seem even more modest (although the *Lenaulieder* had, of course, included a Requiem). Yet they might on their own terms also yearn after salvation.

Example 1:8 'Die Fensterscheibe', bb. 12–31

Example 1:9 'Im Wald', bb. 10–14

The Kulmann and Maria Stuart lieder have, as mentioned, been described as pendants to the Chamisso cycle, but they have not received similar attention. Admittedly the kind of woman's life they evoke is markedly different. Where *Frauenliebe und Leben* follows its protagonist from first love to marriage, childbirth, and widowhood, the Kulmann poems are childlike and visionary, as might be expected of someone who died aged seventeen. The Maria Stuart poems – if written by the deposed Queen at all – are also by someone confronting death; despite spanning the twenty-six years of her life, they do not mention her love affairs or marriages beyond her prayer for the safety of her son.

Crucial to gendered readings of *Frauenliebe und Leben* is the aforementioned notion of Schumann's 'characterlessness', or rather his ability to take on different roles, as they assess his ability to write music for a female protagonist. Chamisso's poems have been described as 'role-playing' that 'portray[s] a man's wishful image of woman', a theme taken up by Ruth Solie, who explores how the music might construct the protagonist's 'gendered self'.[32] Solie concludes that 'the impersonation of a woman by voices of a male culture, [is] a spurious autobiographical act' and that the cycle does 'cultural work' in terms of gender relations, the misogyny of which can make listeners feel uncomfortable today. Jonathan Dunsby's attempt to redeem Schumann by invoking Michel Schneider's suggestion that 'the female voice, clearly expressing a "not-I", allows Schumann to escape from his recurrent melancholia', might be yet another display of the readiness with which we conflate the composer's life and works (in other words, another spurious autobiographical act), but it does raise some interesting points on considering Schumann's preference for female poets in the later works.[33]

If Chamisso's female protagonist appealed to Schumann as a means to escape to himself, poetesses such as Kulmann and Maria Stuart must have been doubly alluring.[34] But it is also true that 'implicit in any sincere impersonation is always also a sympathetic identification with one's subject'.[35] The attraction of female authorial voices did not lie simply in their 'otherness' or nostalgia for better times. Despite the youth of Kulmann and Maria Stuart they shared some of Schumann's concerns. They look forward not to life but to death and all hope for redemption.

Kulmann's family was left in poverty by the father's early death, and Elisabeth helped to support them by working as a translator and as a poet. By her death in 1825 she had written almost 1,000 poems, translated Anacreon, Ozerov, Metastasio, Alfieri, Camoens and Milton, and written hundreds of letters in at least seven languages. Kulmann's fame in 1840s Germany was immense. Schumann seems to have first read her poetry in the spring of 1851.[36] Kulmann's appeal may have lain in her being a kind of real-life Mignon figure, a poor orphan capable of producing simple, moving and slightly mystical poems about nature.[37] She presents the male composer with an opportunity to author the authoress, as Matthew Head has written about with regard to Minna Brandes in the eighteenth century (and there seem to be quite a few parallels between Brandes and Kulmann, not least their being worked to death).[38] Maybe Schumann was attempting to take such a controlling role by an unusual feature of the op. 104 lieder: the composer's preface to each song explaining their biographical context. His dedication to the collection claims:

It is in her poetry that we read how her life, spent in quiet obscurity and the greatest poverty, became richly happy. These few small songs . . . cannot give even an approximate notion of her character.[39]

The first song, 'Mond, meiner Seele Liebling', is said to be one of many poems Kulmann addressed to her mother. The second celebrates 'the beautiful Northern skies' of her homeland by wishing the swallows a safe journey; the third is a retort to children taunting her because of her poverty. The fourth song, 'Der Zeisig', written when Kulmann was probably about eleven years old, is said to exemplify how 'she always reflects reality in the profoundest way' ('Auf das tiefste spiegelt sie überall die Wirklichkeit ab'). Her deceased family returns in a vision in 'Reich mir die Hand, O Wolke'; Schumann explains that 'she has a foreboding that she will soon have to leave [the world]'. The next poem, probably dating from the last year of her life, is also a presentiment of death; the flowers in her little garden are beginning to fade, as will she. In the final song, 'Gekämpft hat meine Barke', probably written shortly before her death, Kulmann is described as seeming certain of her imminent end: only the thought of the mother she leaves behind causes her profound pain. As a postscript, Schumann adds:

She died, writing poetry to the very end, on 19 November 1825, in her seventeenth year. Among her late verse is the remarkable 'A Vision after my Death', in which she describes her own death. It is, perhaps, one of the sublimest masterpieces in all poetry. Thus she departed, as airy as an angel passing from one shore to another, but leaving behind her the luminous trail of a heavenly vision, gleaming afar.

It seems rather strange to refer to a poem – a sublime masterpiece of a poem, no less – at the end of the song cycle rather than setting it. A significant piano postlude would not have been out of character, although in many ways in the Kulmann lieder such an 'artistic' outpouring would be. These are deliberately simple settings.[40] They are syllabic and often strophic. The overall harmonic scheme is limited, alternating between G minor and Bb major before ending in Eb major. Yet within the songs there are harmonically felicitous moments, such as at the end of the fourth and fifth songs, which both move to the tonic major as, in the first, the lonely girl is consoled by the sight of the moon, and in the fifth, as she imagines the clouds raising her to heaven. The return of the opening lines and music at the end of 'Du nennst mich armes Mädchen' after the harp-like figuration of the E flat major middle section when the girl describes the richness of sunrise and sunset proves her point: she may look poor, but she is not. Occasionally the very bareness of the music intensifies its visionary quality. 'Die letzten Blumen starben' makes the dead flowers all the more ghostly by distended harmonic rhythm and odd voiceleading (Example 1:10). The introduction's promise to blossom into a preparatory cadence or melody (leading from the crotchet F sharp in bar 2) is hijacked by an accented falling sixth, B flat to D, which is repeated three times with seemingly little regard to the contour of the vocal melody. This awkward motif is accompanied by a fairly static bass line, which sustains the tonic through most of the verse in tied notes, and unresolved dissonances in the piano's treble part. It is as if the music is almost present; like the girl, its hold on the world is slipping away.

The relative simplicity of the musical setting, apart from making it more other-worldly, also makes the poetry more prominent. Many would argue that this is the reason for the obscurity of the cycle today: we can no longer tolerate such naïve texts without musical distraction. Certain images, however, have a significance that reaches beyond the Kulmann lieder. One of these is the notion of exile, of a desire to return to one's homeland – which

Example 1:10 'Die letzten Blumen starben', bb. 1–8

Schumann gives as the motivation for the second song – or to join one's loved ones in the other world, as in songs 5 and 7. In the latter, the final song of the cycle, the poet's barque struggles in the rough sea but she can see calmer waters on the horizon: in the first of the Maria Stuart lieder, the Queen bids farewell to France as she sets sail for Scotland, carried by the waves of the piano's semiquaver accompaniment. A sense of flight is conveyed still more strongly in the Kulmann lieder by the figure of the bird. The second song wishes the swallows a safe journey south, saying she would like to travel but would always want to return home. Two songs later, another bird – this time a finch – tries to persuade the child to leave her songbooks and come out to play. The song itself is a game, with its diminutive time signature of $\frac{4}{16}$, and the suggestion of a 'Wettgesang' or singing contest captured by the canon and imitation between voice and piano. It is marked to be repeated *ad libitum* – I imagine it could become faster each time. Schumann's prefatory comment to this song, 'she always reflects reality in the profoundest way', implies a deeper reading of the text. The bird may be tempting the child to fly away with it to distant lands, leading, in other words, to death.

As a brief digression, it is worth noting that this is not the first time a bird acts as a poetic symbol of foreboding in Schumann's songs, or indeed in

Example 1:11 'Einsamkeit', bb. 16–21

literature and music more generally: from the owl sounding Dido's deathly lamentation onwards.[41] Birds recur in this sense more frequently in Schumann's late songs, seemingly in preference to more positive associations, such as birds as chirpy companions or as fellow victims of lovesickness. The second stanza of Lenau's poem 'Einsamkeit' speaks of a sombre grey bird alone in the branches ('Grauer Vogel in den Zweigen!'), singing the lover's sorrow.[42] Schumann's music does not mark the birdsong in any obvious mimetic way, unless we take the brief melodic arch in the piano to be some abstract lyricism; the more remarkable result is the change of key to A flat minor, over which the vocal line copies rather than answers the mentioned piano melody (Example 1:11). In 'Warnung' from the op. 119 *Drei Gedichte aus den Waldliedern von Pfarrius*, composed in the autumn of 1851, the little bird is warned to stop singing because it will attract the attention of the owl: 'you are singing yourself into death!' ('Du singst dich in den Tod!'). Again, there is no obvious portrayal of birdsong or the forest. Instead, the sense of foreboding is achieved by a recurring syncopated figure that falls on two minim or crotchet chords and whose harmonic vagrancy is unsettling, particularly at the end, where it is only the voice's final 'Tod!' that provides the tonic, and by the vocal line's occasional high notes (Example 1:12).[43]

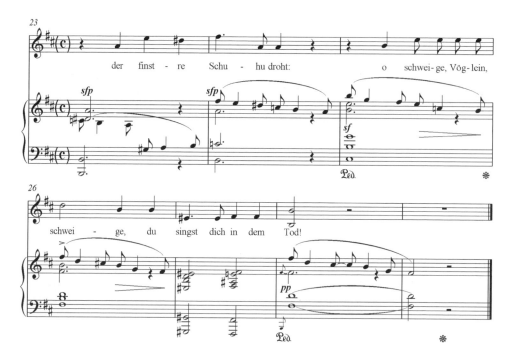

Example 1:12 'Warnung', bb. 23–9

The trepidation identified in the figure of the bird and Kulmann's desire to escape to her homeland recur as themes in the Maria Stuart lieder. Issues of identity become even more complicated with the deposed queen, who led a very creative posthumous life, particularly in England and France. The most famous German version of her life story was by Schiller, who imagined a meeting with her half-sister Elizabeth I that never took place (his play formed the basis of Donizetti's opera). But perhaps the most insidious fictionalization of Mary was the publication of her poems. As part of her schooling, Mary wrote a few poems, and tried sonnets in French and Italian during her long captivity in England.[44] After her death, however, several poems supposedly by her began to circulate, the products of forgery and misattribution. The verses she was said to have composed as she began her return voyage to Scotland (which appear in the first song of Schumann's cycle)

Adieu, plaisant pays de France!
O ma patrie,
La plus chérie!
Qui a nourri ma jeune enfance!

first appeared in the *Anthologie Françoise* of 1756, the work of a French journalist and circulated by Brantôme. Schumann took his texts from Gisbert Vincke's *Rose und Distel. Poesien aus England und Schottland* (Dessau, 1853).[45] These included 'Nach der Geburt ihres Sohnes' a forgery by Anne-Gabriel Meusnier de Querlon (1765) and 'An die Königin Elisabeth', taken from an anonymous wall inscription from Edinburgh castle, mistakenly attributed to Maria by Fanny Lewald in 1852.

However sentimental the Maria Stuart songs may be, they are also some of the most closely linked of Schumann's lieder compositions in terms of motivic and harmonic relationships.[46] The vocal lines of all except the first song begin with stepwise descents; in the second and third songs they begin with a three-note fall to the tonic. Referring to the *Lebewohl* motive is not inappropriate in this context, for these songs represent more than anything Maria Stuart's farewell to the world. A further descending pattern it seems reasonable to invoke is that of the lament, particularly in the fourth song, 'Abschied von der Welt', throughout which there is a falling piano figure. There is also some sharing of material between songs; the contour of the opening two lines of 'Abschied von Frankreich' is returned to in 'Abschied von der Welt', with some variation at the beginning and the end. The fourth bar, though, is an exact copy. So, where in the first song she said, 'Ade, mein fröhlich Frankenland', in the fourth she says: 'Mein Herz erstarb für irdisches Begehren' (Example 1:13). The death of her heart to earthly pleasure might have been caused by her departure from France.

The central song of the Maria Stuart lieder, in every sense, is the third, 'An die Königin Elisabeth'. Mary is writing to her sister, pleading with her to change her destiny. Her determination to break free might explain why this is the one song of the cycle not in E, but in A minor.[47] As in 'Abschied von der Welt', it is punctuated by a distinctive piano figure, one marked by dotted rhythms. And as in 'Abschied von Frankreich' and the final song of the Kulmann lieder, it uses the image of a boat as a symbol of escape and deliverance from earthly suffering. Here the boat is still in harbour, being kept from departing by a storm. Heaven's bright countenance is darkened by night ('Des Himmels heit'res Antlitz nachtumgraut'). Mary claims not to fear her sister, but fate, which often tears trusted sails ('Doch des Schicksals Walten / Zerreisst das Segel oft, dem wir vertraut'). The vocal line borrows for the image of the boat restrained to harbour the rhythm of the piano figure, and straining at the harmonies like a ship pulling at its mooring ropes in a storm. The final verse (Example 1:14) includes the first verbal repetition, of 'vor euch nicht', and, for the first time,

Example 1:13a 'Abschied von Frankreich', bb. 1–4

Example 1:13b 'Abschied von der Welt', bb. 1–5

Example 1:14 'An die Königin Elisabeth', bb. 20–31

the vocal line sings two crotchets, on 'Schwester'. The piano increases the sense of entreaty by a swelling three-quaver figure that both supports and slightly rushes the voice's arch. It matches the following line, about the force of fate, more directly. The final words, 'dem wir vertraut', are also repeated, lending extra emphasis to Mary's attempt to convince Elizabeth of their sisterly bond.

The remaining Maria Stuart songs are prayers, first hoping for the safety of her son; and last a plea for God to rescue her. Mary's prayer is given musical expression of a directness far removed from the earlier cycles. The initial descent of a second followed by a fifth becomes the head motive for the first half. Initially it seems as though we are back in A minor, but we quickly move to the dominant of E – entreaties to Elizabeth have proved

Example 1:15 'Gebet', bb. 12–23

useless, God is the only remaining hope. The vocal line rises sequentially from G sharp up to D, as the bass line moves stepwise; the music yearns for the tonic as Mary does for salvation. Her lament turns around a-b-c-b-a, but release is not given (Example 1:15). The vocal line ends with an interrupted cadence on 'und rette du mich!' – 'Rescue me!' The incarcerated queen is abandoned, for which the piano's resolution of the opening phrase onto the tonic is little consolation.

The historical figure of Maria Stuart of course cannot be saved but only memorialized. Her final prayer, though, might represent the individual's hope for redemption. It might strike us (if in a fanciful mood) that the incarcerated queen resembles the institutionalized composer. Certainly, Schumann seems to have had a strong personal investment in the idea of redemption. Its expression here, though, in the intimate context of the lied, is not often noted. Redemption is the business of the large-scale works, of the triumphant symphonic finale or the celebratory chorus. In other words, the individual can pray for redemption but the collective can grant it. This tension between the individual and the collective runs through writings on Schumann: it is often expressed through other binaries, such as the subjective and the objective, the intimate and the public, song and chorus. As is highlighted by the shared theme of redemption the distance between such poles is sometimes small. After all, how could we have a collective without individuals?

We can still therefore give song and the notion of subjective, individual expression a central place in Schumann's late style. However, the idea of song the late lieder put forward is slightly altered from our usual conception. Through the more declamatory style of vocal writing, simple ternary forms and distilled piano accompaniments, they have lost their lyrical aspect in the conventional sense. Perhaps this suggests that the composer's psyche has changed: that the subjects of these songs are different from those of the earlier cycles or that there is an expressive failure written into the musical style. Or maybe it is that their expression has changed, in recognition of a new decade and a particular poetic manner. I suggested at the beginning of this chapter that a sense of farewell pervades the late lieder. Maybe, though, it is not something within the lieder. Maybe it is that we, as listeners, have to bid farewell to our old image of Schumann, to greet him anew.

Notes

1. On the political overtones of the songs see Ulrich Mahlert, *Fortschritt und Kunstlied: Späte Lieder Robert Schumanns in Licht der liedästhetischen Diskussion ab 1848* (Munich and Salzburg: Katzbichler, 1983).

2. Further discussion of the late songs will be found in Jon W. Finson, *Robert Schumann: The Book of Songs* (Cambridge, Mass.: Harvard University Press).

3. The phrase is John Clare's, from 'How can I forget', one of his late poems written while an inmate of the Northampton General Lunatic Asylum (from 1841 to his death in 1864). *John Clare: Selected Poems*, ed. Jonathan Bate (London: Faber and Faber, 2003), p. 299.

4. Letter to Kistner, 26 August 1850, cited in Beate Julia Perrey, *Schumann's 'Dichterliebe' and Early Romantic Poetics: Fragmentation of Desire* (Cambridge: Cambridge University Press, 2002), p. 151.

5. On the reception of Lenau's poetry during the second half of the nineteenth century, see Rainer Hochheim, *Nikolaus Lenau: Geschichte seiner Wirkung, 1850–1918* (Frankfurt: Lang, 1982).

6. In Lenau's lifetime two volumes of his poetry were published: *Gedichte*, 1822; and *Neuere Gedichte*, 1838. Schumann used the later edition for his songs. See *Robert Schumann: Neue Ausgabe sämtlicher Werke: Literarische Vorlagen der ein- und mehrstimmigen Lieder, Gesänge und Deklamationen*, ed. Helmut Schanze, Serie VII: Supplemente Band 2 (Mainz: Schott, 2002), pp. 279–80.

7. Daverio, *Robert Schumann*, p. 463.

8. The debate began with Arthur Komar's essay 'The music of *Dichterliebe*: the whole and its parts' and Allen Forte's commentary on Heinrich Schenker's

graphs in the Norton Critical Edition of *Dichterliebe* (New York: Norton, 1971), pp. 63–94 and 95–106; which was critiqued by Joseph Kerman in 'How we got into analysis and how to get out', *Critical Inquiry* 7 (1980), 311–31. An overview of subsequent readings alongside her own interpretation is given in Beate Julia Perrey, *Schumann's 'Dichterliebe'* a critique of her approach is given by Berthold Hoeckner in 'Paths through *Dichterliebe*', *19th-Century Music* 30 (2006), 65–80.

9. Graham Johnson suggests that another figure the *Lenaulieder* might have been a kind of Requiem for was Chopin, who had died the previous year. The accompanimental figuration to 'Einsamkeit', he notes, is similar to that of Chopin's Etude in E flat minor, op. 10/vi. Programme booklet to *The Songs of Robert Schumann*, vol. 1 (Hyperion, 1996), p. 47.

10. For such a consideration see Klaus Velten, 'Robert Schumanns Lenau-Vertonungen op. 90', *Robert Schumann: Philologische, analytische, sozial- und rezeptionsgeschichtliche Aspekte* (Saarbrücken: Saarbrücker Druckerei, 1998), pp. 90–6.

11. David Ferris argues that cycles create a 'provocative context' for the interpretation of the earlier song collections; see *Schumann's Eichendorff 'Liederkreis' and the Genre of the Romantic Cycle* (Oxford: Oxford University Press, 2000).

12. Jensen, *Schumann*, p. 297.

13. On which see John Daverio, 'Schumann's "new genre for the concert hall"', *Schumann and his World*, ed. R. Larry Todd (Princeton: Princeton University Press, 1994), p. 139.

14. Perrey gives a rich reading of the two songs in *Schumann's 'Dichterliebe'*, pp. 141–62.

15. Harald Krebs describes 'metrical dissonance' hanging over the end of the song 'like the brooding clouds mentioned in Lenau's text'; *Fantasy Pieces: Metrical Dissonance in the Music of Robert Schumann* (Oxford: Oxford University Press, 1999), p. 164.

16. Perrey, *Schumann's 'Dichterliebe'*, p. 158. Her emphasis.

17. Perrey, *Schumann's 'Dichterliebe'*, p. 159.

18. Perrey, *Schumann's 'Dichterliebe'*, p. 162.

19. Richard Kramer mentions tears as a symbol for the love act, giving examples from *Dichterliebe* (although not, interestingly, 'Ich hab' im Traum geweinet') in *Distant Cycles: Schubert and Conceiving of Song* (Chicago: University of Chicago Press, 1994), p. 127 n. 5. See also Lawrence Kramer, '"Little pearl teardrops": Schubert, Schumann, and the tremulous body of romantic song', *Music, Sensation and Sensuality*, ed. Linda Phyllis Austern (New York: Routledge, 2002), pp. 57–74.

20. On two of Freud's interpretations of tears, see Tom Lutz, *Crying: The Natural and Cultural History of Tears* (London: Norton, 1999), pp. 124 and 216.

21. See Slavoj Žižek, 'Robert Schumann: anti-humanist', *Plague of Fantasies* (London: Verso, 1997), p. 202.

22. Sigmund Freud, 'On transience' (1916); for further discussion see Matthew von Unwerth, *Freud's Requiem: Mourning, Memory and the Invisible History of a Summer Walk* (New York: Continuum, 2005).

23. Adam Phillips, *Darwin's Worms* (London: Faber and Faber, 1999), p. 26.

24. The phenomenon of being moved to tears before visual art has recently been discussed by James Elkins, *Pictures and Tears: A History of People who have Cried in Front of Paintings* (New York: Routledge, 2004).

25. For example, see Lawrence Kramer, '*Carnaval*, cross-dressing, and the woman in the mirror', *Musicology and Difference*, ed. Ruth A. Solie (Berkeley: University of California Press, 1993), pp. 305–25; and Carolyn Abbate on *Carnaval* and disenchantment in *In Search of Opera* (Princeton: Princeton University Press, 2001), pp. 240–2.

26. Perrey, *Schumann's 'Dichterliebe'*, p. 113.

27. On Schumann's response to Lenau's poems see Albrecht Riethmüller, 'Lenaus *Husarenlieder* als Klavierlieder Schumanns (op. 117)', *Schumann und seine Dichter: Bericht über das 4. International Schumann-Symposium* (London: Schott, 1993), pp. 43–54.

28. *Jung Volkers Lied*, the fourth song from op. 125, was also composed in 1851.

29. Recorded after a visit from Ullrich on 26 February 1847; see Robert Schumann, *Tagebücher, Band II: 1836–1854*, ed. Gerd Nauhaus (Leipzig: VEB Deutscher Verlag, 1987), p. 416.

30. Comparing 'Herzeleid' with Berlioz's *La Mort d'Ophélie* (1842) is instructive. On Berlioz's setting as apotheosis of female vocality, see Heather Hadlock, 'Berlioz, Ophelia, and Feminist Hermeneutics', *Berlioz: Past, Present, Future – Bicententary Essays*, ed. Peter Bloom (Rochester, N.Y.: University of Rochester Press, 2003), pp. 123–34.

31. On redemption in the Second Symphony see Michael Steinberg, *Listening to Reason: Culture, Subjectivity, and Nineteenth-Century Music* (Princeton: Princeton University Press, 2004), pp. 129–31.

32. Ruth Solie, 'The gendered self in Schumann's *Frauenliebe*', *Music and Text: Critical Inquiries*, ed. Stephen Paul Scher (Cambridge: Cambridge University Press, 1992), pp. 219–40; here p. 220.

33. Jonathan Dunsby, 'Song', *The Cambridge Companion to Schumann*, ed. Beate Perrey (Cambridge: Cambridge University Press, 2007); and Michel Schneider, *La tombée du jour: Schumann* (Paris: Seuil, 1989), p. 55.

34. Schumann set quite a few texts by female poets (Lily Bernard, Catherine Fanshawe, Wilhelmine Lorenz, Marianne von Willemer), which is something that seems to have gone unnoticed despite the amount of scholarly energy spent on interpreting gender relations in *Frauenliebe und Leben*.

35. For further discussion see Kristina Muxfeldt, '*Frauenliebe* now and then', *19th-Century Music* 25 (2001), 27–48; here 40.

36. He asked Brahms for a copy of her poetry to be sent to him in the asylum; see letter of 20[?] March 1855, *Clara Schumann – Johannes Brahms, Briefe aus den Jahren 1853–1896*, ed. Berthold Litzmann (Hildesheim: Georg Olms, 1989), I, p. 103.

37. On Schumann's relationship with Kulmann, see Olga Loseva, 'Neues über Elisabeth Kulmann', *Schumann und seine Dichter*, ed. Matthias Wendt (Mainz: Schott, 1993), pp. 77–86.

38. Matthew Head, 'Cultural meaning for women composers: Charlotte 'Minna' Brandes and the beautiful dead in the German enlightenment', *Journal of the American Musicological Society* 57:2 (2004), 231–84. There is a question over whether Kulmann's teacher and publisher Karl Friedrich von Großheinrich had a hand in her prolific output.

39. All translations from the Kulmann and Maria Stuart lieder are taken from Richard Stokes's translations for the CD booklet to *The Songs of Robert Schumann*, vol. 3 (Hyperion, CDJ33103, 1999).

40. On their childlike simplicity see Ulrich Mahlert, '"… die Spuren einer himmlischen Erscheinung zurücklassend": Zu Schumanns Liedern nach Gedichten von Elisabeth Kulmann op. 104', *Schumann in Düsseldorf: Werke, Texte, Interpretationen*, ed. Bernhard Appel (Mainz: Schott, 1993), pp. 119–40.

41. The most famous bird image in Schumann's late works is found not in song, but in a piano piece, 'Vogel als Prophet' from *Waldszenen*. For further discussion see Chapter 6 and Laura Tunbridge, 'Piano music II: afterimages', *The Cambridge Companion to Schumann*, ed. Beate Perrey (Cambridge: Cambridge University Press, 2007).

42. On what this *Grauen* may mean see David Ferris, 'Was will dieses Grau'n bedeuten?': Schumann's *Zwielicht* and Daverio's 'incomprehensibility topos', *The Journal of Musicology* 22:1 (2005), 131–53; here 139.

43. Friedrich Hinrich complained that Schumann's choice of text from the late 1840s onwards became increasingly 'mannered in the most melancholy sense of the word'. The examples he gave were from the *Drei Gedichte aus den Waldliedern von Pfarrius* op. 119 and the *Fünf heitere Gesänge* op. 125. 'Zur Würdigung Richard Wagners', *Neue Zeitschrift für Musik* 39:19 (1854), 200.

44. For a recent biography see John Guy's *'My Heart is my Own': The Life of Mary Queen of Scots* (London: Harper Perennial, 2004).

45. Hans Joachim Zimmermann, 'Die Gedichte der Königin Maria Stuart. Gisbert Vincke, Robert Schumann und eine sentimentale Tradition', *Archiv für das Studium der neueren Sprachen und Literaturen* 214 (1977), 294–324.

46. On Schumann's setting more generally see Joachim Draheim, 'Bedeutung und Eigenart der Maria Stuart Lieder', *Archiv für das Studium der neueren Sprachen und Literaturen* 214 (1977), 325–7. Given the wrangling over implicit value judgements in the case of *Dichterliebe*, it is striking that commentators approach *Frauenliebe* and the Kulmann and Maria Stuart lieder unproblematically as

cycles. If anything, the recurrence of music in *Frauenliebe* is considered to increase its aesthetic worth. Perhaps the lack of concern over their status as a cycle is that it is so obvious in terms of their subject matter; perhaps a woman's life is unquestionably cyclic.

47. On the songs' key relationships see Edward Rooker Phillips, 'The Mary Stuart songs of Robert Schumann: key as an aspect of cycle', *Canadian-Association-of-University-Schools-of-Music-Journal/Association-Canadienne-des-Ecoles-Universitaires-de-Musique-journal* 9:2 (1979), 82–7, 91–9.

2 | The sound of legend

'Wo bin ich? Ist's Wahrheit, ist's ein Traum?' ('Where am I? Is this reality; is it a dream?') (Example 2:1). The rose's question, on waking to find herself transformed into a human in Schumann's *Der Rose Pilgerfahrt*, encapsulates on many different levels the musical, dramatic, and contextual issues raised by the large-scale choral works completed in the 1850s.

Based on a poem by Moritz Horn, *Der Rose Pilgerfahrt* tells the tale of a rose who wants to become human, to experience the joys of love and motherhood. The fairy queen warns her of love's sorrows but eventually accedes to her request, giving her a magic rose that will bring joy as long as she keeps it, but death should she lose it. Elves work their magic as she sleeps, much as Ariel and the spirits hover around the slumbering Faust at the beginning of Goethe's Part II. More importantly, the tenor's narration of the rose's transformation creates several frames around her: the first is harmonic, by the prefacing modulation from E flat to G major, one of many examples of Schumann's predilection for – as Eduard Krüger called it – 'the evil mediant'.[1] The second is stylistic, in that the tenor's vocal style predicts the rose's '*rezitativischer Gesang*'; a mingling of recitative and arioso that Schumann had first experimented with in *Das Paradies und die Peri*, earning him some critical disapproval but also signalling the proximity of his late vocal writing to Wagner. The third has to do with the organization of the libretto into scenes of 'action' linked by explanatory narrative, creating a kind of *tableau* effect fundamental to the ballads and of consequence for the dramatic trajectory (and perhaps to the generic categorization) of the whole. The fourth might be thought the frame that frames the frames: Schumann's careful balancing of the naïve or sentimental with more sophisticated and progressive elements. Thus more 'modern' mediant and chromatic harmonies and *rezitativischer Gesang* consort with the very simple melodic and harmonic style of other sections, such as the rose's next entry. This mixture of progressive and conservative elements indicates that, while the poetic themes of the oratorio might seem deliberately backward-looking, their purpose was to create a new future; an aim characteristic of mid-century historicism and nationalism.

Example 2:1   *Der Rose Pilgerfahrt*

Schumann described *Der Rose Pilgerfahrt* as 'more rustic, more German' than *Das Paradies und die Peri*. That it is more German is undeniable; *Peri* was based on a translation of *Lalla Rookh*, a poem set in a fabulous Orient by the Irishman Thomas Moore. *Der Rose Pilgerfahrt*, on the other hand, takes place in the German Romantic forest, whose supernatural inhabitants might be counterparts to the *Peri's* fairies, but which belongs more firmly to the *Volkstümlichkeit* sensibility. A brief introduction to the latter will be useful here.

The German Romantic forest was sometimes a forbidding and forbidden place. Goethe's *Erlkönig* might prise sons from their father's arms; children in search of food might, like Hansel and Gretel, lose their way; struggling hunters might ask the devil to cast them magic bullets, as in Weber's *Der Freischütz*. But, as in the paintings of Moritz von Schwind or Schumann's *Genoveva*, the forest could also be a source of innocence and family values: in *Der Rose Pilgerfahrt*, the rose falls in love with the forester's son, with whom she has a child. Although – as historian Robert Pogue Harrison cautions – it is a cliché to describe the Germanic forest as representing sanctuaries of origins, race and community (or, alternatively, as the source of nightmares), its presence in the stories collected by Jacob and Wilhelm Grimm to Schumann's *Der Rose Pilgerfahrt* attests to its 'mystique' in the

Romantic imagination.[2] However, for the Grimms and many other writers, tales of the forest were not simply to do with perpetuating tradition: they also reflected long-standing philological interests. The mystique of the forest, as Harrison points out, was thus entwined with Romantic historiography and its attempt 'to liberate the past from the grand narrative schemes of classical historiography and to resurrect the inner *life* of the past, in all its concrete fullness'.[3] In and through the forest and its legends, the 'spirit' of the past and the nation could be found with the people rather than their rulers, with their distant wars, banquets and courtly fashions.

Perhaps most importantly, the forest and its inhabitants spoke German. The idea that there was a natural basis for language, as well as customs, was fundamental to claims of German nationhood in the early nineteenth century. Johann Gottfried Herder argued that the nation should be defined in terms of its ethnic and linguistic features. Thus Vienna in 1815 was not only the site for the Congress proclaiming Germany's liberation from France; in the *Wollzeile*, a street near St Stephen's Cathedral, a group of artists, scholars, book dealers and antiquarians (including Jacob Grimm) founded the *Wollzeilergesellschaft*, a society dedicated to the collection and publication of the oral traditions of the German people, including folk songs, rhymes, fairy-tales, superstitions and proverbs.[4] According to Johann Gottlieb Fichte, the *Ur-Volk* 'speaks a language that is alive down to its first emanation from natural force, while the other Germanic tribes speak a language that only twitches at its surface, but is dead at the root'.[5] Hopes of a reunified country inspired a kind of cultural nationalism, to which the notion of the *Volk* and their ways of communicating traditions and legends were key: for example, Arnim von Achim claimed that projects such as his collection of folk tales would not have been necessary had the country been unified.[6]

The 'natural force' of the *Volk* drew most sustenance from the Middle Ages, which for many exemplified the greatest flourishing of German culture, when the Empire was last united. While on one level medievalism reflected a conservative and particularist agenda, its adoption in the service of the nationalist cause (most obviously through festivals of German culture) meant that it also served a purpose for liberals.[7] Although the 1848–9 revolutions might have been an attempt to overthrow traditional and conservative political systems within the German states in favour of a unified, liberal nation, the period immediately afterwards is generally agreed to have seen a retrenchment to conservative values. The 1850s are often described as reactionary, and perhaps for that reason tend to be overlooked by histories, but Hans-Ulrich Wehler has argued that this decade and the following one were breakthrough years for Germany's twin national and industrial revolutions, that deserve closer attention.[8]

In terms of German musical culture, historicist and nationalist concerns were most obviously expressed at the mid-century through regional music festivals and music societies.[9] Both were conceived as a means by which to establish bourgeois identity and national unity – aspirations with which Schumann, as music director in Düsseldorf, and as organizer of the 1853 Lower Rhine Music Festival, was directly engaged in cultivating.[10] 'Chorus and orchestra lift us beyond ourselves', he claimed in a letter to Carl Meinardus.[11] In certain ways all the choral works from the 1850s can be understood as expressions of cultural nationalism, with its associated emphasis on the construction of community spirit.

To start, there is the great care Schumann took over the construction of his libretti, often to the frustration of his collaborators – especially Richard Pohl, who worked with him on *Des Sängers Fluch* and on three projects that came to nothing: an oratorio based on the life of Martin Luther, and the adaptation of Goethe's *Hermann und Dorothea* and Schiller's *Die Braut von Messina*. As important as the dramatic structure, for Schumann, were the poetic attributes of the text, all of which (with the exception of the Mass and Requiem) were in German. For example, he wanted to retain the original metre of Uhland's verse for *Des Sängers Fluch* and for the text of the Luther oratorio to be written in metrical verse, to create a 'volksthümlich-alt-deutsche' effect.[12] Indeed Schumann often consciously invoked *Volkstümlichkeit* aesthetics and recognized their nationalist overtones. Thus the projected *Singspiel* of *Hermann und Dorothea* was to be a simple, *volkstümlich*, German work ('Das Ganze müßte in der Musik, wie Poesie, in einfacher, volkstümlich deutscher Werke gehalten werden').[13] Likewise, the Luther oratorio was to be *volkstümliches* throughout, so that both peasants and the bourgeoisie (*Bauer und Bürgen*) would understand it.[14]

Schumann's concern for the *volkstümlich* aspect of the libretto was matched by his plans for the music. Of the Luther project he wrote:

This oratorio should be popular in its style; something intelligible to everybody, townsman and peasant alike, and thus corresponding to the character of the hero, who was a great man of the people. I will compose the music in the same vein, making it simple and touching, appealing to the listener by its rhythm and melody without anything artificial, complicated, or contrapuntal.[15]

He responded dismissively to Pohl's suggestion that the Luther oratorio should take place over three consecutive evenings; not only was it too ambitious, it was not in the character of the Reformer. Instead, it should value concision, strength, and clarity ('Kürze, Kraft und Klarheit').[16] He asked Pohl to provide openings for choruses wherever possible, with double choruses in the final movements of each part. The model he advocated was Handel's *Israel in Egypt*, which Schumann described as his 'ideal choral work'.[17]

While the influence of *Israel in Egypt* on the Luther project probably centred on its extensive use of choruses rather than Handel's musical style, it is worth acknowledging Schumann's appreciation of the composer, who is often overlooked in histories of nineteenth-century choral music in favour of J. S. Bach. As a student Schumann had seen his law professor, A. F. J. Thibaut, moved to tears when playing Handel at the keyboard – a formative experience that is supposed to have encouraged his decision to study music. And while Schumann was a great admirer of Bach's St John Passion, and conducted it on several occasions, during the 1840s he also studied and conducted most of Handel's oratorios.[18] His respect for Handel was shared by some of his contemporaries, including Mendelssohn, who had hunted out the manuscript for *Israel in Egypt* while in London in the 1830s and invented an organ accompaniment for it.

The greatest significance of *Israel in Egypt* for Schumann, though, probably resided in its tableau-like structure. During the nineteenth century, the oratorio's division into passages of narration and scenes of 'action' (the parting of the Red Sea and various plagues) was reflected in its performance with *tableaux vivants*, which recreated the various scenes from the oratorio with living people. Mendelssohn arranged such a performance in 1833, reporting to his sister that it proved very effective. Schumann did not see *Israel in Egypt*, but he did attend other *tableaux vivants* performances, and even proposed that some could accompany his *Requiem für Mignon*, op. 98b.[19] Further impetus for a tableau-like structure to his choral works might have come from the vogue for illustrated ballad books following the success of Eugen Neureuther's *Randzeichnungen zu Goethes Balladen* (1828), and from engravings based on popular dramatic and literary works, such as the interpretations of Goethe's *Faust* by Moritz Retzsch and Eugène Delacroix, among others.[20] A close link between pictures and words was also established through the illustration of music examples in journals and on the title pages of scores; see, for example, Richter's illustrations for *Album für die Jugend*, the Düsseldorf painter Theodor Minter's design for the title page of *Der Rose Pilgerfahrt*, and the first editions of the four choral ballades.

In musical terms, the influence of *tableaux* might be reflected in the 'frames' proposed at the beginning of this chapter with regard to the scene from *Der Rose Pilgerfahrt*. Often, narrative passages are devoted to describing the events taking place; perhaps as a result, as much time is given to visual details as to the plot. Sometimes that results in musical pictorialism, such as the depiction by violas and cellos of a galloping horse at the opening of the fourth scene of *Der Königssohn*. On other occasions it is more dramaturgical. In the first ballad of *Vom Pagen und der Königstochter*, for instance, the narrator describes the princess's response to the page's declaration of love: 'She did not say yes! She did not say no!' and, for a prolonged moment, the couple stay transfixed in their pose, waiting for her to alight from her horse. At moments like these, emphasis is almost placed more on the narrator than on the characters; or, to put it slightly differently, on description rather than enactment – an inherently visual approach.[21]

Incidentally, that *Vom Pagen und der Königstochter* was made up of four separate ballads increases the sense of the work's division into *tableaux*, something further emphasized by the key scheme of the whole. In broad terms, the first ballad moves from E minor to major; the second – in which the King cross-questions the page and then kills him – is in C sharp minor; the third – the transformation of the page's remains by water nymphs – has an A major key signature but is strongly coloured by E minor, not least because of the bass pedal on E that lasts for the first twenty bars. There is a later move to C sharp major, followed by F sharp major – both of these keys again being established by the use of lengthy pedal points. The fourth ballad begins in B major, with a transformed version of the first ballad's opening melody, representing the return to the court. A description of the princess, sadly preparing for her wedding to another, is cordoned off from the surrounding tonality by a dominant pedal. The interruption to the ceremony – of which more later – brings about a series of rapid harmonic moves, eventually ending in E minor. Each ballad, then, is given a strong harmonic identity, enhanced by the use of pedals, which further contribute to a sense of each scene being framed and made to keep its pose.

The tableau-like organization of *Der Rose Pilgerfahrt* and *Vom Pagen und der Königstochter*, and the possible interchange between Schumann's musico-dramatic conception and contemporaneous visual entertainments, points to an aspect of the choral music that has been problematic for critics – its mixture of genres. *Der Rose Pilgerfahrt* is the only piece that the composer consistently referred to as an oratorio. He described *Das Paradies und die Peri*, written six years earlier, as being in 'a new genre for the concert hall' – somewhere between opera and oratorio.[22] And the three parts of *Szenen aus Goethe's Faust* offer a similar combination of types: Part III (1844) is most like a straightforward oratorio while Part I (1849) is closer in many ways to opera, and Part II (1849) is somewhere in between.[23] Even the religious choral works (including the planned Luther oratorio) were said by Schumann to belong in both church and concert hall.[24]

Along similar lines, the four choral ballades were considered by Berthold Litzmann to be substitutes for opera. In order to introduce the narrative techniques of these larger works, and to give a further example of Schumann's willingness to create hybrid genres, a brief digression is needed. In 1851–2, Schumann composed two 'declamation ballades' for speaker and piano: a setting of Hebbel's 'Ballade vom Haideknaben', and 'Die Flüchtlinge', a translation of Shelley's 'The Fugitives'.[25] Schumann described these pieces as a 'kind of composition that arguably does not yet exist'.[26] Their hyperbole is at odds with most of Schumann's vocal music, which rarely makes explicit what can be implied. Within his oeuvre the declamation ballades were not entirely without precedent, however, falling somewhere between the orchestral melodramatic music to Byron's *Manfred*, the declamatory style of some of the late lieder, the unaccompanied choruses published as *Romanzen und Balladen* (opp. 67, 75, 145 and 146) and the four choral ballades.

In 'Ballade vom Haideknaben', the moorland boy dreams of being beaten on his way to the village: his master does not believe him but sure enough, the boy is robbed and killed by the shepherd's lad he meets on the road. The boy's premonition is conveyed musically by recurrences of a distinctive chromatic descent in the piano accompaniment; first heard in the introduction as a dream. The transition to reality occurs as the shepherd's lad sits the boy down and asks him to recount his dream, with the foreboding aside, 'Ich träumte – Gott soll mich verdammen, / Trifft's nicht mit deinem zusammen!' ('I dreamed too – God damn me if our dreams / Don't turn out to be the same!'). As he says these words the piano, which has been playing only a fragment of its chromatic descent since the introduction, now gives its first bar again in full (Example 2:2). A prolonged tremolando dominant pedal portrays the sinister whispering leaves and sad murmuring stream around them; the boy reveals that he dreamt of a man: 'was it me?' his companion asks. From this point on the chromatic figure vanishes. It is left to birds to explain what happened; ravens describe with glee what the murderer did, while doves are paralysed by fright and can only recount the boy's tears and pleas for his life.

As in Schubert's 'Erlkönig', Schumann's 'Ballade vom Haideknaben' privileges the poems' dramatic trajectories over their strophic structures. It embeds the storyteller in the temporal performance of the text: the repetitions of the chromatic figure track both the narrator's foresight and the acting out of the tale. The ballad thus plays with the time it takes the narrator

Example 2:2 'Ballade vom Haideknaben', bb. 62–71

to tell his story and for it to be heard.[27] But there is another way that these ballads play with time, for they evoke another era.

Such temporal play is extended in the choral ballads, which make the historicist implications of what Adorno referred to as 'the sound of legend' in Schumann's music more explicit.[28] Each has a medieval setting and fantastical elements. The division between courtly life and the people – of the inner life of the past – is of fundamental concern, in keeping with the *volkstümlich* ideals described earlier. Indeed, the four choral ballads have been considered to respond to the uprisings of 1848–9 and their aftermath.[29] Thus, according to Daverio, *Der Königssohn* addresses 'the question of a monarch's divine right to rule'; *Des Sängers Fluch* is concerned with 'tensions between populist demands and monarchical prerogatives'; *Vom Pagen und der Königstochter* is about 'conflicts between bourgeois and aristocratic classes'; and *Das Glück von Edenhall* represents 'the eternal return of repressive regimes'.[30] Each includes a paean to German art and brotherhood, sometimes alongside revolutionary cries of 'Freiheit!' and 'Vaterland!'

Perhaps the strongest indication of the political bias to Schumann's choice of texts is that nearly all were taken from Ludwig Uhland (1787–1862): the exception is *Vom Pagen und der Königstochter*, which was based on Emmanuel Geibel.[31] An outspoken leftist and enthusiastic member of the National Assembly in Frankfurt, Uhland has been called the poetic representative of the Wars of Liberation. His taste for medieval literature resulted in essays on the poetry of Northern France and on Walther von der Vogelweide, a collection of poems entitled *Alte hoch- und niederdeutsche Volkslieder*, and the study of folk-songs. Drawing on such research, and cannily supported by the publisher Cotta, he became one of the leading authors of Romantic ballads.

In a similar manner to the Ossianic poetry popular in the 1830s, Uhland's verse reflects his investment in the genius of the *Volk*, taking folk-tales and the medieval era as models for quasi-Christian purity and harmony.[32] It also promotes an idealized sense of community, locating national consciousness within the people, rather than their rulers.[33] Schumann described *Der Königssohn* as being well suited to mass performance (*Massenaufführung*) for it consists largely of folk choruses. However, from within the collective of the choral ballades can be heard occasional questioning voices.

For example, in *Des Sängers Fluch* the feared king commands visiting minstrels to sing for his queen; they comply with a 'graceful' Provençal song about youthful love, a 'forceful' ballad about a king being killed by his brother, and a 'passionate' duet celebrating freedom and Fatherland.[34] During the second ballad the king fears that the secret of his own route to the throne has been discovered; by the duet he suspects treason. But the queen entreats him to let them sing once more: a song she loved when she was young, called 'Renunciation' ('Entsagung'). The meaning is clear. Forgetting themselves, queen and minstrel sing together:

Ja! Die Zeit ist hingeflogen,
Die Erinn'rung weichet nie
(Though time may have passed,
The memory never faded)

Abandoning his ballad, the minstrel declares his love in an expansive lyrical melody, his accompanying harpist becoming ever more frantic, partly in recognition of his emotional state but also because the young man's life is in danger. Enraged, the king murders the minstrel. At this point, revelations about the past inspired by the ballads are turned against the court; the harpist curses them never to hear music again, never to see plants grow. Years later the castle is no longer standing and the gardens are barren.

Worse still, no song remembers the king's name: lost and forgotten –
that is the minstrel's curse ('Versunken und vergessen. Das ist des Sängers
Fluch').

In *Vom Pagen und der Königstochter*, another distant voice upsets the
court's stability. As already outlined, a young page is executed for loving the
king's daughter. His remains are thrown into the sea where nymphs persuade
a Merman to fashion his bones and golden hair into a harp. The princess
is to be married to another; preparations for the wedding are interrupted,
however, by the sound of the Merman outside the gates. He commands:
'Hey, be quiet! Noble castle by the sea, listen to the Merman's harp' ('Hei
leise! Feines Schloß am Meer, horch auf des Meermann's Harfen!'; marked
in the score 'aus der ferne'). The female chorus comment:

Hear! How up from the sea it surges,
O sweet, sad sound,
It creeps so softly through the Night
Upwards to the halls
It creeps so softly into the ear of the bride;
To her it is as if out of the depths.
It is as if out of the depths with greatest effort
The sweetest lover calls her.
(Horch! Wie's empor von dem Meere wallt!
O süßes, trauriges Schallen,
Es schleicht so sacht durch die Nacht
Herauf in die Hallen.
Es schleicht so sacht in das Ohr der Braut;
Ihr ist, als ob aus der Tiefe,
Er ist als ob aus der Tiefe mit Allgewallt
Der lieblichste Buhle sie riefe.)

The princess recognizes in the sound of the Merman's harp the voice of
her beloved.[35] As in 'Ballade vom Haideknaben', though, it is the return of
previous music that signals the narrative's outcome: once she has recalled
how handsome the page was, we hear the melody that had accompanied the
transformation of his remains into a harp. The chorus brings the ballade to a
close by describing the sound of the Merman's harp fading away ('Morning
dawned grey in the window, the Merman's harp faded away'; 'Im Saal liegt
bleich die Braut, ihr ist das Herz zersprungen; der Morgen trüb' in die Fenster
graut, des Meermann's Harf' ist verklungen'). If the harp is a mediator
between worldly and heavenly realms, it is here made all the more spectral
by not being heard at all.

The disruptive voices of the minstrel and the Merman's harp have been taken to indicate Schumann's disenchantment with the political situation of the 1850s.[36] Such interpretations, though, tend to focus on individual utterances as the source for the composer's 'true' voice – a tendency that, as discussed further in other chapters, implicitly dates Schumann as belonging to an earlier generation. He is often depicted as a solitary Romantic, withdrawn from the world and attuned only to 'Stimmen aus der Ferne'.[37] Such an attitude might have been in vogue in the 1830s and early 1840s, but was out of line with post-revolutionary Germany, as is particularly apparent when Schumann is compared to Wagner. The two composers shared many interests; from medieval settings and the fate of German art to an investment in the idea of redemption. Several critics have noted similarities between *Szenen aus Goethes Faust* and *Tannhäuser*, while *Genoveva* and *Lohengrin* premiered in the same year.[38] However, Schumann seems to stand as a kind of Wolfram to Wagner's Tannhäuser – left behind in Germany while Wagner was exiled to Switzerland after the revolutions, Schumann appears more dutiful and, ultimately, less exciting.

Schumann's relationship with Wagner was, of course, much more complex than that. After attending the Dresden premiere of *Tannhäuser* on 19 October 1845, he complained to Mendelssohn about the score's technical inadequacies – from voiceleading and four-part chorale harmonization to parallel fifths and octaves. On hearing a revised version of the work and meeting the composer the following month, though, his opinion began to change. *Tannhäuser* and other of Wagner's operas, he concluded, were much more successful on stage than on the page. The two composers met while Schumann was working on *Genoveva*; Wagner found him taciturn and unwilling to listen to his advice, despite his experience in preparing his own libretti.[39] However, Schumann read *Oper und Drama* with interest in 1851, describing it to Liszt as very important ('sehr bedeutend'), but saying he was amazed that Wagner did not mention *Fidelio*.[40] He thought less of 'Kunstwerk der Zukunft' (read in 1853), commenting that it was a contradiction in terms; the best artwork of the future, in his opinion, was the masterwork ('Das beste 'Zukunftswerk' ist eben das Meisterwerk').[41] Around the same time he complained that Wagner's music lacked a sense of form and melodiousness, and that it was often almost 'dilettantisch, gehaltlos und widerwärtig': dilettantist, empty and disgusting.[42] Why did there have to be so many performances of his works, when there were many German masterworks that could be put on instead?

Schumann's objections to Wagner no doubt reflect his distaste for critics' support of the composer, and respond to the growing animosity he himself felt from the musical press. Had Schumann composed another (more successful) opera after *Genoveva*, the situation might have been different; his focus on choral music, though, reinforced the sense that he was writing for a conservative audience rather than devising music for the future. Despite the similarities noted between the *Faustszenen* and *Tannhäuser*, and the declamatory vocal writing of many passages in the choral ballades, it is noticeable that the choral music from the 1850s is decidedly un-Wagnerian in its strongly characterized accompanimental figures and instrumental themes, and clearly delineated key schemes. Rather than using myth to reinvigorate German art – as Wagner claimed – the stories of the choral ballades and *Der Rose Pilgerfahrt* can seem merely sentimental. The 'sound of legend' becomes associated with a kind of nostalgia – a determination to '*preserve the art of storytelling*', as Daverio puts it, instead of a drive to reinvigorate the form.[43] Like the German Romantic forest, then, late Schumann becomes ringed with loss.[44] What once provided sustenance for the *Volk* was forgotten by subsequent generations: lost and forgotten; that was the singer's curse.

Church music of the future

With his black attire and reserved countenance, Schumann was often mistaken for a clergyman as he walked around Düsseldorf. Yet his relationship to the Church was not straightforward, not least because he was a Protestant working in a Catholic province. His decision to set the Ordinary of the Mass to music, and to complete a Requiem, in 1852, has further perplexed critics who remain uncertain whether these pieces are intended to serve a liturgical function or are better suited to the secular setting of the concert hall. Schumann himself described the Mass as 'suited both to the divine service and to the concert platform', implying it to be as much a hybrid genre as the crossbreed of oratorio and opera found in *Das Paradies und die Peri*, the *Szenen aus Goethes Faust* and the four choral ballades.[45] Such mixing of the sacred and the secular, Catholic and Protestant, reflects the complicated position of religion not only in the composer's outlook but also more generally in German culture post 1848.

Schumann's knowledge and appreciation of the Lutheran Bible was attested to by many of his contemporaries – not least by Brahms who, according to the reminiscences of Arthur M. Abell, claimed: 'it was Schumann who first aroused my deeper interest in the Holy Writ . . . [He] always was quoting the Bible.'[46] While that might have been the case, Schumann seems also to have contributed to a loosening in the younger composer's religious attitudes, encouraging an intellectual and humanistic approach to theology.[47] Despite the affinity often sensed between Romanticism and Catholicism (as in the writings of Novalis and Eichendorff), it seems that Schumann and his circle thought of religion in a broader, non-dogmatic sense, rather than adhering to any particular tenet of Christianity.

Religion in nineteenth-century Germany was inextricable from questions of nationhood and society. The ceremony of the Church was valued, according to Ernest Gellner, 'as an aid to community, and not so much in itself'; loyalty to the nation should transcend confessional allegiances.[48] Investment in the *Volk* as the spiritual root of all German culture, high and low, had a quasi-Christian aspect, as did its partnering medievalism. At stake was an ideal of purity – of an earlier nation state and of morals.[49]

The question of purity was raised with regard to church music, not only with regard to the Protestant-Catholic divide, but also in terms of sacred and secular genres. Herder had argued that church music needed to retain the basic distinctions between the sacred and the profane: mixing elements from operatic style with church style, he argued, caused the latter to lose dignity.[50] His objection to operatic elements was also nationalistic; why sully German art with Italian frippery? However, Schumann's old professor, Thibaut, in his 1824 treatise *Über Reinheit der Tonkunst* (*On Purity in Musical Art*), had proposed that composers should rescue oratorio from the clutches of opera and return to a morally pure church style. That purity, we might assume, would have meant for Thibaut an exclusively Protestant type of composition; generally speaking, Catholicism was associated with theatricality, in opposition to Protestant inclinations towards inwardness.[51] Thibaut thought, on the other hand, that Protestant composers would benefit from adopting the Catholic aesthetic of Palestrina and Lotti. He mourned the loss of musical inspiration in the Lutheran Church, pointing out that Luther himself had argued for the retention of Catholic music.[52]

Schumann might have reminded himself of Thibaut's openness to both Protestant and Catholic musical styles while exploring repertoire with the Dresden *Chorverein*, which under his direction performed Palestrina, Lassus, J. S. Bach and Jommelli. His engagement with church music intensified at Düsseldorf, where his duties included conducting four Masses and two performances in church in Holy Week. By the time he wrote to August Strackerjan that 'it is surely the artist's supreme goal to apply his creative powers to sacred music' on 13 January 1851, he had already completed settings of Friedrich Rückert's *Adventlied*, op. 71 (1848) and *Verzweifle nicht im Schmerzensthal*, op. 93 (1849) and the *Neujahrslied*, op. 144 (1849/50), which ends with the chorale *Nun danket alle Gott*.[53] Many other sacred works were planned by him in the 1850s: there was to be a *Stabat Mater* and Requiem to words by Rückert (planned with the completed *Missa sacra*); settings of religious songs by Clemens Brentano; and the already mentioned oratorio based on the life of Martin Luther (which prompted thoughts of a German Mass based on the Protestant liturgy). The *Projektenbuch* also mentions the possibility of setting a text from the Old Testament, a Maria, a German Requiem, and a Psalm (from the Latin vulgate).

Schumann's reason for setting the Ordinary of the Mass, though, remains unclear. He completed the score fairly quickly and, while still working on the piece, organized a run-through with piano accompaniment by the Singekränzchen on 18 April 1852; two days later he rehearsed the Mass with the whole *Gesangmusik-Verein*.[54] Work on the Requiem began a week later. It is not a complete setting of the liturgical text of the Mass of the Dead as found in the *Missale Romanum*; like Mozart (K. 626) he omitted the Gradual and the Tract. Schumann also reordered some sections of the text, thereby removing them from their functional role within the liturgy.[55] He completed a draft on 8 May, and played it through on the piano for Clara the next day. While Peter Fuchs (also the copyist of the Mass) made a copy of the score, he added an orchestral accompaniment to the motet for men's double chorus *Verzweifle nicht im Schmerzensthal*. Schumann then orchestrated the Requiem.

A performance of the first two movements of the Mass was planned for one of the Music Society's May concerts but for reasons unknown was later removed from the programme.[56] Schumann was keen that the whole Mass be performed, but perhaps because of its length, he found this hard to arrange. It also proved difficult to find a publisher. Eventually the Kyrie and Gloria were performed in Düsseldorf under Schumann's direction on 3 March 1853, alongside Beethoven's Piano Concerto in G major, lieder by Mozart, Schubert, and Mendelssohn, and Schumann's Symphony in D minor and *Vom Pagen und der Königstochter*. There were no lengthy reviews, but a notice in the *Düsseldorfer Journal und Kreis-Blatt* referred to the music as noble, profound and edifying, while the orchestra's concert master Ruppert Becker noted in his diary that the sections were 'both full of the most wonderful harmonies, of a kind only Schumann could write'.[57] Performance of further movements was probably discouraged by Schumann's conducting duties being taken away from him after his disastrous direction of Moritz Hauptmann's Mass in G minor (op. 30) in St Maximilian's Church on 16 October 1853.

While at Endenich, Schumann enquired whether any progress had been made with regard to publishing the Mass and Requiem.[58] A few years later

Clara remained uncertain whether they should be published, and sought the advice of Brahms, Joachim and Franz Wüllner. Brahms responded:

[The Mass and Requiem] are not from Schumann's final period. Indeed, he himself intended to publish them and prepared them fully for publication. Who, then, has the right to interfere? But, once again, apologies must be made, and it will never be taken amiss if, in an excess of immodesty, we ensure that the garland of immortality which such a well-loved and respected man wove for himself should consist only of imperishable blooms. But what we perform is the work of mortal men. The world almost demands to see the weakness of those who are greater than us, and sooner or later it will uncover them.[59]

Brahms suggested a trial performance be arranged before a final decision was made. Eventually Wüllner conducted the Kyrie, Sanctus, Benedictus and Agnus Dei from the Mass in Aachen on 25 July 1861. Clara wrote to Brahms:

You cannot imagine how beautiful it all sounds. The Kyrie is deeply affecting and wonderfully unified, while the Sanctus contains individual sections of such marvellous tonal effect that they make your spine tingle. Apart from a few individual passages, the music is really deeply religious, churchlike, which I had not imagined would be the case . . . Naturally, I no longer have any doubts about having it printed.[60]

The Mass was published by Rieter-Biedemann at the beginning of 1863 and soon after was performed in Leipzig and Vienna. Individual movements were included in concert programmes over the following decades, particularly at memorials (such as at the centenary celebrations of Schumann's birth in Zwickau). The Requiem was not performed before its publication in 1864, when it was given, symbolically, the final opus number in the official list of Schumann's works.

Predictably, reviewers of the Mass tended to focus on its ambiguous religious aspect; or its 'indecisive character', as an anonymous critic in the *Signale für die musikalische Welt* put it, explaining that the 'idiosyncratic splendour of Schumann's colourful imagination, a Romantic effusiveness which finds expression in the most elegant and modern form, [excludes] religiosity almost entirely'.[61] Selmar Bagge, editor of the *Allgemeine Musikalische Zeitung* and the first critic to review the Mass after its publication, thought that the Kyrie and Gloria had a 'certain churchlike character' but that the Credo suffered from 'trivial-sounding rhythms and melodies' and from 'false declamations'.[62] The Offertory belonged more to *Liebesfrühling* than to a Mass and the Sanctus was secular in part. That the Sanctus, Benedictus and 'O salutaria hostia' were through composed, ending with a fugal

'Amen', offended liturgical conventions. The treatment of the chorus in the Agnus Dei was a failure. Only if the Sanctus was rewritten would the Mass become suitable for liturgical use, Bagge concluded, but even then the work as a whole, with its many slow sections and overall length, was 'not exactly uplifting' ('nicht eben sehr erquicklich'). Ferdinand Peter Graf von Laurencin found fault with the Protestant's decision to set the Mass at all.[63] While the Kyrie, Offertory and Agnus offered an 'atmospheric composer' ('Stimmungsmusiker') such as Schumann opportunity for subjective interpretations, the Gloria and Credo did not. Laurencin ultimately declared the work respectable from a purely musical standpoint – in terms of its orchestration, rich harmonies and contrapuntal density – although its thematic writing was unproductive.

Others were convinced by Schumann's ability to write church music, however, and this included Eduard Hanslick, who sent a copy of the Mass to Anton Bruckner. Some expressed surprise – and satisfaction – that the work was not more complicated, despite being posthumous.[64] Similar comments were made about the Requiem, which had several private performances for small forces in Leipzig during the winter of 1864–5. After the first public performance (19 November 1864), a critic for *Signale* wrote:

The Requiem is not . . . an especially outstanding example of Schumann's work; only in certain movements, such as the *Dies irae*, do the inspiration and execution approach the highest levels of the composer's genius; the Requiem does not display true religious and sacred depth, nor the compelling creative power and original imagination, that we find in other works of the master. Nevertheless, the work is well worth hearing and the music is nowhere difficult to follow.[65]

Rudolf Weinwurm in Vienna was less equivocal, declaring: 'Schumann has rarely written such insignificant music as this Requiem.'[66] Bagge, however (in stark contrast to his view of the Mass a year earlier), found that, although 'many of Schumann's *last* compositions had not been such as to encourage a favourable opinion of the state of his productive powers during that period', the Requiem was 'quite free of scholastic convention' and heralded 'a new style'; one purer than Cherubini.[67] This was a Requiem as work of art, to be praised for its rich and sometimes daring harmonies and for its highly expressive melodies. Bagge's major reservation was that 'the gentleness of the style may give rise to a feeling that one has yielded unduly to sentiments of melancholy and that a true sense of *exaltation* has failed to arrive'.[68]

Two points from the criticism deserve further elaboration: the first has to do with Schumann's treatment of themes and harmony in light of secular and sacred genres; the second concerns the 'sentiments of melancholy' detected by Bagge. As is to be expected of music for the church, much of the writing is imitative, creating the sense of cohesion Clara admired in the Mass's Kyrie. But it is in movements such as the Sanctus that the tensions between secular and sacred elements come to the fore. As Bagge noted, this movement from the Mass is through composed and ends with a fugal Amen. Perhaps the most striking passage, though, is the opening (given in its recapitulation in Example. 2:3). Sustained, *pianissimo* chords by the choir, wind section, and low strings, are accompanied by a repeated crotchet figuration from the first violins and cellos. It is very simple, but effective, in a manner similar to the Offertory from Berlioz's Requiem that also features a repeated instrumental melody which Schumann had particularly admired.[69] The real magic, though, lies not in the repetitions of the melody but in the harmonic progressions (often featuring the submediant) that surround them, and by subtle motivic transformations: while in its opening phrase the bass line descends by step (moving through I, I flat 7, VI, VI flat 7, V, I), in the next phrase the movement is reversed. Later, the return of this material is prepared by the adaptation of the first violins' triplet crotchet melody to reintroduce an emphasis on the interval of a fourth and on the note D flat (Example 2:3). It is difficult to listen to this music and not think of Schumann's secular choral works; the limited tonal range of the movements of the Mass bears comparison to the tableau-like arrangement of keys outlined earlier with regard to the choral ballades, while the fugal writing in the final verse of the *Faustszenen's* 'Gerettet ist das edle Glied' and the second version of the *Schlusschor* would not be out of place in either Mass or Requiem.

Indeed, Franz Brendel had found in Part III of the *Faustszenen* sounds of the 'church music of the future', echoing not only Wagner's famous essay but also Liszt's 1834 *Manifesto on the sacred music of the future.*[70] Liszt had argued that the Church needed music that was 'mystical, forceful and readily intelligible'. He continued that 'it should unite theatre and church in one great synthesis which is at once dramatic and holy, solemn and plain, joyful and serious, passionate and restrained, stormy and restful, clear and mystical'.[71] Few texts provided such an opportunity for synthesis as the ending of Goethe's drama, when the spirit of Faust is redeemed by the penitent Gretchen – a scene Schumann entitled in his setting 'Faust's Transfiguration' (*Fausts Verklärung*). Yet Goethe's *Faust* is not simply 'super-Christian'; as Jaroslav Pelikan has discussed, Goethe wanted to be seen 'as standing, in some sense, within the Christian tradition – *and* within

Example 2:3 Mass, 'Sanctus'

the Classical tradition *and* within the humanistic tradition *and* within the scientific tradition!'[72] Thus Christ does not appear to free Faust's soul from hell, nor is he prayed to directly; instead, he is saved by Eros and Nature, united in Mary as Virgin, Mother, Queen and Goddess: the Eternal Feminine.[73] The manner in which *Faust* straddles traditions provides a useful model for the combination of sacred and secular styles in Schumann's choral music. While the quasi-operatic passages of the Mass and Requiem, and the ecclesiastical overtones of the *Faustszenen* or *Der Rose Pilgerfahrt*

Example 2:3 (*cont.*)

might have made critics anxious, they seem to have reflected a willingness on the composer's part to combine not only musical genres but also literature and liturgy, all for the sake of creating great German art: 'mystical, forceful and readily intelligible', as Liszt would have it.

Ultimately, though, the Mass and Requiem were criticized less for their secular aspects than because they were heard as late works. Schumann commented in response to Richard Pohl's (a.k.a. 'Hoplit') attack on him in *Das Karlsruher Musikfest im Oktober 1853* (discussed in the Introduction):

Example 2:3 (*cont.*)

'why, this might induce me to lay everything aside and strike up my Requiem, which is actually still lying on my desk!'[74] While he was surely joking, Brahms recalled that Schumann had often had premonitions of death, which had alarmed Clara, even claiming that: 'At the time of the *Requiem* he thought that, like Mozart, he had written it for himself, and during his illness he used to tell me how often he had similar fears.'[75] Wasielewski circulated a similar tale in his biography, quoting the composer as having said: 'a work of this nature is written for oneself'. Such a notion gained currency in the nineteenth century with the myth surrounding Mozart's Requiem.[76] And, of course, some composers did intend their Requiems to be performed in their memory: for example, Cherubini intended his *Deuxième Messe de Requiem* in D minor (1836) to be played at his funeral, as it was in 1842. Yet the association of Schumann with his Requiem had a pernicious edge, as is apparent from Wasielewski's interpretation of the composer's remark:

[He was thinking] less of the glorification of the church than of his own transfiguration. This isolated instance is of lesser significance in light of the fact that Schumann's views were no longer entirely free in the year 1852 but had already acquired a morbid character that, with the onset of his mental derangement, degenerated into a form of mysticism.[77]

Coeuroy similarly linked Schumann's turn to religious music with his impending illness: 'Schumann is much more of a mystic than Bach or Beethoven, but his mysticism was personal. It turns inward to the point of ending up with auditive hallucination. Hallucination is not communicable.'[78] Brahms complained that Schumann was for the most part not allowed a Bible in the asylum, because 'this desire was understood by his doctors to be a new symptom of his mental illness'.[79]

Tragic as all this seems, it is also apparent that long before the 1850s, Schumann was attracted by the possibility of redemption – as, of course, were many others.[80] As already mentioned, several choral works end with the spiritual transfiguration of their protagonists: from *Das Paradies und die Peri*, to the *Szenen aus Goethes Faust*, *Requiem für Mignon*, *Der Rose Pilgerfahrt* and the choral ballades, not to mention the Requiem that closes the op. 90 *Lenaulieder*. Schumann recognized that the *Schlussszene* of *Faust* and *Das Paradies und die Peri* both had protagonists who 'attain to heaven after much straying and striving'.[81] The notion that striving might lead to salvation is made explicit in Goethe's 'Prologue in Heaven', as the Lord and Mephistopheles make their wager over Faust's soul. Men will stray as long as they keep striving, the Lord explains. But it is their striving that will eventually save them. Thus the angels who bear Faust's immortal part to heaven proclaim: 'Wer immer strebend sich bemüht, den können wir erlösen!' ('For him whose striving never ceases / we can provide redemption'). There are few better epitaphs for the prolific Schumann. In his choral music from the 1850s he constantly strove to construct from the past – be it the Middle Ages, seventeenth-century counterpoint, or his earlier compositions – 'something absolutely valid which might be realized here and now just as at any other time', in Adorno's words: if not the sound of heaven, then perhaps the sound of legend.

Notes

1. Eduard Krüger, *Allgemeine Musikalische Zeitung* 47 (1845), cols. 609–10. He explained: 'This usage has become so common with recent Italian composers that one might want to ban it on patriotic ground.' See Daverio, 'Schumann's "new genre for the concert hall": *Das Paradies und die Peri* in the eyes of a contemporary', *Schumann and his World*, ed. R. Larry Todd (Princeton: Princeton University Press, 1994), p. 155.

2. Robert Pogue Harrison, *Forests: The Shadow of Civilization* (Chicago: University of Chicago Press, 1992), pp. 164–5.

3. Harrison, *Forests*, p. 164.

4. For more on which, see Volker Schupp, '"Wollzeilergesellschaft" und "Kette": Impulse der frühen Volkskunde und Germanistik', *Zeitschrift für deutsche Philologie* 100 (1981), 4–31.

5. J. G. Fichte, 'Reden an die deutsche Nation', *Johann Gottlieb Fichtes sämtliche Werke*, ed. I. H. Fichte (Berlin, 1845/46), vol. VII, fourth speech, p. 325.

6. Quoted in Susan M. Crane, *Collecting and Historical Consciousness* (Ithaca and London: Cornell University Press, 2000), p. 173.

7. For further discussion see Abigail Green, *Fatherlands: State–Building and Nationhood in Nineteenth-Century Germany* (Cambridge: Cambridge University Press, 2001).

8. He dates the beginning of this revolution to 1845; see Hans-Ulrich Wehler, *Deutsche Gesellschaftsgeschichte*, Vol. III, *Von der 'Deutschen Doppelrevolution' bis zum Beginn des Ersten Weltkrieges, 1849–1914* (Munich: Beck, 1995), pp. 4–5; and Wolfram Siemann, *Die 'Polizverein' deutscher Staaten: eine Dokumentation zur Überwachung der Öffentlichkeit nach der Revolution von 1848/9* (Tübingen: Niemeyer, 1983).

9. On the political activities of the choral societies see Dieter Düding, 'Nationale Oppositionsfeste der Turner, Sänger und Schützen im 19. Jahrhundert', *Öffentliche Festkultur, Politische Feste in Deutschland von der Aufklärung bis zum Ersten Weltkrieg*, ed. Dieter Düding, Peter Friedemann and Paul Münch (Reinbeck: Rowohlt, 1988), pp. 166–90; Friedrich Brusniak and Dietmar Klenke, 'Sängerfeste und die Musikpolitik der deutschen Nationalbewegung', *Musikforschung* 52 (1999), 29–54; and Hans-Werner Boresch, 'Der "alte Traum vom alten Deutschland": Musikfeste im 19. Jahrhundert als Nationalfeste', *Musikforschung* 52 (1999), 55–69.

10. See Conrad L. Donakowski, *Music for the Masses: Ritual and Music in an Age of Democratic Revolution* (Chicago and London: University of Chicago Press, 1972).

11. Letter of 28 December 1853, *Briefe. Neue Folge*, p. 388.

12. Letter to Richard Pohl, 14 February 1851, *Briefe. Neue Folge*, p. 337.

13. Letter to Moritz Horn, 8 December 1851, *Briefe. Neue Folge*, p. 353.

14. Letter to Richard Pohl, 25 June 1851, *Briefe. Neue Folge*, p. 344.

15. Letter to Richard Pohl, 14 February 1851, *Briefe. Neue Folge*, pp. 336–7.

16. Letter to Pohl, 13 May 1851; *Robert Schumann in his Letters*, 138–9. For the sake of the drama, Schumann suggested, Hutten, Sackingen, Hans Sachs, Lucas Kranach, the Electors Friedrich and Johann Philip of Hessen must be given up as soloists, but could be in the narrative.

17. Letter to Richard Pohl, 14 February 1851, *Briefe. Neue Folge*, p. 337.

18. About the St John Passion, see Schumann's letters to Moritz Hauptmann, 21 February 1851 and 8 May 1851; *Briefe. Neue Folge*, p. 337 and pp. 341–2. The list of Handel oratorios Schumann studied is included in Gerd Nauhaus, 'Schumanns *Lektürebüchlein*', *Robert Schumann und die Dichter*, ed. Bernhard R. Appel and Inge Hermstrüwer (Düsseldorf: Droste, 1991).

19. See Bernhard R. Appel, '"Mehre Malerei als Ausdruck der Empfindung" – Illustrierende uns illustrierte Musik im Düsseldorf des 19. Jahrhunderts', *Akademie und Musik: Erscheinungen und Wirkungen des Akademiegedankens in Kultur- und Musikgeschichte-Institutionen, Veranstaltungen, Schriften. Festschrift für Werner Braun zum 65. Geburtstag*, ed. Wolf Frobenius, Nicole Schwindt-Gross and Thomas Sick (Saarbrücken: Saarbrücken Druckerei, 1993), pp. 255–68.

20. For further discussion, including the connection between *Das Paradies und die Peri*, *Requiem für Mignon*, and *Szenen aus Goethe's Faust*, and an idea of *tableaux vivants*, see Laura Tunbridge, *Euphorion falls: Schumann, Manfred and Faust* (PhD Princeton, 2002), pp. 103–30.

21. Daverio makes a similar point for slightly different reasons in 'Einheit', p. 74.

22. For further discussion see Daverio, 'Schumann's "new genre"', *Schumann and his World*, pp. 129–55.

23. For further discussion see Tunbridge, *Euphorion Falls*, pp. 93–147.

24. Of the Luther project Schumann wrote 'Das Oratorium müßte für Kirche und Concertsaal passend sein'; see letter to Richard Pohl, 14 February 1851, *Briefe. Neue Folge*, p. 336.

25. Three years earlier Schumann had set Hebbel's 'Schön Hedwig' in a similar vein.

26. Letter to van Bruyck, 17 December 1852, *Briefe. Neue Folge*, p. 363. Christian Strehk points out that Schumann was anticipated by Schubert's 'Leb wohl, du schöne Erde', D829; see 'Eine "Art von Composition, die wohl noch nicht existiert": Friedrich Hebbels Ballade *Schön Hedwig* in Robert Schumanns Sicht', *Hebbel-Jahrbuecher* 50 (1995), 155–91. Liszt completed two accompaniments to declamation within a decade of Schumann's: a setting of Lenau's *Der traurige Mönch* and Bürger's *Lenore*.

27. Carolyn Abbate discusses these temporal distinctions as *Erzählzeit* and *erzählte Zeit* in *Unsung Voices: Opera and Musical Narrative in the Nineteenth Century* (Princeton: Princeton University Press, 1991), p. 54.

28. Adorno, 'On the Social Situation of Music', *Essays on Music*, p. 403.

29. For example, see Reinhard Kapp, 'Schumann nach der Revolution: Vorüberlegungen, Statements, Hinweise, Materialien, Fragen', *Schumann*

Forschungen, vol. 3, *Schumann in Düsseldorf: Werke – Texte – Interpretationen*, ed. Bernhard R. Appel (Mainz: Schott, 1993), pp. 315–415; and Michael Struck, 'Kunstwerk – Anspruch und Popularitätsstreben – Ursachen ohne Wirkung? Bemerkungen zum *Glück von Edenhall* op. 143 und zur *Fest-Ouvertüre* op. 123', same volume, pp. 265–314.

30. Daverio, 'Einheit', p. 64.

31. On 28 May 1851 Schumann also set Uhland's *Der Sänger* as a choral partsong (op. 145:3).

32. On Schumann's treatment of Ossianic themes see Jonathan Bellman, '*Aus alten Märchen*: the chivalric style of Schumann and Brahms', *Journal of Musicology* 13 (1995), 117–35; and Daverio, 'Schumann's Ossianic Manner', *19th-Century Music* 21 (1998), 227–73.

33. For more on this see Liah Greenfeld, *Nationalism: Five Roads to Modernity* (Cambridge, Mass.: Harvard University Press, 1992), p. 3.

34. The adjectives are taken from the score: 'mit Anmuth', 'mit großer Kraft', 'mit Begeisterung'. The minstrels' songs were taken from other poems by Uhland, which caused problems for the flow of narrative solved by writing some connecting links; see Schumann's letter to Pohl, 25 June 1851, *Briefe. Neue Folge*, pp. 141–2.

35. On the harp's function as a symbol of disembodiment see Daniel Beller-McKenna, 'Distance and Disembodiment: Harps, Horns, and the Requiem Idea in Schumann and Brahms', *Journal of Musicology* 22:1 (2005), 47–89.

36. For further discussion see Daverio, '*Einheit-Freiheit-Vaterland*', pp. 59–77.

37. Slavoj Žižek writes about absent melodies in Schumann's *Humoreske* in *The Parallax View* (Cambridge, Mass.: MIT Press, 2000), pp. 365–6.

38. Eduard Hanslick likened Faust's answer to Care in Part II to the Sängerszenen from *Tannhäuser*, while Eduard Krüger objected to Schumann's declamatory style of vocal writing, complaining: 'In writing *hardly any memorable melodies…* Schumann takes the same path as Wagner; the predominantly psychological recitation, tone painting, and orchestral texture all impede melodic memorability.' Alfred Ehrlich damned Faust's monologue 'So ist es also' as a 'perfect example of endless melody according to Wagnerian principles'. See Gisela Probst, *Robert Schumanns Oratorien* (Wiesbaden: Breitkopf und Härtel, 1975), p. 559.

39. Wagner recounts their meeting in *Mein Leben*.

40. Letter to Liszt, 6 December 1851, *Briefe. Neue Folge*, p. 352.

41. Letter to August Strackerjan, 24 July 1853, *Briefe. Neue Folge*, p. 376.

42. Letter to Carl Debrois van Bruyck, 8 May 1853, *Briefe. Neue Folge*, p. 373.

43. My emphasis. *Robert Schumann*, p. 433.

44. Harrison refers to the German Romantic Forest being 'ringed by a halo of loss' in *Forests*, p. 156.

45. Letter to Schott, 10 December 1852, cited in Bernhard R. Appel, 'Kritischer Bericht', *Neue Ausgabe sämtlicher Werke Serie IV: Bühnen- und Chorwerke mit Orchester, Werkgruppe 3: Geistlicher Werke Band 2: Missa sacra*, op. 147 (Mainz:

Schott, 1991), p. xxiv. Philipp Spitta wrote: 'He cannot have imagined, when composing these works, that they might be used at church services, since they contain idiosyncrasies in matters of form which run counter to the fixed order of the mass.' *Ein Lebensbild Robert Schumann's* (Leipzig: Breitkopf und Härtel, 1882), pp. 98–9. A similar view was held by Herman Abert, *Robert Schumann* (Berlin: Harmonie, 1903), 77; while Eugen Schmitz argues that the Mass could be performed in a liturgical context; see *Robert Schumanns c-moll-Messe*, *NZfM* 111 (1950), 644–6.

46. Arthur M. Abell, 'Brahms as I knew him', *Etude* 49 (1931), 852.

47. For more on which see Daniel Beller-McKenna, *Brahms and the German Spirit*, p. 34; and Hans Christian Stekel, *Sehnsucht und Distanz: Theologische Aspekte in der wortgebundenen religiösen Kompositionen von Johannes Brahms* (Frankfurt: Peter Lang, 1997).

48. Ernest Gellner, *Nationalism* (New York: New York University Press, 1997), p. 77.

49. Frederick C. Beiser, ed., *The Early Political Writings of the German Romantics* (Cambridge: Cambridge University Press, 1996), p. xxii. As an extension of that interest in purity, Schumann's decision to add the Offertory 'Tota pulchra es, Maria' to his Mass in April 1853, despite not being Catholic, might be explained by his interest in the subject of the Virgin Mary – perhaps roused by contemporary discussions of the Immaculate Conception, made dogma by Pius IX the following year. Schumann may also, though, have added the Offertory to take part in a competition for a newly composed Mass; see Appel, 'Kritischer Bericht', pp. xxvi–xxvii.

50. For further discussion see James Garratt, *Palestrina and the German Romantic Imagination* (Cambridge: Cambridge University Press, 2002), 36–61.

51. See Michael Steinberg, *Listening to Reason: Culture, Subjectivity, and Nineteenth-century Music* (Princeton: Princeton University Press, 2004), p. 123. On the tension between Catholicism and Protestantism in nineteenth-century Germany see Donakowski, *A Muse for the Masses*, pp. 122–31.

52. For more on Luther's attitudes see Walter Buszin, *Luther on music* (Minneapolis: Saint Paul, 1958), pp. 119–20.

53. Schumann, *Briefe. Neue Folge*, p. 335.

54. Schumann sketched it out between 12 and 24 February 1852, and orchestrated it from 25 February to 30 March. A visit to Leipzig from 5–22 March interrupted work, as did moving apartments on 15 April. For more on Schumann's the compositional and performance history of the Mass, see Bernhard R. Appel's 'Werkgeschichte' in the 'Kritischer Bericht' to the *Neue Ausgabe sämtlicher Werke: Serie IV: Bühnen- und Chorwerke mit Orchester, Werkegruppe 3: Geistliche Werke Band 2: Missa sacra, op. 147* (Mainz: Schott, 1991), pp. xv–xxxvii.

55. A reviewer later derided the 'dismemberment and displacement of the text' ('Zerstückelung und Versetzung des Textes'). G. Carlssohn, *NZfM* 60:32 (5 August 1864), 277–9.

56. Schumann later explained that ill health had prevented him from completing several works, including the Mass, Requiem, and *Vom Pagen und der Königstochter*. Letter to Julius von Bernuth, 17 October 1852, cited in Hermann Erler, *Robert Schumanns Leben* (Berlin, 1887), II, p. 178.

57. Both cited by Appel, 'Werkgeschichte', pp. xxii–xxiii.

58. See letters to Clara, 14 and 26 September 1854. *Briefe, Neue Folge*, pp. 397 and 400. After consulting with Brahms Clara eventually decided not to send the score; see Brahms to Clara 6 December 1854; *Clara Schumann – Johannes Brahms: Briefe aus den Jahren 1853–1896*, ed. Berthold Litzmann (Leipzig: Breitkopf und Härtel, 1927), I, p. 46.

59. Letter of 6 August 1860, *Schumann–Brahms Briefe*, I, pp. 318–19.

60. Letter of 29 July 1861, *Schumann–Brahms Briefe*, I, p. 372.

61. *Signale für die musikalische Welt* 21:24 (14 May 1863), 382–3.

62. *Allgemeine Musikalische Zeitung* 1:4 (21 January 1863), cols. 61–8.

63. *NZfM*, 60: 30 (22 July 1864), 257–61.

64. *Signale für die musikalische Welt* 21: 24 (14 May 1863), 382–3.

65. *Signale*, 22:50 (2 December 1864), 942.

66. Review of concert by the Vienna *Singakademie* 9 April 1865; cited in Appel, 'Kritische Bericht' to Requiem, p. 143.

67. *AMZ* 2:39 (28 September 1864), 664–70. Hermann Kretzschmar's influential concert guide contradicted Bagge's evaluation of the Mass and Requiem, describing the former as an important work but that the Requiem was too hastily composed: 'There is a strange confusion of idioms: serious, strictly worked passages are followed by others which seem like Italian products from the notorious age of the guitar orchestra.' *Führer durch den Concertsaal*, Div. II, Part I, *Kirchliche Werke* (Leipzig: Liebeskind, 1888), p. 238. Schumann, incidentally, greatly admired Cherubini's C major Requiem.

68. Ibid., cols. 669–70. A further problem was the orchestration. Bagge argued that because the Requiem was primarily conceived for voices, the orchestra was understandably left in the background; he also claimed that a planned organ accompaniment had not been included. August Reissmann similarly suggested the Requiem was 'unfinished work. Much of the orchestration, in particular, is only sketched and the master would certainly have completed it; indeed, much else would have assumed a somewhat different form had he set his hand to making improvements.' Reissmann, *Robert Schumann*, p. 19.

69. See entry for 23 February 1843 in *TB* III, p. 238; and *TB* II, p. 533, n. 585.

70. Franz Brendel, *Geschichte der Musik in Italien, Deutschland und Frankreich von den ersten christlichen Zeiten bis auf die Gegenwart* (Leipzig: Heinrich Matthes, 1878), p. 359.

71. Cited in Donakowski, *A Muse for the Masses*, pp. 72–3.

72. Jaroslav Pelikan, *Faust the Theologian* (New Haven: Yale University Press, 1995), pp. 3–4. His emphasis.

73. Pelikan, *Faust the Theologian*, p. 119.

74. Letter to Richard Pohl, 6 February 1854; cited in F. Gustav Jensen, 'Ein unbekannter Brief von Robert Schumann', *Die Musik* 5:5 (1905–6), 112.

75. Brahms to Clara, 29 January 1855, *Schumann-Brahms Briefe*, I, p. 24.

76. Friedrich Rochlitz in the *AMZ*, i (1798), refers to Mozart 'writing this piece for his own funeral' (thanks to Barry Cooper for the reference). According to Gregory W. Harwood, Schumann had read Nissen's biography of Mozart, which describes the composer as being transfigured by his own exequies, in December 1838. See 'Kritischer Bericht', p. 140.

77. 'Dieser vereinzelte Fall ist daher um so weniger von Gewicht, als Schumann's geistige Richtungen im Jahr 1852 nicht mehr ganz frei waren, sondern bereits einen krankhaften Charakter angenommen hatten, der mit Beginn seiner Geistesumnachtung in eine Art von Mysticismus ausartete.' *Robert Schumann. Eine Biographie* (Dresden, 1858), pp. 250–1.

78. Cited in Marcel Brion, *Schumann and the Romantic Age*, trans. Geoffrey Sainsbury (London: Collins, 1956), p. 321. The connection between Catholicism and mental illness made here was perhaps prefigured in Schumann's often cited joke on moving to Heidelberg in 1829: 'My lodgings face the asylum on the right and the Catholic church on the left, so that I'm really in doubt whether one is supposed to go crazy or become Catholic'. Peter Ostwald, *Schumann: Music and Madness* (London: C. Gollancz, 1985), p. 51.

79. Rudolf von der Leyen, *Johannes Brahms als Mensch und Freund* (Düsseldorf: Karl Robert Langeweische, 1905), pp. 31–2.

80. Dieter Borchmeyer has recently complained that Wagner's *Tannhäuser* is transformed at the end of its second act into a Romantic opera of renunciation and redemption. *Drama and the World of Richard Wagner*, trans. Daphne Ellis (Princeton: Princeton University Press, 2003), p. 146.

81. See Daverio, *Robert Schumann*, p. 304.

3 | Collecting thoughts

'Memory is preserved in a number of things'[1]
'It is invariably oneself that one collects'[2]

Every collection carries a story; the reason for its gathering, the source and process of it.[3] On contemplating a collection – even one of our own from long ago, a box of ribbons and ticket stubs saved for who knows what purpose – we become detectives, piecing together evidence to find the most convincing narrative. Then we become curators: repackaging, classifying, and neatening loose ends. Such a pattern is apparent in Schumann's collecting habits, which in later years began to exhibit more strongly a desire not simply to gather objects together but also to edit and arrange them. In 1850 he returned to earlier works, cutting certain passages from the piano cycles. He also prepared for publication songs and piano pieces he had written almost twenty years earlier. These included songs originally composed as part of *Dichterliebe*, which as mentioned in Chapter 1 finally appeared as op. 142, and the piano collections *Bunte Blätter*, op. 99 and *Albumblätter*, op. 124, which assembled pieces written between 1832 and 1849. In April 1852 he continued the *Dichtergarten* project begun some twenty years earlier, returning to his favourite authors (Goethe, Jean Paul, Shakespeare) and extracting passages on music. In the summer of the following year, he made a catalogue of his music library and an index to his compositions.

Borrowing from Walter Benjamin, John Daverio described the effect of Schumann assembling objects into a collection as imbuing them with 'an aura, an indefinable quality compounded of nearness and distance that inspires the beholder with awe'.[4] The pieces he claims exemplify this process are the accompaniments to Bach's Sonatas and Partitas and Cello Suites, completed in spring 1853. According to Daverio, Schumann 'provided Bach's works for solo strings with an aura in the form of accompaniments that are generally discreet and often transparent, as transparent as the glass case through which we might view a collection of rare coins or stamps'.[5] While he may not have touched Bach's violin or cello parts, his 'glass cases' – the keyboard accompaniments – fundamentally alter the nature of the music, in terms of harmony and texture. These are very much personal rather than historical collections, as are the accompaniments to Paganini's Caprices (begun in 1853 and continued in the asylum), pieces that Schumann had used as a basis for piano études in the 1830s. Paganini had, of course, been one of the inspirations towards his taking up a career in music. Perhaps in 'collecting' the Caprices, along with cataloguing his library, extracting his favourite authors and editing his works, Schumann was creating the archive of his musical life.

If so, a more fitting model for Schumann's collecting habits in his final years might be found in Benjamin's *Charles Baudelaire*, which describes the collector as 'the true inhabitant of the interior . . . The collector dreamed that he was in a world which was not only far-off in the distance and in time, but was also a better one.'[6] There are few truer inhabitants of the interior than Schumann, particularly when we consider the more prosaic collecting projects undertaken at Endenich, such as the lists of city names taken from an atlas. These may have been a symptom of Schumann's illness, or may have indicated a desire to escape it (visitors reported that he spoke of travelling a great deal). The composer might simply have been trying to collect his thoughts by pondering the outside world or even by the process of listmaking itself. Perhaps he reminded himself of the character in Jean Paul who compulsively makes lists. Before pathologizing Schumann's collecting habit, though, it is worth bearing in mind that there were other models for collecting in the nineteenth century; and that what may seem to us like worthless ephemera may then have held a different aesthetic value. This chapter is, then, concerned with exploring Schumann's collecting habits in context, in terms of the art, literature and museums around him; his sense of history and the preservation of memory; and as part of the composer's creative approach.

Collecting oneself

Arguments that Schumann became more conservative in middle age find their strongest support in the revisions he made to his earlier music from 1849 onwards. He prepared new editions of the *Impromptus* (op. 5), *Davidsbündlertänze* (op. 6), the Symphonic Etudes (op. 13), the Third Sonata (op. 14), and *Kreisleriana* (op. 16). Many of the changes seem minimal: the op. 14 *Concert sans orchestre* became *Grande Sonate*; *Etudes Symphoniques* (op. 13) became *Etudes en forme de Variations*; and *Davidsbündlertänze* became *Davidsbündler: Achtzehn Charakterstücke*. Yet in all these alterations there is a down-playing of poetic aspect: a grand sonata is very different in aspiration from a concerto without orchestra, as are piano studies in the form of variations rather than symphonically conceived. The transformation of the *Davidsbündlertänze* into 'eighteen character pieces' – a more demure prospect than the characters dancing themselves – was completed by stripping the collection of its poetic motto and the ascription of individual movements to Florestan and Eusebius. Repeats were also added, it has been suggested, to facilitate the listener's understanding of the sudden changes of mood within and between pieces.[7] And then there were what seem to be more brutal revisions: the excision of movements from the *Impromptus* and *Etudes Symphoniques*, while the *Grande Sonate* regained a movement (having lost two on being revised in 1836–40).[8] The fifth movement of *Kreisleriana* had its oblique dominant ending replaced by a firm cadence on to the tonic. 'Der frohe Wandersmann', which had originally begun the Eichendorff *Liederkreis*, op. 39, was replaced by 'In der Fremde' for its second edition – a change seemingly intended to sustain the cycle's poetic and harmonic unity.[9]

Why all these revisions? Schumann explained in a letter to the publisher Friedrich Whistling, à propos of the new edition of *Kreisleriana*, that: 'Unfortunately, I spoiled my pieces so often in earlier times, wantonly so. All that has now been eliminated.'[10] Wasielewski attributed Schumann's editorial activities in the 1850s as evidence of a growing attunement to his prospective audiences and thus to composerly maturity. More recent scholars acknowledge that market forces had a role to play, but bemoan the music's 'bowdlerization'. Jon W. Finson comments: 'the composer softened clashing harmonies, regularized peculiar phrases, clarified cadences, and generally removed their more bizarre (some would say original and astonishing) features.'[11] Charles Rosen advocates returning to earlier versions, pointing out that despite the fashion for *Urtexts* most performers still use the later edition.[12] Along similar lines, Beate Perrey has argued that the four songs omitted from the first edition of *Dichterliebe* should be reinstated for the sake of the cyclic organization.[13]

At stake in returning to these earlier versions is a privileging of the younger Schumann's Romantic eccentricities over the relatively 'classical' and objective late style. Both Rosen and Perrey are attracted by the fragmentary, postmodern aspects of the earlier works, which become more apparent on allowing the movement from *Kreisleriana* its dominant ending, and by disrupting the much-analyzed cycle of *Dichterliebe* with other songs. Yet deciding that the composer's first thoughts should take precedence over subsequent revisions, according to literary critic Zachary Leader, also reveals the lingering influence of Romantic ideas about organicism; the notion that a work enters the world spontaneously, in complete form, rather than being part of a process that may never be finished.[14] An author's attitude to revision, Leader continues, is also bound up with issues of personal identity:

> To some Romantic authors – to some people – personal identity is single and continuous, something indivisible with which we are born . . . To others, personal identity is a creation, the sum of a series of discrete 'selves', both over time and at any one time. When the self is thought of as inherently indivisible and continuous, revision is often seen as a simple matter of refinement or clarification . . . When the self is thought of as something towards which one works, an aspiration or value rather than something given, revision is as much an attempt to establish personal identity as to reveal it.[15]

With regard to the construction of Schumann's authorial identity, the example of Wordsworth is perhaps most relevant. During his lengthy career he constantly revised his works; the first collected edition was published in 1815, the final one overseen by the poet appeared in 1849–50. Recent editors have tended to prefer earlier editions of his poems, arguing that they represent the texts his contemporaries (Keats, Shelley, Hazlitt and Lamb) would have known, and that by preserving original versions a clearer understanding can be gained of Wordsworth's development. However, according to Leader, Wordsworth made revisions 'not out of indifference to – or to repudiate – the intentions of a former self, but to assert his identity with that self'.[16] His purpose was often to bring into focus and clarify an original meaning or intention sometimes obscured by his earlier more performative and experimental style, rather than altering or denying it: 'as a reviser, [Wordsworth] was neither mad nor senile, nor did he conceive of revision as the creation of new works'; revision was no violation to his past or present self, but preserved the affinities between them.[17] Through his revisions, in Leader's formulation, Wordsworth reveals himself to be 'a single and continuous person over time'.[18]

Schumann's career might have been much shorter and the number of revisions he made fewer than the example of Wordsworth, but there are some similarities between poet and composer in terms of scholarly attitudes towards them. As discussed, Schumann's revisions have been considered to neutralize the more vivid and experimental aspects of his earlier works. In a similar manner to Leader, we might suggest that this was with the intention of clarifying their structure and meaning. But what of the composer's personal identity is revealed through the revision process? Like Wordsworth, Schumann did not conceive of revision as the creation of new works; however, scholars have been quick to interpret his impulse to revise as an attempt to suppress – or, if we formulate it in more extreme terms, to destroy – the music's most original features. For example, Richard Taruskin explains that Schumann was 'morbidly sensitive to symptoms of 'irrationality' in his early output, [which] caused him to revise some of his most remarkable compositions to render them more conventional, hence less threatening to his peace of mind'.[19] However – whatever his fears – Schumann was neither mad nor senile in 1850, raising the question why we cannot resist interpreting the revisions as a shift in his aesthetic. Could they not be a refining of his thoughts in the same manner as Wordsworth?

The assumption that Schumann's return to earlier works in the 1850s was an attempt to keep 'irrational' elements under control is apparent in the reception of his most major revision; that of the D minor Symphony, originally composed in 1841, and finally published by Breitkopf und Härtel in 1853 as Symphony no. 4, op. 120. The motivation for the revision might have been a recent, unsuccessful performance of the original version (along with the *Ouvertüre, Scherzo und Finale*, op. 52) and Schumann's orchestration of the Scherzo from Norbert Burgmüller's unfinished Second Symphony. In its initial version, the D minor Symphony was criticized for its lack of 'outward finish' and found wanting in content and form.[20] Many of the alterations made on its revision in December 1851 seem at first glance cosmetic, being primarily concerned with orchestration; also, Italian tempo indications were replaced with German ones, and the note values of the first movement's *Lebhaft* section were halved. However, as in his revision of the *Ouvertüre, Scherzo und Finale*, which gave drastically slower metronome markings for each movement (particularly for the Scherzo, designated dotted crotchet = 112 in 1846, and = 84 in 1854), Schumann requested slower tempi throughout the Fourth Symphony.[21] Wasielewski considered this general slowing down of tempi to parallel Schumann's tendency as a conductor, at around the same time, to claim that performances were too quick.[22]

Schumann also considered giving the revised version the title 'Symphonistische Phantasie für grosses Orchester'. His use of the word fantasy acknowledges its unusual form; all movements of the Symphony are linked.[23] What is more, a determination to emphasize the interconnectedness of the whole might have lain behind his most substantive musical alterations: the deletion of the brass chorale at the opening of the third movement, and the recasting of the transitions into the *Lebhaft* section of the first movement and the finale. The opening of the finale now referred back to the semiquaver theme of the earlier *Lebhaft*. Such cross-referencing, along with the relatively tight motivic working throughout, has encouraged interpretation of the Symphony as proto-Brahmsian. However, Brahms himself preferred the earlier version of the Symphony, mostly because of its orchestration; he described the music as having been overwhelmed by cumbersome clothing ('aber alle seine schöne, freie und anmutige Bewegung ist in dem schwerfälligen Kleid unmöglich geworden').[24] On revising the Symphony, Schumann had cut some of the score's most striking features, such as the inclusion of a guitar amidst the pizzicato strings of the Romanze.[25] He also doubled most of the strings' melodic lines – mixing an orchestral palette, it has often been complained, of 'grey on grey'.

Against such criticisms, Schumann defended his revision of the Symphony's orchestration as being better and more effective than the earlier version.[26] Whether or not critics and listeners have agreed with him, it is apparent that his concern, throughout the revision process, was to make structure and themes more intelligible. As discussed with regard to Wordsworth, it is an understandable attitude for a more experienced and mature composer revisiting an earlier work. But according to Ludwig Bischoff, reviewing a performance of the revised Symphony at the *Niederrheinischen Musikfestes* in May 1853, Schumann's attitude towards contemporary composition was disappointingly retrogressive; the composer was intent on looking backwards, Bischoff surmised, preferring to retreat to the past rather than engage with the present by creating new works.[27]

In many different ways, the process of collecting his works, and the production of new, 'improved' editions, did – as Bischoff concluded – allow Schumann to contemplate his achievements. Any attempt to portray the composer as exclusively regressive or nostalgic, however, is complicated by considering the role historicism played in nineteenth-century German culture. This topic has already been touched on in Chapter 2, with regard to the choral music, but there were many less obvious but no less critical ways in which a composer such as Schumann could engage with the historicizing process. The revision and collection of his works, for example, can be understood as self-historicizing. In an age of Romantic biography and nascent musicology, the need increased for a composer to provide information and materials about his life, views and works, so that others could assess his importance. By preparing editions and so forth, Schumann can be considered to have transformed himself into a historical object, in turn becoming part of material, collectable, culture.

Schumann complemented the revision of his earlier musical works by collecting and cataloguing his compositions and writings. He had first considered making a catalogue of his works in 1847; four years later one was published by Whistling, listing all works with opus numbers up until op. 92 and a few without (including the *Introduction und Allegro appassionato* and the 'Patriotisches Lied').[28] Given the rate at which new works were emerging, the catalogue was soon out of date and Schumann hoped that Breitkopf und Härtel would produce another, explaining: 'When one is getting older one begins to look back on the past life and wishes to leave one's intellectual affairs [*seinen geistigen Hausrath*] in good order.'[29] He continued to ask after the status of the thematic catalogue and other unpublished works while at Endenich. In 1860 Alfred Dörffel's *Thematisches Verzeichnis* appeared (published by J. Schuberth). Eduard Hanslick commented in a review that 'nothing can more helpfully introduce the precise knowledge of a master than such a catalogue; and nothing, in turn, can so securely complete that study'.[30]

Of his contributions to the *Neue Zeitschrift für Musik* Schumann wrote to the publisher Härtel: 'I would collect those scattered leaves – which are a lifelike reflection of that eventful time, and contain many an instructive hint to younger artists in the way of personal experiences of life – into a volume, as a remembrance of that time and of myself.'[31] Were we tempted to speculate on psychological motivations for Schumann's turn to collecting, we might remember Jean Baudrillard's claim that after adolescence, collectors are most commonly men over forty, for whom collected objects are projections of the self.[32] While this seems to fit with the composer's gathering of his scattered leaves, it is worth remembering that Schumann made collections and lists throughout his life; the Robert-Schumann-Haus archive in Zwickau holds catalogues the composer made of compositions in 1833, 1843, and 1853, suggesting that he was concerned with maintaining a sense of his own history throughout his career.[33]

Schumann was not the only collector in the nineteenth century, nor were all his collecting projects entirely focused on himself. As Judith Pascoe, among others, has recently discussed, the sense of passing time and human loss expressed so eloquently in Romantic poetry was partnered by a more general interest in the past, in the recovery and preservation of old objects and documents.[34] A passion for historical objects resulted in the proliferation of antiquarian societies, the development of the historical novel, and the rise of national libraries and museums.[35] In the process, collecting became democratized; no longer the preserve of the extremely rich, everyone (in theory) could visit museums or, through the many periodicals devoted to collecting, imagine them. A more democratic view of history was also presented by the historical societies, which celebrated the people and their culture through the display of popular artistic and technical artefacts, rather than royal collections.[36] Music had its own part to play in this enthusiasm for history: from the establishment of the concert hall and canon, to the founding of the Bach Gesellschaft, with which Schumann was involved.[37] As such, music was also a vital force in the establishment of a culture of German nationhood, with its concomitant commitment to education (*Bildung*). Schumann's collecting impulse can be understood as pedagogical on a small and a grand scale, encouraging the performance and appreciation of particular pieces of music while simultaneously increasing the understanding of music history in broader terms.

Stones talk

Schumann's original title for the opp. 99 and 124 collections of piano pieces was *Spreu*: chaff or worthless stuff.[38] While Daverio observes that by 'bringing together the rags and tatters of the earlier parts of his career' he saved them from being binned, another motivation is suggested by the first collection's eventual title, *Bunte Blätter* (*Many-Coloured Leaves*). It echoes Jean Paul's favoured title for *Beiwerke* or subsidiary works in his novels – *Extrablätter* – and the title of a collection of short stories by Adalbert Stifter (1805–68) published in 1853: *Bunte Steine* (*Many-Coloured Stones*).[39] Although there is no direct connection between Schumann's and Stifter's volumes, further examination reveals some shared interests in an aesthetics of collecting that values the everyday – 'Spreu' – as much as or even more than the artful.[40] Schumann might not simply have been gathering the detritus of his career into sellable volumes, but have had a more serious purpose in mind.

Schumann met Stifter in the mid-1840s and read a number of his works.[41] The appeal of *Der Condor*, *Feldblumen* and the 1844 collection *Studien* might have been their similarity to Jean Paul. There is no record of Schumann reading *Bunte Steine* but, as will become clear, various features bear comparison to the composer's late style, particularly with regard to collecting. The stories in *Bunte Steine* were written and revised between 1845 and 1853. Each is named after a common stone: fool's gold, granite, limestone, rock crystal, tourmaline, and bergmilch. Each centres on an enigmatic character, such as the frugal pastor attached to expensive linen in 'Limestone' or the nameless, flute-playing girl with an abnormally large head in 'Tourmaline'.

In collecting together the stories, Stifter hoped the stones' value would be revealed to all. Through banal objects, he thought it possible to gain direct access to essential life: 'as it is in external nature, so is it also with inner nature' ('So wie es in der äußeren Natur ist, so ist es auch in der inneren'), he claimed in the preface to *Bunte Steine*. Literature was thus conceived as a continuous natural process rather than as a rhetorical or aesthetic strategy; unlike realist writers such as Wilhelm Raabe and Theodor Fontane, Stifter did not aim to transfigure the everyday but to allow it gradually to reveal its qualities.[42] He was guided by 'das sanftes Gesetz' (gentle law), a kind of narrative butterfly effect that placed as much value on everyday trivialities ('beetles and buttercups', Hebbel complained) as on those guided by 'much higher laws'. According to Stifter the same force that causes milk to boil over in a poor woman's saucepan leads a volcano to erupt and stream lava; one is not more important than the other.[43]

Stifter's 'sanftes Gesetz' is embodied in the circular narratives of the *Bunte Steine* stories, most of which move from order to threat and then back into order. He was fond of *Rahmenerzählung* or framing narratives, which prevent the central – often quite disruptive – event from disturbing the story's overall continuity. For example, in 'Tourmaline', the Rentherr's world is shattered by his wife's seduction by his best friend. She disappears without explanation and, soon after, so does her husband, along with their baby. The woman from whom the narrator had heard the tale then takes up the story. She had been disturbed one night by the haunting sound of a flute in the street, played by a young girl with an unusually large head, accompanied by an old man. The girl is discovered with her flute and a jackdaw at the doorkeeper's apartment of the derelict 'Perronsche Haus'. The old man – who was the Rentherr – had committed suicide. The woman and her husband try to educate the girl so that she can earn a living as a seamstress. Gradually her head shrinks and she becomes a respectable member of society.

Another framing narrative, which lasts even longer than family bonds, is the stone of the stories' titles. 'Tourmaline' begins: 'Tourmaline is dark, and what is being told here is very dark'. Granite is mentioned only at the beginning of its tale, as the scene is set – 'The stone is very old, and nobody remembers hearing when it might have been laid' – and at the end, as order is restored: 'Since then many years have passed, the stone still lies before my father's house, but now my sister's children play on it'.[44] There is more talk of stones in 'Limestone', perhaps because the central narrator is a surveyor. He and the priest sit among the stones, and there are several descriptions of the landscape. For instance, after heavy storms:

The infinite quantity of rain the night before had washed the limestone hills smooth and they lay white and gleaming beneath the blue of the sky and the rays of the sun. As they stretched away one behind the other, they exhibited their broken shining colours in soft gradations of grey, yellowish, reddish and pink, and between them lay the long sky-blue shadows, more and more beautiful the further away they were.[45]

Although beautiful, the heavy rains cause the river to break its banks, meaning that the local schoolchildren have to wade through flooded meadows. The priest guards them from deep holes where a farmer had removed some stones – an act of kindness that uncovers further details about his past. Looking back, the narrator remembers the priest primarily through the objects associated with him; with the fine linen he had kept from his previous worldly life to 'the stones whose reflections shimmered so gently and softly'. As he leaves 'the lonely stones' for the last time, 'tears flowed from my eyes'.

The stones of *Bunte Steine* thus reveal something of characters' histories and psychological states. Later in the nineteenth century, Freud would compare the way 'stones talk' to archaeologists to the buried memories uncovered by psychoanalysis.[46] Eva Geulen put this another way, explaining that for Stifter the stones and banal objects are endowed with 'the allure of future significance. Writing amounts to excavating, collecting, and ordering the world of things in such a way that, ideally, nothing is left out or lost.'[47] The narratives of *Bunte Steine* often consist of the collection of things and their recollection: 'memory is preserved in a number of things', comments the grandfather in 'Granite'. Stifter's extensive descriptions of objects – and his commentaries on the act of describing – create, in Geulen's words, 'the pervasive impression of a paralyzing quietude'. People become objects, as in 'Tourmaline', where the Rentherr's child is listed among the room's effects:

Below this tent there stood on a table a fine basket, in the basket there was a small white bed, and in the bed was the child of the two married people, the girl next to whom they often stood observing the tiny red lips and the rosy cheeks and the closed eyes.[48]

(Unter diesem Zelte stand auf einem Tische ein feiner Korb, in dem Korbe war ein weißes Bettchen, und in dem Bettchen war das Kind der beiden Eheleute, das Mädchen, bei dem sie öfter standen und die winzigen roten Lippen und die rosigen Wangen und die geschlossenen Äuglein betrachteten.)

Stifter's paradoxical poetical goal – to make stones speak – led to the disjointed repetitiveness of his late prose, which in turn influenced Nietzsche, Kafka, Thomas Mann and Hofmannsthal, but it had roots in another tradition that might be thought antithetical to any modernist project.[49] Stifter explained *Bunte Steine* as 'a collection of little games and gimmicks for young people, so that they may delight in it'. The volume was intended to be 'A Holiday Gift' for Christmas 1852 but publication was delayed by a year. These are children's stories not only because their protagonists are youngsters or somehow childlike, but also because they depict an educational process – albeit one less idealized than the notion of *Bildung* conceived by Goethe.[50] Stifter's focus on the mysteries of everyday life and his privileging of the child's view might have created a new mode of writing, but it can also be seen as a retrogressive move; as an attempt to exempt himself from 'the experiences of the last few years', as he puts it in the preface to *Bunte Steine*: in other words, from the aftermath of the failed revolutions of 1848. This is the collector as inhabitant of the interior, as Benjamin explained – concerning himself with the 'paralyzing quietude' of the domestic.

The potential parallels between Stifter and Schumann are obvious. In the 1850s both escaped to the world of children's stories and fairy-tales, and their late styles have both been characterized as disjointed and repetitive. Schumann's opp. 99 and 132 collections further complicate matters because they consist not simply of childlike music but of what is also, relatively speaking, juvenilia: several of the pieces in *Albumblätter* were composed in 1832; others make use of the famous A-S-C-H motto; and *Bunte Blätter* includes a piece originally intended for *Carnaval*.[51] There is little sense that either collection is to be played as a cycle; although the harmonic relationship between movements is usually smooth (dependent on thirds and fifths), there is no apparent thematic progression either musically or poetically.[52] Also, with the exception of the final movements, which in both collections are the most recent, the pieces do not seem to have been ordered by date of composition. *Bunte Blätter*, however, was assembled into groups: an opening set of three small pieces from 1838 ('Drei Stücklein'), 'Fünf Albumblätter' and six separate movements. So how does the music from the 1830s sit with 'Canon' of 1845, which ends *Albumblätter*, or with 'Geschwindmarsch' (composed in 1849) that closes *Bunte Blätter*? Once collected and published in the 1850s, do we hear these pieces as early works or late?

Perhaps, in collecting his earlier works, Schumann was sifting through his *Spreu* with an eye to its future significance, excavating aspects of his late style from his previous efforts, ordering and preserving them. Because these are relatively small-scale pieces (on the whole those in *Bunte Blätter* are longer than those in *Albumblätter*) and not part of an overarching cycle, structures tend to be less complex than Schumann's other piano pieces from the 1830s and early 1840s. This might explain the prevalence of ternary forms (as in *Bunte Blätter*'s 'Novellette', 'Abendmusik' and 'Marsch') that, as discussed in Chapter 6, might be compared to the framing narratives of Stifter's stories. The point here is obviously not that Schumann suddenly began to write in ternary forms, for these movements were mostly written in the 1830s and early 1840s, but that his willingness to

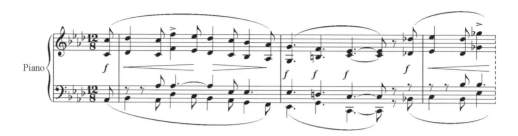

Example 3:1 'Larghetto', bb. 1–3

publish them in the 1850s suggests a confidence in simple structures that would bear further fruit in the *Fantasiestücke* op. 111 and in his music for children.

Other movements from *Albumblätter* exhibit traits that predict defining features of Schumann's late style, particularly the manipulation of thematic repetition and sequences, and the doubling of melodic lines. No. 11, 'Romanze', doubles the melody throughout and begins and ends with the same two-bar cadential arabesque in a similar manner to 'Herberge' from *Waldszenen*. The oddest movement is the 9-bar-long F minor 'Larghetto' (1832), whose right hand melody is doubled at the octave, with the bass line in parallel thirds (Example 3:1). The melody (a close relation to the theme of the second movement of op. 41 no. 2) accents the second beat of the bar but the peak of the crescendo as marked in Clara's edition occurs a beat later. Bizarrely, given the material, the first four bars are marked *forte*, the remainder *piano*. Odd too is the treatment of the two-bar melody; it is repeated immediately a semitone higher and then broken in half, its first bar played three times before the final cadence.

In comparison to these movements, the 16-bar Canon that closes *Albumblätter* is remarkable for its regularity. The tenor line follows the treble at the distance of a bar throughout. The low bass line suggests the Canon was conceived for the pedals of an organ, a feature that recurs in later piano works as discussed in Chapter 6. The 'Geschwindmarsch' of *Bunte Blätter*, the other 'later' piece in the collections, exhibits a similar use of sequence and repetition as found in movements from the *Album für die Jugend* (op. 68) and the later piano cycles. However, there is a greater emphasis on the exact repetition of sections than in Schumann's earlier piano pieces.

In conclusion, the music in *Albumblätter* and *Bunte Blätter* sits quite comfortably with the late music, because of its tendency towards simple forms, sequence and repetition. It might be argued, then, that the collections prove that Schumann's works from the 1850s were a late blooming of his style, the seeds for which were sown some twenty years earlier. The peculiarity of a movement such as the 'Larghetto' ('regularized' in the op. 41 quartet, much as Schumann had smoothed out the irregularities of *Kreisleriana* for its second edition), however, suggests that we are dealing here not with an unbroken line between the earlier and later periods, but with a particular affinity between the juvenilia and the final works. In the former he may have been moving towards his mature style, in the other away from it: 'turning again towards childish treble', as Shakespeare has it. The question, really, is how knowingly we listen to this music. One reason the 'Larghetto' is so striking is that – as a precursor of op. 41: 2 – it might also be an ancestor of the *Geisterthema* discussed in Chapter 6. And then there is Brahms's use of the first of the 'Fünf Albumblätter' (composed in 1841) from *Bunte Blätter* as the theme for his op. 9 Variations, which has certainly lent a melancholy cast to the melody, compounded by Brahms having written his Variations in 1854, after Schumann had entered the asylum.

The influence of context on the interpretation of the composer's collecting habits is further evident on contemplating his list-making practices. Throughout adulthood Schumann had made efforts to record his daily life.[53] In the *Tagebücher* he noted his family's expenses and travels, concerts performed and attended, books read, the progress of his career, his sexual activities and his feelings. He also often excerpted passages from literature he found resonant. These functioned partly as sources for epigraphs and mottoes in the *Neue Zeitschrift für Musik* and his compositions. Daverio considers this 'obsession with lists' to 'represent attempts on Schumann's part to keep the ever-threatening chaos of an uncertain future at bay'.[54] The practice of collecting, as evident in his revisions of earlier works and the gathering together of his writings and unpublished pieces, might have helped him to re-engage with the past, which he might indeed have found comforting. But there is also a sense in which recording and organizing things could have not only protected him from chaos and uncertainty but helped to control and make sense of it: and how different is that, really, from the writing of history, or the careful arrangement of facts and thoughts for a pedagogical purpose?

In the late spring of 1852, Schumann returned to a project he had begun with Clara during the early days of their marriage: excerpting passages on music from Shakespeare's plays.[55] He also searched out other literary references to music, from Homer and Plato to Goethe's correspondence and poems from Arnim's and Brentano's *Des Knaben Wunderhorn*. The process was systematic: after completing his survey of Shakespeare on 6 April 1853 he turned to Jean Paul, re-reading *Titan*, *Die unsichtbarer Loge*, *Hesperus* and *Siebenkäs* before, over Christmas, turning to Schiller's poetry and E. T. A. Hoffmann's *Kreisleriana*. He also provided some explanatory commentary.[56]

Schumann was not alone in making 'motto books'. In many ways his selection of musical passages from literature is a continuation of the collection of folk tales, local legends and sayings undertaken most famously by the Grimms. Brahms also collected excerpts from Jean Paul, Goethe, and Novalis, as well as quotations from friends such as Joachim and, while staying with the Schumanns in Düsseldorf in 1854, compiled a collection of proverbs (*Deutsche Sprichwörter*).[57] And over the next two decades, collections of *Sprüche* as expressions of the *Volk* became increasingly popular, suggesting a connection between the collecting process and the assertion of national and regional language and culture.[58]

However, the status of quotations as collectable material is slightly different from plastic objects, such as antiques or paintings, whose material aspect is tangible, and the collection of which is more obviously fetishistic (prizing the object above all and aiming to gather as many of them as possible) or systematic (driven by an intellectual interest in complete sets).[59] The quotation, in comparison, seems more like a souvenir, to some extent evoking the collector's personal history.[60] Its fragmentary nature defies any attempt to create a 'complete' collection, for that would simply mean a return to its original source. Quotations also sidestep the question of authenticity, for they are undeniably copies.[61] Assembling them into a collection for the perusal of others (such as Schumann intended with *Dichtergarten*, and historical societies did on a larger scale by transcribing and reproducing ancient documents in their journals), in Susan Crane's words, provided 'a museal site rather than the site of origin'.[62] By making texts available in places other than their original locations, their instructional value could be emphasized over their inspirational qualities. The 'free-floating use value' of works of literature and quotations from them (to borrow from Crane again), might also apply to arrangements of music. For example, Schumann's accompaniments to Bach and Paganini might be understood not as a 'misunderstanding' of the original musical objects but as creating a kind of imaginary museum, to frame and explain them. That the collector did not ascribe a 'fixed value' to the original versions such as we are inclined to give today, is in keeping with nineteenth-century attitudes towards restoration, to which I now turn.

Bachiana

Having searched in vain for the grave of J. S. Bach in Leipzig in 1836, the following year Schumann wrote that 'the German nation' should 'gather the lost, forgotten, and hidden-away treasures of Bach into a publicly available collection'.[63] His recommendation finally became reality with the foundation of the Bach Gesellschaft in 1850, at the heart of which was the production of a new complete edition that involved, in the words of Celia Applegate, 'gathering scattered manuscripts, authenticating them, making copies, compiling lists'.[64] However, the historicist projects of the nineteenth century did not always approach the composer's music with the reverence for 'authenticity' we expect today. This is most obvious in the treatment of the Sonatas and Partitas for solo violin, which were adapted and transcribed for alternative forces. For example, Mendelssohn and Schumann (among others) provided piano accompaniments for the famous D minor Chaconne. Subsequently Schumann explained to the publisher Härtel that he found many of the Sonatas 'would decidedly gain by a pianoforte accompaniment' and he completed the whole set from late December 1852 to February 1853, in March also providing accompaniments for the Cello Suites.[65]

Comparing Mendelssohn's and Schumann's accompaniments for the D minor Chaconne suggests that they had slightly different conceptions of what kind of piano accompaniment would best suit Bach's music. If, as Daverio proposed, the accompaniments act as 'glass cases' for the violin line, they are not wholly transparent; the listener stands at a slightly different angle with each version, so some passages can be seen clearly through the glass, while others seem obscured by reflected light. Mendelssohn, for example, tends to smooth over Bach's rhythms; he provides a first beat for the opening bar, and often underpins the violin with regular repeated chords that could have been taken from a song accompaniment. Schumann follows the violin line much more closely in terms of rhythm, figuration and tessitura. Often he keeps the piano part in the upper register of the violin, allowing their lines to intertwine like two solo instruments. Although both composers treat certain passages in virtually the same way, others contrast greatly. Take, for example, the D major section beginning in bar 177 (Example 3:2), which Mendelssohn marks *forte*, doubling the violin's lower line (at a third) in parallel octaves in the bass register. The presentation of the Chaconne theme in bar 185 is accompanied by an onbeat tonic pedal in the bass, and repeated quaver chords in the right hand. Schumann conceives both sections differently. His accompaniment from bar 117 also doubles the lower line at a third, but with quavers in the treble, and marked *piano*. The quavers continue in bar 185, joined by a tonic pedal in the bass that follows the chaconne rhythm, keeping with the offbeat violin line from bar 189, while Mendelssohn continues to stress the first beat of the bar.

Although Schumann's accompaniment might seem more sensitive to Bach's rhythmic pulses than Mendelssohn's, not all of the Sonatas and

Example 3:2 Schumann's and Mendelssohn's accompaniments to Bach's D minor Chaconne, bb. 177–86

Partitas received the same treatment. Schumann provided strong downbeats for the Prelude to the E major Partita and ignored the movement's sarabande rhythm, while adding a 'lilt' to the Andante of the A minor Sonata by introducing syncopated crotchets and a new bass line.[66] Joel Lester has criticized Schumann's approach by making comparative readings of eighteenth-century transcriptions and adaptations. The Romantic composer is said to be left 'at a loss' by the contrapuntal complexities of the G minor fugue, adding and abandoning countersubjects in a manner that might have suited the thematic foreclosure of the op. 17 *Fantasie* but that is 'not pertinent to Bach'.[67] Where Schumann probably intended to promote and make palatable Bach's music for nineteenth-century performers and listeners, Lester hears him as misunderstanding its structure and even *Affekt*. A parallel might be made to Schoenberg's complaint that in his criticism Schumann 'underlaid Bach with everyday images and feeling', distracting readers' attention from the more unusual aspects of the music. As Schoenberg acknowledged, however, the latter 'would have put people off: too much brain was needed to produce them'.[68] In other words, while Schumann may have 'misunderstood' Bach according to the precepts of today's performance practice, his purpose might have been geared less towards 'authenticity' and more towards pedagogy and *Bildung*, helping the nineteenth-century musician come to terms with the music of another era.[69]

Schumann's purpose in preparing the accompaniments to the Sonatas and Partitas and Cello Suites can be better understood in the context of the age's reinvestment in historical and national cultural identity. Although the increased interest in city art museums and the recording of folk-tales, as well as the collecting of ancient manuscripts and the preservation of ancient buildings, is considered by James J. Sheehan to express 'the need to preserve and protect the threatened residues of the past' in the face of 'destructive forces of change', the manner in which monuments and so forth were preserved was very different from today's reverence for *Urtexts* and 'authentic' practices.[70] Indeed, Schumann's Bach accompaniments most closely resemble Romantic restoration projects – meaning not refurbishment, but 'restoration to completion'. This was, after all, the time when preservationists campaigned to put arms on the Venus de Milo and the twin towers of Cologne Cathedral were finally being built.[71] According to Crane, restoration represented not only contemporary aesthetics but also the principle of historical collecting: supplementing fragments by imagining a whole that may have preceded them, and then positing the original rather than the fragments as what was found, saving and restoration had less to do with damage repair and more to do with restitution, 'returning' to an imaginary original state of completeness.[72] In this light, Schumann's Bach accompaniments resemble not so much glass cases, as Daverio proposed, as a once missing limb.

Unfortunately, Schumann's Bach accompaniments were not thought to attain a renewed state. The composer tried to persuade the publishers Kistner to purchase the accompaniments to the Cello Suites in 1853, but they declined, explaining that according to their account books 'these Sonatas have been particularly unsuccessful' and that they were very well provided for with regard to them anyway, with an edition (probably by Bernhard Molique) about to appear.[73] In 1860, Clara sought the advice of Joachim and Brahms about whether the accompaniments should be published. They thought not; as Clara explained in a letter to the publisher Schuberth, 'because they were not by any means finished'.[74] Along with the Violin Concerto, Third Violin Sonata and Five Cello Romances, the accompaniments to the Cello Suites thus became casualties of Clara's, Brahms's and Joachim's determination to prevent the public from seeing works that seemed to bear the marks of Schumann's creative failure too clearly.[75] Their attempt to preserve a more 'perfect' view of the composer in some ways is a review as drastic as the completion of the Venus de Milo. Schumann may not be made more beautiful by the addition of these 'late' works to the Collected Edition, but awareness of them aids our understanding of his engagement with music history on many different levels.

In a magic circle

On 21 October 1853, three days after completing his 'last' piano cycle, *Gesänge der Frühe*, Schumann began a series of piano accompaniments to Paganini's Caprices for solo violin. In so doing he was returning to a musician who had first captured his imagination in 1830, when he attended a concert by the virtuoso violinist in Frankfurt. Two years later, while he was completing the *Studien nach Capricen von Paganini* (op. 3), Schumann noted in his diary that he was visited by 'a picture that made a shocking impression – Paganini in a magic circle – the murdered wife – dancing skeletons and a train of dim, mesmerizing spirits . . . While making the arrangement of the G minor Presto [Caprice no. 16; no. 6 in op. 3] the picture often hovered before me, and I think that the close [of the arrangement] reflects it.'[76] His *Sechs Concert-Etuden nach Capricen von Paganini* (op. 10) followed the next year, in 1833.

While the opp. 3 and 10 studies are without doubt virtuosic, reflecting Schumann's then aspirations as a concert pianist, as responses to Paganini's Caprices they are almost coy; the original music is treated with reverence, for the most part simply having been transcribed into a pianistic equivalent. In this regard Schumann was unlike composers such as Liszt and Brahms, who absorbed the Caprices as material for displaying their virtuoso techniques rather than presenting the music virtually in its original form.[77] Liszt seems to have acknowledged as much by the inclusion of Schumann's more temperate version of the G minor Caprice as an ossia above his own pyrotechnic

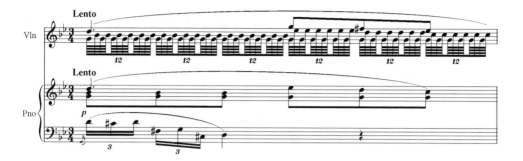

Example 3:3   Schumann's accompaniment to Paganini's Caprice in G minor, b. 1

response in the first edition of the *Grandes Etudes* (dedicated to Clara in 1839–40).[78] Perhaps it was receipt of Liszt's revised version, in 1851, without ossia, that prompted Schumann to return to the Caprices the following year.

Actually, Schumann's treatment of the G minor Caprice had varied Paganini's original to a greater extent than other adaptations in op. 10. The violin's melodic line was maintained, but its original hemidemisemiquavers were converted into semiquaver triplets, the whole being underpinned by a new descending triplet figure in the bass. Although, as with the accompaniments for Bach, Schumann's 1853 treatment of the Caprices, as Joachim described, is conceived 'in a very simple harmonious mode, very clearly written and logical', the accompaniment for the sixth Caprice retains the bass figure devised for op. 10 (Example 3:3).[79] Some of the left hand's syncopations (e.g. bar 15) are smoothed out, and the offbeat accentuation of the bass semiquavers in op. 10's bars 31–4 omitted.

Generally speaking, Schumann's accompaniments are not adventurous. With a few exceptions, such as the G minor Caprice, the piano part is mostly made up of simple chords, as if beginning to improvise an accompaniment – an effect akin to the 'unfinished' aspect of the Cello Suites Clara referred to in her letter to Schuberth. There is a sense throughout the accompaniments that the piano resembles the composer's ear, listening to the harmonic implications of the various arpeggios, trills and ricochet figures. In the accompaniment for the middle section of the third Caprice the piano's chords seem barely able to keep up with the frantic violin line. Schumann's approach to the same Caprice as the last movement of op. 10 had been markedly different: the piano had taken up the violin's challenge, chasing its semiquaver line in kind. Maybe the younger composer had more energy to take on Paganini's virtuosity; in the accompaniments there is a sense instead that he was now prepared to sit back and contemplate the violinist's wizardry.

Example 3:4   Schumann's accompaniment to Paganini's Caprice in E major, bb. 1–3

If – as Harald Krebs suggests – Paganini's Caprices were an early influence on Schumann's exploration of metrical dissonance, by the 1850s they proved more of a challenge.[80] For example, Paganini's first caprice in E major took as the source for its fast-moving arpeggio motive Pietro Locatelli's seventh Caprice, exploring some of its chromatic implications and shifting its opening from the downbeat to the upbeat.[81] A further layer of rhythmic and metrical complexity was added by changing the metre from $\frac{3}{4}$ to $\frac{2}{4}$ while retaining the motive's original duration. Schumann did not include the E major Caprice in opp. 3 or 10. In his accompaniment, rather surprisingly, the piano provides the upbeat with a tonic chord; particularly because a dominant chord falls on the downbeat and the tonic, again, on the upbeat, in effect he returns to Locatelli's metrical pulse (Example 3:4).

On resuming his work on the accompaniments while at Endenich (March–June 1855), Schumann had explained to Joachim that he intended 'to harmonize the Caprices by Paganini, and not in a complicated canonical way like the A minor Variations, but simply'.[82] When asking Brahms for copies of his opp. 3 and 10, he explained that he had harmonized five Caprices already:

but the work seems to me harder than my free arrangements of old. The reason is that in the violin he often has such a peculiar bass. In any case my previous piano solo arrangements would greatly assist my present work.[83]

(Es scheint aber die Arbeit schwerer, als meine freie Bearbeitung von früher. Der Grund ist, in der Violine liegt so oft der Baß nach seiner Weise. Jedenfalls würden meine älteren Piano-Solo-Arrangements mir die jetzige Arbeit sehr erleichtern).

As outlined above, Schumann's struggle with some of the Caprices is evident. The simplicity of his accompaniments, and the way in which they occasionally alter the harmonic rhythm of the originals, are where his imagination most obviously failed him. There is something all the more moving about the fact that it was with Paganini's Caprices that this happened; the dream of the violinist in a magic circle that had mesmerized him back in 1830 seeming so distant from the composer trying to find in his earlier musical experiences a way in which to collect his thoughts.

Collecting thoughts

Although Schumann's collecting practices in the 1850s can be understood as manifestations of the historicizing process, from the gathering together of his life's achievements to the preservation of masterworks by other writers and musicians, the collections he made during his years at Endenich (with the exception of the Paganini accompaniments) took a slightly different and more troubling form.

Dr Richarz's logbook for 6 September 1855 notes that the previous evening Schumann had had trouble enunciating – his tongue seemed heavy and thick, as if he were speaking with his mouth full, and his consonants were unclear, slurred and blurred ('undeutlich, verschliffen und verschwommen').[84] His sleep was a little disturbed. The next morning he busied himself with making geographical excerpts from a map ('bei der Visite mit einem geographischem Auszug nach der Karte beschäftigt'). Brahms reported to Joachim on 10 April 1856 that Schumann had greeted him as joyfully and warmly as ever, but that Brahms could not understand a word he said. Schumann was reading an atlas, from which he was making extracts in a childlike manner ('Er war ein Atlas und er eben beschäftigt, Auszüge zu machen, freilich kindische').[85]

The process of collecting seems to have overtaken, in Schumann's mind, its purpose. While the assembling of ephemera is perhaps no less worthy, in historical terms, than the framing of masterpieces in gold, the enumeration and classification of objects, without narratives about their origins or the reconstruction of the(ir) past, is near impossible for anyone apart from the collector to understand.[86] At a certain point, Susan Stewart argues, it is necessary to distinguish between 'the "proper" collection and the insane collection, which is a collection for its own sake'.[87] The psychological impulses behind such collections are generally theorized as regression to a childlike state, an anal retentiveness that attempts to protect body and soul from the outside world. Schumann in the asylum undoubtedly fits such a model. But this is not to say that all of his collecting practices should be seen to lead to the moment when he began to pore over an atlas. It is crucial that we try to disentangle the different projects he embarked upon in the 1850s from the trawler net of his final illness, for otherwise we risk drowning everything in 'lateness', rather than considering the implications of the historicist movement or the composer's self-awareness of his changing style. Let us not unthinkingly 'collect' the composer: putting him in a particular box along with other 'mad', Romantic artists who outlived their time; classifying, repackaging, and neatening loose ends.

Notes

1. Adalbert Stifter, *Limestone and Other Stories*, trans. David Luke (New York: Harcourt, Brace and World, 1968), p. 38.
2. Jean Baudrillard, 'The system of collecting', trans. Roger Cardinal, *The Cultures of Collecting*, ed. John Elsner and Roger Cardinal (London: Reaktion Books, 1994), p. 12.
3. See Stanley Cavell's essay on collecting, 'The world as things', in *Philosophy the day after tomorrow* (Cambridge, Mass.: Belknap Press, Harvard University Press, 2005), pp. 236–82; here pp. 238–9.
4. Daverio, *Robert Schumann*, p. 477.
5. Daverio, *Robert Schumann*, p. 477.
6. Walter Benjamin, *Charles Baudelaire: A Lyric Poet in the Era of High Capitalism*, trans. Harry Zohn (London: Verso, 1983), p. 168.
7. Daverio, *Robert Schumann*, p. 138.
8. On the *Grande Sonate* see Linda Correll Roesner, 'Schumann's "parallel forms"', *19th-Century Music* XIV (1991), 268–72.
9. For further discussion of the substitution's implication see Jon W. Finson, 'The intentional tourist: romantic irony in the Eichendorff *Liederkreis* of Robert Schumann' in *Schumann and his World*, ed. R. Larry Todd (Princeton: Princeton University Press, 1994), pp. 156–70.
10. 'Ich verdarb mir leider in früheren Zeiten meine Sachen so oft, und ganz unmuthwilliger Weise. Dies ist nun alles ausgemerzt'. Letter to Friedrich Whistling, 20 November 1849, *Briefe. Neue Folge*, p. 464.
11. Jon W. Finson, 'The intentional tourist', p. 156.
12. Charles Rosen, *The Romantic Generation* (Cambridge, Mass.: Harvard University Press, 1995), p. 692.
13. Beate Julia Perrey, *Schumann's 'Dichterliebe' and Early Romantic Poetics: Fragmentation of Desire* (Cambridge: Cambridge University Press, 2002), pp. 116–22.
14. Zachary Leader, *Revision and Romantic Authorship* (Oxford: Clarendon Press, 1996), pp. 2–3.
15. Leader, *Revision and Romantic Authorship*, pp. 4–5; for further discussion see Roger Parker, who quotes the same passage in *Remaking the Song: Operatic Visions and Revisions from Handel to Berio* (Berkeley: University of California Press, 2006).

16. Leader, *Revision and Romantic Authorship*, p. 38. Wordsworth's career spanned from 1785–1850; the last collected edition he worked on himself was published in 1849–50.

17. Leader, *Revision and Romantic Authorship*, p. 74.

18. Leader, *Revision and Romantic Authorship*, p. 73.

19. Richard Taruskin, *The Oxford History of Western Music: The Nineteenth Century* (Oxford: Oxford University Press, 2005), vol. III, p. 318.

20. *AmZ* 43 (1841), cols. 1100–01.

21. Marc Andreae, 'Die vierte Symphonie Robert Schumanns, ihre Fassungen, ihre Interpretationsprobleme', *Ein romantisches Erbe in neuer Forschung. Acht Studien*, ed. Robert-Schumann-Gesellschaft Düsseldorf (Mainz: Schott, 1984), pp. 39–40.

22. Wasielewski, *Robert Schumann*, p. 484. For further discussion of Schumann's attitude to tempi see Reinhard Kapp, *Studien zum Spätwerk Robert Schumanns* (Tutzing: Hans Schneider, 1984), pp. 106–25.

23. 'Z' (Maria Heinrich Schmidt) singled out the transitions between the Symphony's movements as a notable formal innovation in her review of the 1841 premiere for the *Neue Zeitschrift für Musik* 15 (1841), 198.

24. Letter December 1889, *Johannes Brahms im Briefwechsel mit Franz Wüllner*, ed. Ernst Wolff (Berlin: Deutsche Brahms Gesellschaft, 1921), p. 167. Against Clara's wishes, Brahms had the 1841 version published by Breitkopf und Härtel in 1891.

25. For further discussion see George Asher Zlotnik, *Orchestration Revisions in the Symphonies of Robert Schumann* (PhD diss., Indiana University, 1972).

26. Letter to Verhulst, 3 May 1853, *Robert Schumann's Briefe. Neue Folge*, p. 372.

27. Ludwig Bischoff, *Rheinische Musikzeitung*, cited in Wolfgang Boetticher, *Robert Schumann: Leben und Werk; Quellen, Daten, Dokumente* (Wilhelmshaven: Florian Noetzel, 2004), p. 367.

28. For further discussion see Margit L. McCorkle's introduction to the *Thematisch-Bibliographisches Werkverzeichnis, Robert Schumann: Neue Ausgabe sämtlicher Werke* (Mainz: Schott, 2003), vol. VIII: 6.

29. Letter to Breitkopf und Härtel, 3 November 1853, *Briefe. Neue Folge*, p. 485.

30. *Deutsche Musik–Zeitung* 1:29 (14 July 1860), 225. Dörffel's catalogue received three reprintings and a fourth, revised and expanded edition. Meanwhile, further works by Schumann emerged, as Clara, Joachim and Brahms decided which of the later works merited publication.

31. Letter of 3 June 1852, *Briefe. Neue Folge*, p. 474. Schumann's *Gesammelte Schriften* were initially published by Wigand; the second edition was produced by Breitkopf und Härtel in 1883.

32. For such men, Baudrillard continues, collecting is 'a regression to the anal stage, which is characterized by accumulation, orderliness, aggressive retention, and so on'; see Jean Baudrillard, *The System of Objects*, trans. James Benedict (London: Verso, 1996), p. 87.

33. According to McCorkle, p. 58, there is a three-page list of compositions from 1824–43 (4871/VII C, 2-A3); a list of compositions from 1833 in a book of letter drafts (the so-called *Briefkonzeptbuch*, 4871/VII C, 9-A3); and a compositional overview (*Kompositionsübersicht*) in the *Projektenbuch* (4871/VII C, 8-A3), the last entry in which are the Cello Romances, composed in November 1853, that Clara apparently destroyed forty years later.

34. See Judith Pascoe, *The Hummingbird Cabinet: A Rare and Curious History of Romantic Collectors* (Ithaca and London: Cornell University Press, 2006), pp. 4–5.

35. On historical societies see Hermann Hempel, *Geschichtsvereine einst und jetzt. Vortrag gehalten am Tag der 70. Wiederkehr der Gründung des Geschichtsvereins für Göttingen und Umgebung* (Göttingen, 1963).

36. Abigail Green explains how, after 1848, government policy actively promoted history, museums, monuments and festivities as cultural activities; *Fatherlands*, pp. 97–147.

37. See Celia Applegate, *Bach in Berlin: Nation and Culture in Mendelssohn's Revival of the 'St. Matthew Passion'* (Ithaca, New York: Cornell University Press, 2005); and William Weber, *Music and the Middle Class: The Social Structure of Concert Life in London, Paris, and Vienna* (London: Holmes and Meier, 1975).

38. Schumann began to collect together his *Spreu* over Christmas 1850, noting its progression alongside the season's snowfall in his diary. *Tagebücher, Band III: Haushaltbücher 2*, p. 548.

39. In fact, Schumann's collection was published in January 1852, before Stifter's volume (*Albumblätter* was published in January 1854).

40. On the relationship of Stifter's writings to 'the dynamics of collecting' see Peter M. McIsaac, 'The museal path to *Bildung*: collecting, exhibiting and exchange in Stifter's *Der Nachsommer*', *German Life and Letters* 57 (2004), 268–89.

41. See J. van Heukelum, *Das Künstlerehepaar Robert und Clara Schumann und der Dichter Adalbert Stifter*, in *Vierteljahresschrift des A. –Stifter-Instituts* Linz 34 (1985), 61–90.

42. The similarity of Stifter 'stressing the ultimate continuity of nature' with Schopenhauer's thoughts is pointed out in Martin and Erika Swales, *Adalbert Stifter: A Critical Study* (Cambridge: Cambridge University Press, 1984), p. 17. In the essay 'Die Kunst und das Göttliche' (1867), Stifter claimed the task of art was to reveal the divine as a heightened form of reality: 'die wirklichste Wirklichkeit'; see John Walker, 'Two realisms: German literature and philosophy', *Philosophy and German Literature, 1700–1990*, ed. Nicholas Saul (Cambridge: Cambridge University Press, 2002), p. 132.

43. As James J. Sheehan explains, although the plots sometime seem 'almost static, no mid century writer was more aware of the power of change than . . . Stifter'. *German History, 1770–1866* (Oxford: Clarendon Press, 1989), p. 829.

44. In its first version 'Granit' was entitled 'Die Pechbrenner' ('The Pitch Burner'), which would have lent the arrangement of the narrative a different emphasis.

45. Adalbert Stifter, 'Limestone', *Brigitta and Other Tales*, trans. Helen Watanabe-O'Kelly (London: Penguin, 1990), p. 213.

46. See Sigmund Freud, 'The aetiology of hysteria' (1896) and John Forrester, 'Freud and Collecting', *The Cultures of Collecting*, ed. John Elsner and Roger Cardinal (London: Reaktion Books, 1994), pp. 224–51. Jacques Derrida critiques Freud's assumptions about the stones in *Archive Fever: A Freudian Impression*, ed. Eric Prenowitz (Chicago: University of Chicago Press, 1996), pp. 94–5.

47. Eva Geulen, 'Tales of a collector', *A New History of German Literature*, ed. David Wellbery (Cambridge, Mass.: Belknap Press, 2004), p. 588.

48. Translation, Swales, *Adalbert Stifter*, p. 177. Adorno wrote, perhaps thinking of a passage such as this: 'The complaints about [Stifter] as a harmonistic, affirmative writer have been exaggerated, especially in reference to his late works, where objectivity is reduced to a lifeless mask and where the alleged evocation of life reads more like a ritual to keep life at a distance'; 'The Autonomy of Art', *The Adorno Reader*, ed. Brian O'Connor (Oxford: Blackwell, 2000), p. 250. On realism in *Bunte Steine* see also Eric Downing, *Double Exposures: Repetition and Realism in Nineteenth-Century German Fiction* (Stanford: Stanford University Press, 2000), pp. 24–40.

49. According to Geulen ('Tales of a collector', p. 587), Stifter's new strategy also 'established his fame as the most boring German-language writer'. Stifter's alleged boringness and sentimentalism – and his celebration by literary critics – is the target of a long diatribe in Thomas Bernhard's 1985 novella *Alte Meister*, in which the musicologist Reger devises a 'Stifter test', demanding from readers an honest answer whether they had liked what they read. None do. *Old Masters*, trans. Ewald Osers (Chicago: University of Chicago Press, 1992), pp. 34–41.

50. For further discussion see Geulen, 'Tales of a collector', pp. 590–1.

51. The pieces from 1832 in *Albumblätter* are nos. 1 ('Impromptu'), 3 ('Scherzino'), 12 ('Burla'), 13 ('Larghetto'), 15 ('Walzer'). Nos. 4 ('Walzer') and no. 11 ('Romanze') use the A-S-C-H motto. The third of the 'Fünf Albumblätter' in *Bunte Blätter*, 'Ziemlich langsam, sehr gesangvoll', was composed for *Carnaval*.

52. The collections have tended to be excerpted in piano tutors, adding to their pedagogical associations. Reimann claims that *Albumblätter* and *Album für die Jugend* 'are driven by educational and commercial purposes incompatible with the experimental nature of the earlier cycles', *Schumann's piano cycles and the novels of Jean Paul* (Rochester, NY: University of Rochester Press, 2004), p. 8.

53. On Schumann's compulsion to record every aspect of his life see Peter F. Ostwald's review of *Tagebücher*, vol. II in *19th-Century Music* (1984), 176–80.

54. Daverio, *Robert Schumann*, p. 219.

55. The collection has been published as *Robert Schumanns Dichtergarten für Musik* (Bonn: Stroemfeld, 2007).

56. Peter Kross observes that – even taking into account the help of Clara and a copyist in compiling *Dichtergarten* – Schumann's entries showed no disturbance in order or handwriting; cited in Ostwald, *The Inner Voices of a Musical Genius*, p. 272.

57. Brahms filled four notebooks with quotations, each named after E. T. A. Hoffmann's fictional music master Kreisler: *Schatzkästlein des jungen Kreislers*, *Des jungen Kreislers Schatzkästlein*, *Schöne Gedanken über Musik*, and *Schöne Gedanken über Musik*, book 2. Later in life he added further excerpts from Goethe, Jean Paul, Bismarck and others. They were subsequently published as *Des jungen Kreislers Schatzkästlein: Aussprüche von Dichtern, Philosophen und Künstlern, zusammengetragen durch Johannes Brahms*, ed. Karl Krebs (Berlin: Verlag der Deutschen Brahmsgesellschaft m.b.h., 1909); Krebs suggests that they might be considered a companion piece to Schumann's *Dichtergarten*.

58. For more on which see Ryan Minor, 'Occasions and Nations in Brahms's *Fest- und Gedenksprüche*', *19th-Century Music*, 24 (2006), 266.

59. On the three types of collecting (souvenir, fetishistic and systematic) see Susan M. Pearce, *On Collecting: An Investigation into collecting in the European tradition* (London, New York: Routledge, 1995), p. 32.

60. On the collection of musical souvenirs see J. Q. Davies, 'Julia's Gift: The Social Life of Scores, c. 1830', *Journal of the Royal Musical Association*, 131(2006), 287–309. Clara Schumann's *Blumenbuch für Robert*, ed. Gerd Nauhaus and Ingrid Bosch (Bonn: Stroemfeld, 2006) – pressed flowers she collected for her husband while he was at Endenich – seems a further example of keepsakes representing personal history.

61. According to Susan M. Crane, 'written documents resisted the stigma of "copy" (as opposed to "original"), because they were re-presented in the same textual form as they occurred (plastic objects could only be drawn or described in two dimensions).' *Collecting and Historical Consciousness in Early Nineteenth-Century Germany* (Ithaca and London: Cornell University Press, 2000), p. 121.

62. Susan M. Crane, *Collecting and Historical Consciousness*, p. 121.

63. Robert Schumann, 'J. S. Bach: Gesamtwerke', *Gesammelte Schriften*, II, p. 77.

64. Celia Applegate, *Bach in Berlin: Nation and Culture in Mendelssohn's Revival of the 'St Matthew Passion'* (Ithaca, New York: Cornell University Press, 2005), pp. 241 and 254.

65. Letter of 4 January 1853 and 17 January 1853, *Briefe. Neue Folge*, pp. 265–7.

66. On Schumann's flattening of Bach's surface rhythms see Joel Lester, 'Reading and misreading: Schumann's accompaniments to Bach's Sonatas and

Partitas for solo violin', *Current Musicology*, 25–7, 30; see also Wilhelm Geibler, 'Robert Schumanns Klavierbegleitungen', *Robert-Schumann–Tage* (1984), 27–9.

67. Lester, 'Reading and misreading', 43.

68. Arnold Schoenberg, 'Robert Schumann as Critic', *Style and Idea*, trans. Dika Newlin (London: Williams and Norgate, 1951), p. 473.

69. Ostwald explains Schumann's motivation for the accompaniments as resulting from a desire 'to get his mind in order'; a 'wish to make Bach's music accessible to the public'; and from his new friendship with the violinist Becker, who visited the Schumanns' home several times to play the pieces through. *The Inner Voices of a Musical Genius*, p. 255.

70. James J. Sheehan, 'The museum age, 1830–1880', in *Museums in the German Art World: From the End of the Old Regime to the Rise of Modernism* (Oxford: Oxford University Press, 2000), pp. 83–137; here p. 84.

71. Dolf Sternberger discusses proposals to complete Venus in *Panorama of the Nineteenth Century*, trans. Joachim Neugroschel (New York: Urizen Books, 1977), pp. 55–6.

72. Crane, *Collecting and Historical Consciousness*, p. 41.

73. Letter from Carl Gurckhaus, 21 November 1853, Correspondence vol. 26/no. 131; in 'Kritischer Bericht' to *Robert Schumann Neue Ausgabe sämtlicher Werke I: Orchesterwerke, Werkgruppe 1: Symphonien Band 5, Ouvertüre, Scherzo und Finale, op. 52*, ed. Sonia Gerlach and Matthias Wendt (Mainz: Schott, 2000), p. 119.

74. Letter of 25 May 1863, Zsch, archive no. 12170-A2, cited in the 'Kritischer Bericht' to the *Neue Ausgabe* of the violin sonatas, p. 393. See also Joachim's letter against publication of 5 July 1860; *Briefe von und an Joseph Joachim*, ed. Johannes Joachim and Andreas Moser, vol. 2, *Die Jahre 1858–1868* (Berlin, 1912), p. 105.

75. Joachim Draheim prepared an edition of the Third Suite (BWV 1009) in 1985, using a copy of Schumann's piano accompaniment made by Julius Goltermann.

76. 4 June 1832, *Tagebücher, Band I: 1827–1838*, ed. George Eisman (Leipzig: VEB Deutscher Verlag, 1971) p. 404.

77. According to Edward T. Cone, Brahms's left-hand version of Bach's D minor Chaconne 'subordinates the transcriber's voice to the composer's', while Liszt's transcriptions sometimes keeps faithfully to the original, at other times express 'the voice of Liszt', and occasionally achieve a hybrid of the two personae. *The Composer's Voice* (Berkeley: University of California Press, 1974), p. 76.

78. Kenneth Hamilton points out that Liszt might have realized the *Grande Etudes* were hardly suitable for Clara's performance style or taste; he interprets the inclusion of Schumann's restrained version as a gesture of respect and friendship. 'Liszt's early and Weimar piano works', *The Cambridge Companion to Liszt*, ed. Kenneth Hamilton (Cambridge: Cambridge University Press, 2005), p. 64.

79. Hanslick, 'Schumann at Endenich', *Schumann and his World*, p. 278. Similarly, the accompaniment for the Fourth Caprice, in C minor, replicates the treatment of the same movement as op. 10 no. 4.

80. Harald Krebs, *Fantasy Pieces*, pp. 69–70.

81. For further discussion see Jeffrey Perry, 'Paganini's Quest: the Twenty-four *Capricci per violino solo*, Op. 1', *19th-Century Music* 27 (2004), 208–30; here 215–26.

82. Letter of 10 March 1855, *Briefe. Neue Folge*, p. 405.

83. Schumann to Brahms, March 1855, *Briefe. Neue Folge*, p. 407.

84. *Robert Schumann in Endenich (1854–1856): Krankenakten, Briefzeugnisse und zeitgenössische Berichte*, ed. Bernhard R. Appel (Mainz: Schott, 2006), p. 325.

85. *Johannes Brahms im Briefwechsel mit Joseph Joachim*, ed. Andreas Moser (Berlin: Deutsche Brahms Gesellschaft, 1921), I, p. 134.

86. See Sue Waterman, 'Collecting the nineteenth century', *Representations* 90 (2005), 98–128, especially 108–9.

87. Susan Stewart, *On Longing: Narratives of the Miniature, the Gigantic, the Souvenir, the Collection* (Durham: Duke University Press, 1993), p. 154.

Affirmative art may become a cipher for despair.[1]

Schumann celebrated his new post as Director of the Allgemeine Musikverein in Düsseldorf by completing two major orchestral works: the Cello Concerto (op. 129, 10–24 October 1850) and the E flat major Symphony (op. 97, 7/2 November–9 December of the same year), otherwise known as the Third or 'Rhenish'. While seeming to spring from the same well of enthusiasm, the Cello Concerto and Third Symphony represent opposite poles of Schumann's 'public' style. The Third Symphony is one of the composer's most respected works, celebrated for its evocation of the Rhineland and Cologne Cathedral, and as much part of 1850s nationalist *Volkstümlichkeit* as the choral ballades discussed in Chapter 2. The Cello Concerto, on the other hand, was not published until 1854 and is often considered flawed, despite having been championed by soloists in the twentieth century. Behind critical responses there have often lain suspicions that Schumann was incapable of the kind of virtuosic display expected of the conventional Romantic concerto – the most extrovert of public styles – a view also apparent in the reception of his other late concerted works, the *Phantasie* for violin and orchestra, op. 131 and the Violin Concerto WoO 23.

The difference between the Third Symphony and the Cello Concerto, and their differing receptions, can also be explained as representing a shift in conceptions of subjectivity with regard to Schumann's music. That shift in turn can be mapped on to changing attitudes towards – perhaps changing generations of – Romanticism at the mid-century, attitudes that have already been touched on in earlier chapters, but which are worth outlining more explicitly here. In an 1830 self-portrait, Schumann described his artistic temperament as melancholy, responding to the world with feeling rather than reflection; in short, he thought himself more subjective than objective in approach.[2] Many have agreed with him.[3] For instance, Franz Brendel claimed that the characters of *Kreisleriana*:

reveal a subject focused entirely on itself, one that lives and breathes exclusively in its own inwardness and only moves outward from this center into the external. This subject is not connected directly and intimately with the external, and it does not

experience external circumstances personally and immediately; rather, it appropri-
ates them through fantasy. It is an individuality that expresses only itself and its
personal emotional states, but it depicts the world only as far as the Self has been
touched by it. It is a subjectivity evolving ever more concretely as part of the historical process and now manifesting itself to the extreme in a fashion governed by
fantasy and humour.[4]

We have here both a portrait of the Romantic artist as a young man and
a portrait of the composer as a young Romantic; for in his later works,
Brendel perceived Schumann to move away from subjectivism, describing
him as emerging from his inwardness. 'Restless, passionate agitation gives
way to a more restrained type of expression, traditional forms replace the
self-generated ones', Brendel explained.[5] And whereas Schumann had once
written only for the piano, he now turned to choral and orchestral works.
Despite his admiration for some of those later pieces, Brendel complained
that in them 'The sharp edges of [Schumann's] subjectivity are deflected,
his ruggedness softens, and the composer descends from the isolation of his
former height.'[6] The composer 'seems no longer true to himself when he
has to step outside himself', Brendel continued: 'The foundation of Schumann's creativity is his subjectivity'.[7] Hegelian that he was, Brendel wondered
whether this new objective phase would give way to a third, higher stage that
would reconcile and unify everything.

It was by no means only Brendel who perceived a different approach to
composition in the Schumann of the mid-1840s. The composer himself
admitted to having adopted a 'new manner', claiming that he now devised
music in his head rather than letting it out in a white heat.[8] That new
approach seems to have emerged in tandem with Schumann's recovery from
a period of severe depression, but it also resulted from some crucial changes
in his method of composing. Up until 1845 he had depended heavily on
improvising at the piano, making it hard for us to differentiate between preliminary plans and compositional elaboration; afterwards he began to use
sketches more extensively. The Second Symphony and Piano Concerto show
the fruits of this 'new manner', as perhaps do his studies in counterpoint
(discussed in Chapter 6); transitions become smoother and there is a more
emphatic focus on the development of motivic cells rather than on thematic
elaboration. As well as describing this as 'objective', as discussed in the Introduction, commentators have seen Schumann's approach as becoming more
classical, with conventionally abstract forms such as the symphony and
concerto replacing the poetic Romanticism of the pieces for voice and piano.

Works such as the Second Symphony and Piano Concerto were also significant because of their scale. In writing for larger forces, Schumann was

clearly in search of his public voice. (A similar aim is demonstrated by the time he spent in the mid-1840s looking for subjects for an opera.) Brendel's image of the composer descending 'from the isolation of his former height' implies that interaction with the rest of the world was not necessarily to Schumann's advantage; his relationship with large groups of people was never easy, as will become apparent from later discussion of his reputation as a conductor. However, it was necessary for him to maintain a public profile, particularly at this stage in his career with a reputation to consolidate and a family to support. As will be seen, the notion that the best of Schumann can be found in solo music – and, within that, in passages of inwardness – in many ways continues into the reception of the orchestral music; however grand and ceremonial the piece, it is in those occasional tender solos for wind or strings, or the momentary recollection of a previous theme, that the composer's 'true' voice has been heard.

Inevitably, Brendel's uncertainty over the success of Schumann's public style on the basis of his inherently private creativity over the years has been overlain with awareness of the composer's incipient mental illness. It might be assumed that the subjective impulse would result in Schumann's 'madder' music and to an extent that is true: his earlier works are famous for their eccentricities. However, it is the 'objective' approach that is aligned with the onset of his illness. For instance, Richard Taruskin describes the effect of Schumann's increasing public duties as acting 'as a restraint' on his later compositions, which might show greater mastery of technique 'but also a tendency to conform to public expectations'.[9] That tendency to conform, Taruskin continues, became a means by which Schumann felt he could regain control over his increasingly irrational thoughts: '"Classicism", for him, was a retreat from a threatened abyss.'[10] In a similar manner to the collecting habits discussed in the previous chapter, then, Schumann is deemed to have sought refuge from the world by making his experience of it more regular and manageable. As a result, the 'classical' forms of his music from the 1850s are diagnosed as dissociative, masking inner turmoil; thematic focus becomes repetition–compulsion; and the reminiscence of melodies is no longer thought a means to achieve coherence but a manifestation of aural hallucination. In a strange reversal of Goethe's famous dictum, Schumann's late orchestral music makes Romanticism healthy, and Classicism sick.

Subjectivity thus regains the upper hand. Recent literary scholars such as Marilyn Butler and David Aram Kaiser, however, have critiqued the tendency to foreground subjectivity in studies of Romanticism; to do so, they argue, ignores the role of politics or institutions.[11] While Butler's and Kaiser's concern is with English Romanticism, a similar argument can be made about its manifestation in Germany, particularly when the effect of the revolutionary spirit of the late 1840s is brought into play.[12] The 1848–9 uprisings might not have been matched by an immediate revolution in aesthetics, but ideas about Romanticism did begin to change in their aftermath, and with them conceptions of subjectivity.[13] The kind of individualistic approach prized by earlier Romantic generations (Novalis, Fichte, Friedrich Schlegel) increasingly seemed outdated. Instead, according to historian Brian Vick, 'the apparatus of the public sphere' now served as the 'locus of identity'; the envisioned nation had to be made real through action and to reach a conscious level of experience.[14] Not least because of his post in Düsseldorf, Schumann was part of that public sphere. As discussed in Chapter 2, many of his choral works explored political and nationalistic themes, reflecting the sense that artists needed to re-engage with politics and society.[15] That political awareness was extended into the orchestral works – most notably the Third Symphony, with its Rhenish associations, but also perhaps in Schumann's turn to larger and popular forms more generally. Schumann's 'public style' might then be understood not as a kind of strait-jacketing Classicism but as an attempt to make real shared aspirations for a unified nation, as an individual voice calling for a communal response.

Early in his career Schumann had described the subjective and objective as completely separate entities within him: 'as if I stood between my appearance and my being, between figure and shadow'.[16] There can be no shadow without a figure, of course, and the binary of subjective and objective is more often blurred than clearly defined: Schumann wrote that he stands somewhere between them. It is worth keeping this ambiguity in mind as we consider the late orchestral music in more detail, although discussion will divide the symphonic works from the concertos. There are several reasons for the division: as mentioned, the orchestral works were generally more popular – both in tone and with audiences. They without question represent the public style. The concertos do too, but without the same success, partly because their unavoidable emphasis on the soloist tends to be understood along similar lines to the lieder and choral ballades discussed in the first two chapters. In other words, the composer's voice is heard in solo utterances, undercutting the effectiveness of the collective. A piece such as the Violin Concerto also brings with it other, more sinister shadows. 'Affirmative art may become a cipher for despair', Adorno warned with reference to Adalbert Stifter (whose late style is compared to Schumann's in Chapters 3 and 6) and, rightly or wrongly, a similar suspicion hangs over Schumann's public works. There is a tendency to always listen for his 'unsung' voices.

The risk in so doing is that it is we, rather than Schumann, who start to hear things.

Fest music

Few rivers have evoked as strong a sense of nation as the Rhine did for nineteenth-century Germany. Prussia's acquisition of the Rhineland in 1815, after the Wars of Liberation, helped to strengthen a natural – and long contested – border against the French (who unsuccessfully attempted to claim the region again in July 1840). The Rhine corridor was important because of the wealth brought by its commerce and industry. It also brought together German-speaking Catholics in the west with Protestants in the east – although, as discussed in Chapter 2, not without problems.[17] The Rhine's greatest significance, though, was as a symbol for the hopes of unified Germany, as best shown by Cologne Cathedral, the two towers of which finally began to be built in the 1840s.[18] In 1848 Archduke Joseph described the cathedral as 'a symbol of the great fatherland that we are to construct'.[19]

Schumann's imagination had been captured by the river even before he came to live in Düsseldorf, as is apparent from two very different songs he composed in 1840: 'Im Rhein, im heiligen Strome' from *Dichterliebe*, with its description of Cologne Cathedral, and his setting of Nicolaus Becker's patriotic Rheinlied, 'Sie sollen ihn nicht haben'.[20] Ten years later, Clara described herself and Schumann as having been instantly enchanted by Cologne Cathedral on visiting it in autumn 1850, and Wasielewski claimed in the first edition of his biography that the Third Symphony – begun immediately after the Schumanns' second trip to the city – deserved to be called the 'Rhenish' for it had been inspired by their first sight of the Cathedral.[21] The composer apparently had told him that the fourth movement reflected the celebrations of the elevation of Cologne's archbishop, Johannes von Geißel, to Cardinal. Wasielewski's assertion seemed to be supported by Schumann's original title for the movement, 'In the character of an accompaniment to a solemn ceremony' ('Im Charakter der Begleitung einer feierlichen Zeremonie'), printed in the programme for the first performance. However, as Linda Correll Roesner points out, it is unlikely that the Schumanns could have attended a service in Cologne, because of the timing of their visits.[22] Indeed, there is a sense that Schumann's emphasis on the Rhenish elements of his score was done with an eye to its popular success; to the publisher Simrock he described the music as reflecting 'local colour' and, tellingly, asked that the French words on the title page be removed so that it would be kept 'as German as possible'.[23] To Wasielewski, Schumann commented that in the Third Symphony 'popular elements should prevail'.[24]

Despite the homage paid to the cathedral, the Third Symphony was appreciated by audiences in Düsseldorf to a far greater extent than by those in Cologne (the Symphony was premiered in Düsseldorf on 6 February 1851; the Cologne performance took place on 25 February). According to one review in the *Signale für die musikalische Welt*, the 'usually phlegmatic' Düsseldorf listeners applauded; the orchestra cheered at the end of each movement.[25] The reviewer stressed the popular character of the symphony, with its reliance on the simple strength of folk-song in the second and fifth movements, while the contrapuntal complexities of the fourth movement were said to form a halo over the whole. However, later issues described the audience as indifferent to the Schumann and far more excited by a set of variations by the virtuoso violinist (and teacher at Cologne conservatory) Theodor Pixis, while the orchestra was said to have been better in a rendition of the overture to Spontini's *Olympie*. Ludwig Bischoff, editor of the *Rheinischen Musikzeitung*, complained about the intellectualization in Schumann's late music, demonstrated by the Symphony's contrapuntal excesses: the audience could not be expected to understand such a complex work at only one hearing.[26]

After publication of the score in October 1851, and with three successful performances in Leipzig, the Third Symphony was considered in more detail. Theodor Uhlig reported:

This work not only is couched in the well-known style of the composer in general, but also in the specific musical manner that characterizes the compositions of his latest period. At the same time within this mannered [style] it appears relatively clear – at the very least much clearer than the reports from the Rhine had led us to believe. The work bears witness to the extraordinary strength of form of the composer (a strong melodic invention, however, is less [evident]), and has to make a significant effect as a whole as well as in its individual [movements].[27]

In contrast to the reviews of the Düsseldorf performances and to Schumann's own comments about the work, Roesner observes that Uhlig makes no reference to the popular, *volkstümlich* elements in the Symphony. Indeed, Uhlig avoids the poetic implications of the music almost altogether, instead choosing to focus on the inappropriate church-music character of the fourth movement. By bringing such a style into the secular sphere, Uhlig argues, Schumann did not achieve the spiritual heights of the adagios in Beethoven's symphonies but was entering into the world of programme music:

[Schumann's] more recent large instrumental works (in our opinion already beginning with his Second Symphony) are founded on particular ideas whose artistic representation goes far, far beyond the means that are available to absolute music. In point of fact: just as Schumann has exchanged an earlier genuinely more pleasing style for a disagreeable, mannered musical style, so has he also exchanged an earlier artistic naïveté for aesthetic speculation.[28]

The debate between programme and absolute music, in the case of Schumann, is thus entwined with criticism of his late style – which Uhlig characterizes as disagreeable and mannered (the op. 89 lieder and the Violin Sonatas were similarly rejected by critics as mannerist, as mentioned in Chapters 1 and 5). The different stylistic interpretations of the Third Symphony indicate the extent to which judgement of Schumann resulted from contemporary musical and aesthetic developments: it was not simply a question of works being 'late' but also that they engaged with current issues, such as the programmaticism of Liszt or Berlioz. It is an obvious point, but one still worth making: whatever the composer's intentions, the 'meaning' of his music has changed according to the attitudes of particular generations of critics.[29]

For example: as mentioned, although Schumann described the Third Symphony as featuring 'local colour', the connection he saw between his work and Cologne Cathedral was closer to Beethoven's Sixth Symphony – with its evocation of the emotions aroused by a landscape, rather than the landscape itself – than to the narratives of, say, the *Symphonie fantastique*. In his famous review of the Berlioz, Schumann had advocated that listeners appreciate the music without the aid of its programme.[30] A similar attitude was taken by Richard Pohl, who wrote to Schumann after the Leipzig performance of the Third Symphony:

To me it was a festival-drama in five acts that reached its culmination point in the fourth act. I might give [that movement] the caption 'in Cologne Cathedral', and the second [movement] 'Rhine Journey'. – But that is a play of ideas. One cannot give words to music, for music is simply music; therefore all of the sensations that a masterpiece such as this evokes also cannot be expressed in words.[31]

Pohl's almost Mendelssohnian idea about music's ability to convey what words cannot was increasingly questioned in the 1850s, as advocates of programme music gained sway. (Pohl would, of course, change his opinion as he became more familiar with the music of Liszt.) As symphonic forms expanded during the second half of the nineteenth century, Schumann's explanation to his publisher that a programme might be necessary to help explain the unusual structure of the Symphony seemed unnecessary.

Wasielewski, for one, became increasingly convinced that the Third Symphony's programme was more concrete than Schumann had admitted; in a later edition of his biography, he claimed that the fourth movement made *specific* reference to the elevation of Archbishop von Geißel to Cardinal.[32] By the early twentieth century, Roesner observes, the Third Symphony's 'programme' had come to be accepted as established fact.[33]

More recent critics – particularly John Daverio – have tended to concentrate less on the programmatic aspect of the Symphony, instead emphasizing its motivic and thematic unity. As discussed in Chapter 5 with regard to the chamber music, such a change in attitude indicates a desire to assert Schumann's role as precursor to Brahms. Thus the Third Symphony's most notable features are not simply the Archbishop and his Cathedral, but the way in which popular elements are fused with high art. The similarity between the contours of the Scherzo's sequentially rising semiquaver motive and the E flat minor subject of the fourth movement, and the recurrence of the latter theme in the parallel major in the coda of the final movement, indicate for Daverio the Third Symphony's status as 'a popular epic'.[34]

The tension between 'abstract' form and extra-musical meaning comes to the fore on considering the Concert Overtures Schumann composed in the 1850s, which have specific literary sources: Schiller's *Die Braut von Messina*, Shakespeare's *Julius Caesar* and Goethe's *Hermann und Dorothea*. Each of these pieces is formally intriguing, particularly because of their thematic juxtaposition and contrast. For example, Michael Struck thinks the Overture to *Julius Caesar* redefines the basic sections of sonata form.[35] The way in which it does so, though, is not unique to this work, as it bears some similarity to the 'parallel forms' Roesner proposed with regard to much earlier works, such as the original finale of the G minor Sonata op. 22 and the first movement of the *Concert sans orchestre* op. 14.[36] Namely, much of the 'development' section is recapitulated. Unlike in some of the earlier works, there is no doubt about the tonality of the opening – F minor is established via a quasi-militaristic theme that descends through tonic and dominant. The theme recurs to an unexpected degree; it appears at the beginning of the development in its original key, but at a faster tempo, and at the beginning of the recapitulation and coda. There is a less strongly defined sense of a second subject area; the material contrasts in terms of figuration but until the development – and with the exception of the glance at the mediant in the transitional passage discussed below – it rarely strays far from the opening key.

The repetition of themes and the use of sequential figures in the Overture to *Julius Caesar* are partly what makes the music sounds like late Schumann.

Example 4:1a Overture to *Julius Caesar*, bb. 15–16

As in his comments on the Third Symphony, Daverio argues that some of that repetition contributes towards a sense of coherence. For instance, the transitional motive first heard in bars 27–28 draws on the distinctive rising third motive of the preceding two bars, which in turn derives from the oboe motive of bars 15–16. This is not a case of literal repetition, but of motivic development: initially, the oboe's rising thirds are just minims (Example 4:1a); then the flute quickens the harmonic rhythm and provides quaver embellishment (Example 4:1b); in its third version, the original three-note ascent is reversed, so that it reads c-b♭-a♭ before moving to a B flat chord with appoggiatura (Example 4:1b, bars 27–28). The ascending figure

Example 4:1b   Overture to *Julius Caesar*, bb. 25–9

may be recognizable throughout its adaptations, but perhaps because of its transitional function, it does not seem to act as thematic glue. Instead, it unsettles the structure, almost as though it were a spirit visitation in one of Schumann's choral dramas. This 'otherworldly' aspect is partly a result of the motive's orchestration: by its third manifestation, it is mostly in the upper registers of the woodwind. I am pointing it out here, because separation of wind and strings often happens in the late concertos, with consequences for the interpretation of their form and, loosely speaking, poetic content. Whatever arguments are made for this music's thematic consistency, it is worth remembering that it can sound otherwise simply because of the orchestration; and, as will be discussed at greater length with regard to the concertos, that sonic surface can feed into the understanding of the music's presentation of solo and collective forces.

Struck argues that the concert overtures are fundamentally different in form from the overtures attached to dramatic works (*Genoveva, Manfred* and *Faust*). However, the juxtaposition of themes in the Overture to *Hermann und Dorothea* probably reflects the composer's initial intention to treat Goethe's short epic poem as a *Singspiel*. As with the Third Symphony, the setting is the Rhineland, but on slightly less celebratory terms – the romance of the eponymous characters is set against a backdrop of the expulsion of Germans from the Western bank of the Rhine by French revolutionary armies. The Overture opens with two contrasting themes: the first is a descending triplet melody played by violas, cellos and bassoons in parallel thirds, which stresses the second beat of the bar; the second, played by wind and brass, is the *Marseillaise*. He had included the latter in previous pieces; it appears at the end of *Faschingsschwank aus Wien* (op. 26) and in the song 'Die beiden Grenadiere' (op. 49 no. 1). In both cases the famous hymn is ironic: in *Faschingsschwank aus Wien* it has been interpreted as 'a sardonic reflection on Austrian censorship' (the tune being banned there at the time), while in 'Die beiden Grenadiere' its use as accompaniment to the dying soldier's patriotic speech indicates the futility of war and the price paid in battle.[37] Schumann explained the presence of the *Marseillaise* in the Overture with a note on the score, saying that the first scene of *Hermann und Dorothea* features soldiers from the French Republic. In a way, its appearance is realistic: the tune is cut off abruptly by the return of the first melody (Example 4:2). For some, the *Marseillaise* had retained positive associations as a symbol of republicanism: Jonathan Sperber observes that festivities in honour of the first year of the Parisian uprising in February 1849 (and the next month to commemorate the barricade fighting in Berlin) adopted as symbols red flags and Phrygian caps, sang the *Marseillaise*, and toasted the memory of Robespierre, St Just and Marat.[38] Whatever its political or dramatic implications, the anthem's presence in the Overture to *Hermann und Dorothea* has generally been interpreted as a populist move. A similar impulse is detected in Schumann's final Rhenish piece, the *Fest-Ouvertüre mit Gesang über das 'Rheinweinlied' für Orchester und Chor* (op. 123), which also included a familiar melody, Wilhelm Müller's version of Johann André's 'Rheinweinlied', which is itself a setting of Matthias Claudius's poem 'Bekränzt mit Laub'. This celebration of Rhine wine, which ends with a jubilant rendition of the melody by tenor and chorus, would seem to show Schumann at his most out of character, even if it remains more modest than similar moments in, say, Beethoven's Ninth Symphony or Wagner's *Tannhäuser*; a better point of comparison would be

Example 4:2 Overture to *Hermann und Dorothea*, bb. 9–12

Brahms's Academic Festival Overture, with its quotations from student drinking songs.[39] In terms of communal sentiment, it is worth pointing out that the *Fest-Ouvertüre* primarily expresses a sense of local and regional identity, rather than a broader sense of the German nation.

A major reason for the *Fest-Ouvertüre*'s concentration on Rhenish themes was that it was composed in April 1853, while Schumann, Julius Tausch and Ferdinand Hiller were planning the Lower Rhine Music Festival. Despite the *volkstümlich* aspect of the *Fest-Ouvertüre*, Schumann's one year in charge of the Festival marked the beginning of a different approach: whereas emphasis had previously been placed on local amateur and communal music (through choral groups such as the *Männerchor*), the Festival now became more concerned with 'serious' music – particularly symphonies and oratorios – and featured an increasing number of professional and international performers.[40] The three-day event in 1853 included Handel's *Messiah*, Beethoven's Violin Concerto (played by Joachim) and the Ninth Symphony. There were also premieres of Schumann's re-orchestrated Fourth Symphony and the *Fest-Ouvertüre*, and a performance by Clara of the Piano Concerto.

The Lower Rhine Festival was probably Schumann's greatest public success as a composer.[41] As a conductor, though, his skills were questioned; the effect his failure in this field had on his life and career means that it is worth a brief digression. According to one observer at rehearsals for the festival, Schumann was unable to keep the large chorus and orchestra together in *Messiah*.[42] His conducting had been under fire for some time. A local newspaper had published an anonymous report by a member of the General Music Society's executive committee in March 1851. The Choral Society did not like Schumann's habit of rehearsing from a desk, with Clara providing accompaniment on the piano. His conducting style was said to be unintelligible, and many balked at the extra rehearsals he scheduled. Even Clara noted that Schumann sometimes lost himself in the music, forgetting to give performers their cues and then becoming irritable when their entrances were imprecise. All this reduced discipline and regular attendance. Matters worsened: on 6 September Clara recorded that the meeting to plan the next season had been stormy. She complained that at rehearsals of Bach's St Matthew Passion in March 1852, many members of the dilettante chorus were poorly behaved and impolite.[43] Amid increasing criticism from the General Music Society, performers and audiences, Schumann's ill health caused him to pass over his conducting responsibilities to his deputy, Julius Tausch, in the summer.[44] Two days after Schumann's return in December, according to the leader Ruppert Becker, the concert directors of the Choral Society wrote 'an uncivil letter in which they sought to rid themselves of his conducting'.[45] He was criticized for not giving the orchestra 'solid, sure indication of tempi, even beats, clear, definite and comprehensible directions'.[46] Tempos began to seem too fast to him as his health declined through the concert season. By the beginning of the 1853–4 season he was under attack for not consulting the Executive Committee about changes to programmes and the hiring of out-of-town artists, and for altering the orchestra's rehearsal schedule. Matters came to a head after a disastrous performance of a mass by Moritz Hauptmann under Schumann's direction: in rehearsal he continued to conduct after the music had ended. The Choral Society refused to sing under him any longer, and the General Music Executive Society voted that Tausch should take on all Schumann's conducting apart from that of his own works.

Schumann's tenure as conductor in Düsseldorf was certainly hindered by dealing with dilettantes and bureaucracy, but the complaints about his absent-mindedness, uncommunicativeness and odd behaviour are numerous enough to suggest that he really was not up to the job.[47] Some of these criticisms invidiously feed into the reception of his orchestral pieces: the slowness of tempi (discussed in Chapter 3), the difficulty of following the score and, of course, those 'imagined' melodies. Interestingly, it seems that it was through the performance of the 'public style' that Schumann was thought to fail, rather than in the works themselves; a further – more literal – example of the composer's state of mind being mapped on to the understanding of his music. With the concertos to which I now turn, however, some works do not even get to the stage of performance before awareness of Schumann's illness affects their reception.

Ghost music

As crucial for Schumann as the success of his music at the Lower Rhine Festival were the inspirational performances he heard there. Most noteworthy was Joachim's account of Beethoven's Violin Concerto, which resulted first in a *Phantasie* for violin and orchestra, and then the Violin Concerto. At the beginning of this chapter, I mentioned that Schumann's genius is generally agreed not often to reside in virtuosic writing, particularly for stringed instruments (the showmanship of the Piano Concerto and his earlier keyboard works is more appreciated; as is the *Introduction mit Allegro* for piano and orchestra, op. 134). Perhaps one cause for that is the model he chose: Beethoven's Violin Concerto, while a magnificent and difficult work, is not a flashy showpiece. In it, the soloist's role frequently verges on the contemplative, particularly in the slow movement, with its filigree responses to the opening horn calls. As such, Beethoven's Concerto modifies the typical dynamic between soloist and orchestra in the Romantic era, according to which the soloist – virtuosic, expressive, alone – weighs in against the forces of the orchestra, usually ending the fight bloody but victorious. In the final rondo, Beethoven's solo violinist joins with the orchestra rather than fighting against it; the emphasis is on the work's musical development rather than surface decoration.

To lean on the *musical* stature of Beethoven's Violin Concerto implicitly attempts to redeem the work from a common association of virtuosic genres with artistic shallowness. As a critic, Schumann was known to advocate a more thoughtful approach to technical display. His aesthetic stance can be seen to express a Romantic conception of subjectivity, for it privileges psychological depth and inner meaning. To do so, however, risks not meeting the demands of the genre – as in the case of Berlioz's *Harold en Italie*, which was initially rejected by its commissioner, Paganini, because he thought it would not sufficiently showcase his talents. That piece, however, has in Byron's poem a poetic reason for the character of its soloist. Schumann's late concertos do not – at least not explicitly. They take on conventional forms, with the usual number of movements, and while the linking of movements is noteworthy it is not without precedent in Schumann's other symphonic works. Despite the late concertos being 'absolute' music, though, a poetic interpretation of the work is implicit in their reception. Most strikingly, there is the tendency to think of lyrical passages as being typically Schumannian, which encourages the conflation of the soloist with the composer, despite the fact that he played neither cello nor violin (nor piano in public any longer). The soloist thus becomes not only the individual subject against the world, but also subject–Schumann: the lone voice struggling to express itself while the orchestra and audience fail to understand him.

The question of subjective voices in Schumann's orchestral music is not raised only in the concertos; indeed, an example from recent commentary on the Second Symphony provides a useful introduction to the issues. Michael Steinberg describes the slow movement as follows:

> The exquisite *adagio espressivo* unfolds in a confessional, first-person mode. The music says 'I'; the investment in the musical first person of Robert Schumann is certain but not readily decipherable . . . The adagio's first-person utterance offers a consistent melancholic mood but does not progress in a unified voice; multivocality is made clear by varied orchestration and the use of solo instruments, especially the oboe and bassoon, in sequences that appear and withdraw.[48]

Quite how this music 'says "I" ' is unclear. Its minor key and chromatic main theme might sound melancholic, but these are offset almost immediately by a turn to the relative major, E flat. Most importantly for our consideration of the concertos, though, is that Steinberg seems to align 'the adagio's first-person utterance' with instrumentation, particularly the use of soloists. He continues: '[the movement's] inscription of melancholy works as well through invocations of Mozartean as well as Schubertian gestures, especially in solo wind lines, in the fragmentary quality of phrases passed from one instrument to another, supported by syncopations'.[49] Imagining solo instruments as voices is far from unusual: on first hearing Schubert's C major 'Great' Symphony in 1839, Schumann had reported to Clara that 'the instruments are made to sound like *human voices*'; and Berlioz, in his treatise on instrumentation, often refers to instruments as voices with different characters.[50] The kinds of voices Steinberg hears in the adagio, however, are very particularly Schumannian: they appear only to withdraw; their fragmentation is inscribed with melancholy. The finale 'reclaims an extroverted, public voice, yet it does so not by transcending the private, interior, unresolved melancholy of the adagio but rather by momentarily suppressing it'. The 'authenticity of the melancholic state it has somewhat glibly left behind' makes a reading of the Symphony as a salvation narrative unconvincing, Steinberg concludes. True Schumann, it seems, can only be heard in narrative fractures; in the multiple voices of the melody shared between soloists.

By finding Schumann's 'authentic' voice in ruptured narratives, we might simply be continuing the tendency to think of the composer in terms of the split or multiple personalities of Florestan, Eusebius and the other members of the Davidsbündler: imaginary harbingers of the hallucinations he suffered from later in life. So strong is the association that it cannot be discounted, as outlined elsewhere. However, such emphasis on fragmentation and melancholy – and even on lyricism – tends to write failure into many of Schumann's large-scale public works. In their meditation on subjectivity in music, philosophers Gilles Deleuze and Félix Guattari comment: 'In a concerto, Schumann requires all the assemblages of the orchestra to make the cello wander the way a light fades into the distance or is extinguished'.[51] Allowing the soloist to wander into the distance is far from the standard approach to concerto writing. Yet this is – almost – what happens in the Cello Concerto, in which soloist and orchestra seem strangely independent and removed from one another.

Schumann initially described the Concerto as a *Konzertstück* for cello with orchestral accompaniment, which partly explains the gulf between soloist and orchestra. However, the divide seems more far-reaching, as it extends to the other late concertos, which according to Struck work formally in fundamentally different ways from Schumann's earlier pieces.[52] Soloist and orchestra often oppose one another in a block-like manner (expanding the divide between groups of instruments mentioned with regard to the overtures); figurative solo sections sometimes replace and even take the function of 'thematicism'; and development sections become less substantial.

Only towards the end of a movement – or even, in the Violin Concerto, at the end of the whole piece – do soloist and orchestra come together in a sustained way.

The Cello Concerto certainly opens with soloist and orchestra in different realms: the former reflective, the latter – when not providing discreet accompaniment – striving to establish other, livelier themes. As the movement progresses, the orchestra takes up fragments of the cellist's melody (especially the head motive of the opening theme). Some of the new motives introduced in the tuttis (such as the accented crotchet theme) are taken up by the soloist but invariably then transformed for rhapsodic purposes – figurative solo sections taking the function of thematicism, Struck would say. Indeed, the cellist's response to the orchestra is almost dissociative, a fugue state in the psychological sense. Only one motive seems to halt it in its tracks: a varied return of the opening chords (Example 4:3). As in the Overture to *Julius Caesar*, these chords are distinctively scored for upper woodwind (on their initial appearance they include pizzicato strings). Their reappearance marks the transition into the second movement. A similar prompting brings about the third movement: the orchestra reminds the cellist of its opening theme, its recitative-like response apparently causing a chordal reverberation through the orchestra (Example 4:4).

As Deleuze and Guattari proposed, the orchestra does seem to make the cello wander here. The potential for the relationship between soloist and orchestra to be described in terms of the subjective–objective dualities described above is obvious. In the process, it is difficult to avoid thinking that the way in which the orchestra comes to 'disturb' the soloist's reveries resembles our image of Schumann hearing sustained tones, haunted by melodies from elsewhere. It is somewhat of a relief, then, that once we reach the final movement, cellist and orchestra join forces in a fairly conventional rondo, one that refers back to motivic fragments from the earlier movements without losing a sense of direction.

Schumann read through the Concerto with the principal cellist of the orchestra in Düsseldorf, Christian Reimers, on 23 March 1851. Clara praised the work for its Romanticism, verve, freshness and humour.[53] However, the Frankfurt cellist, Robert Emil Bockmühl, and the Director of the *Cäcilienvereins*, Franz Messer, thought the work too hard to perform.[54] Schumann was reluctant to simplify the more difficult passages, although he did reduce the tempo of the first movement and alter the cadenza. He also prepared a version for violin, intended for Joachim, perhaps in the hope that he would be more willing to tackle it.[55] On being put to bed after his

Example 4:3   Cello Concerto, bb. 240–8

Example 4:4 Cello Concerto, bb. 281–9

suicide attempt of 1854, Schumann began to make corrections to the original score, which Clara noted seemed to calm him. The voices in his head were becoming friendlier.[56]

The Concerto was finally published in August 1854, but no review appeared until the following year. The *Neue Berliner Musikzeitung* considered it alongside a cello concerto by Bernhard Molique (probably the composer whose accompaniments to Bach's Cello Suites were preferred to Schumann's by Kistner, as mentioned in Chapter 3).[57] Strikingly, Schumann's work was described as representative of the so-called new-Romantic school ('der sogenannten neuromantischen Schule'). While praised for its clear, careful and fluent arrangement of ideas, the harmonic progressions

Example 4:4 (*cont.*)

were occasionally thought bizarre. The Cello Concerto was not as rhapsodic as the *Phantasie* for violin, and was difficult for the player to make effective: in that regard, the reviewer concluded, the accompaniment was more of a hindrance than a help.

Schumann's Cello Concerto was finally performed in public, with Ludwig Ebert as soloist, on 9 June 1860, as part of the celebrations commemorating the composer's fiftieth birthday. It was not, though, one of his most performed pieces in the nineteenth century. In 1963, Dmitri Shostakovich reorchestrated the Concerto for much larger forces, explaining that he thought its instrumental writing reflected the composer's severe depression.[58] Arguably, Shostakovich's revision simply makes the Concerto more like his own music; the addition of trumpets in the finale lend the repeated fanfare motive a sinister edge further accentuated by the woodwind. The new harp part in the second movement, on the other hand, makes the sound more luxurious. Recently the cellist Steven Isserlis produced a video of the Concerto in its original version being performed 'deep in the bowels of an evocatively derelict submarine bunker'.[59] The educational intention of the video – it is supposed to introduce audiences to a Romantic master-piece – demonstrates how strongly late Schumann is associated with ideas of impenetrability; his music is a submerged capsule, its meaning lurking beneath the surface.

In the above description of the Cello Concerto, I noted that the lyri-cal solo part seems to express subject–Schumann. While, as noted above, that expression seems intimately connected with ideas about the composer's personality and illness, it is not all that marks the concertos as belonging to the late period. The passages in which the composer's creative powers are thought to show signs of waning in fact usually occur in the faster movements, with their repetitive themes and bravura passagework. Ironi-cally, the virtuosity of Schumann's concertante works for strings is one of the primary reasons given for their failure – not so much because of the semantic lack such embellishment is supposed to veil, but because these pieces are not just flashy: they are very difficult to play.[60] As mentioned above, Bockmühl asked for passages in the Cello Concerto to be made easier. Perhaps remembering his earlier experience, Schumann consulted Joachim while composing the *Phantasie*, asking him to say what was impractical or difficult, and he also requested advice about bowing arpeggios.[61] The violinist willingly responded (he was more reluctant to discuss the Violin Concerto, as shall be seen later), and after his premiere of the *Phantasie* the piece was praised in the *Neue Zeitschrift für Musik* as a 'splendid piece' which allowed 'the performer an opportunity to show himself as a multifaceted artist'.[62] Later reviews, though, were less positive; Richard Pohl declared that the work was 'poorly conceived for the violin' and 'insignificant in terms of its inner musical value'.[63] Hanslick described the *Phantasie* as 'a dark abyss across which two great artists clasp hands. Martyr-like, gloomy, and obsti-nate, this Fantasy struggles along, depending upon continuous figuration to make up for its melodic poverty.'[64] According to Struck, the negative attitude of these later reviews was the result of critics' awareness of the composer's illness, which was thought to have affected his creative ability.[65] However, as mentioned with regard to other late works by Schumann, some felt that it was a question of finding new ways to understand his music; Franz Brendel wrote of Ferdinand David's interpretation of the *Phantasie* that it 'lent the work a surprising effectiveness, demonstrating that it really can be successfully performed for a cultured audience receptive to Schumann's compositions'.[66]

The quest to find a cultured audience receptive to Schumann's compositions took a few peculiar turns in the case of the Violin Concerto, whose performance and reception is one of the late period's more convoluted tales. It was composed shortly after the completion of the *Phantasie* and the two works share some musical features.[67] Again, it was written for Joachim. After Schumann's death, Clara asked Joachim to improve the difficult last movement, which he declined to do. In 1859 they decided that the Concerto should not be published. In a much later letter to his biographer Andreas Moser, Joachim explained that it could not be ranked among Schumann's best creations:

My concern for the reputation of the beloved composer kept me from allowing this work to be printed . . . It must sadly be acknowledged that a certain weariness and lack of mental energy is undeniable. Certain parts (how could it be otherwise!) give evidence of the composer's deep feeling, so it is all the more distressing that these contrast with the work as a whole.[68]

The autograph thus remained in the care of Joachim until his death in 1907, and the manuscripts were left untouched in libraries in Berlin and Zwickau until Joachim's nieces, Nelly d'Aranyi and Adila Fachiri, sought them out in the early 1930s, claiming that they were acting on instructions given to them by Schumann and Joachim from beyond the grave.[69] In 1937 a score of the Concerto was prepared by Georg Schünemann and published by Schott Verlag. Despite the protestations of Schumann's daughter Eugenie, the Concerto was premiered on 26 November 1937, at Berlin's Deutsche Opernhaus as part of the *Gemeinsam Jahrestagung der Reichskulturkammer und der NS-Gemeinschaft 'Kraft durch Freude'*.[70] It is ironic that a work that had been hidden from public view because it was thought to be damaging to Schumann's reputation as a composer was first performed in front of Robert Ley and Joseph Goebbels in a celebration of Germany's musical supremacy.[71]

Schumann's 'last work', as it was erroneously referred to, did not meet with unqualified praise. The one part that gained approval – even from Joachim – was the middle movement. Joachim exclaimed in response to the violin's entry at the end of bar 4:

Example 4:5 Violin Concerto, ii, bb. 4–6

Ließe sich das selige Träumen doch festhalten – herrlicher Meister! So warm, so innig – Wie nur je!

If only the holy dream would let itself be held – heavenly master! So warm, so intimate![72]

Unfortunately, according to Joachim, the life-blood of these moments gives way to brooding. Other commentators have similarly singled out the slow movement's theme (Example 4:5).[73] Importantly, it resembles other melodies by Schumann, including the slow movement of op. 41 no. 2, the opening vocal line of 'Frühlings Ankunft', op. 79:19, and the middle section of 'Vogel als Prophet' from *Waldszenen* (it also recalls the Allegro of Burgmüller's Second Symphony, which Schumann had recently orchestrated). Its contours are also recalled in the Eb major theme allegedly dictated to him by the spirit of Schubert, just before Schumann's suicide attempt in 1854 (discussed in Chapter 6). The melody thus is not simply an example of a lyrical fragment being thought of as Schumannian; it has become one of the composer's voices.

The theme is assembled from falling thirds that in themselves might carry a further message: the *Lebewohl* motive famous from Beethoven's *Les Adieux* Sonata. More striking, though, is the unusual accompaniment; a syncopated figure played by the strings. It appears throughout the movement – in the introduction, accompaniment and in transitions; it is even played by the soloist – but despite its distinctive rhythmic nature it is not a dynamic force. Instead, the syncopated theme has a strangely static quality and a gentle persistence that eventually comes to unsettle the atmosphere of the movement. In part its unsettling effect comes from the fact that the rhythms of the two themes do not coincide, as is apparent in the second bar of the

Example 4:6   Violin Concerto, iii, bb. 136–44

violin's melody, shown in the example. The slow moving bass line – which sustains a tonic pedal throughout the opening bars of the violin's entry – does not help the music to gain momentum. A similar effect is found in the transition into the final movement (discussed later as Example 4:7); the rhythm continues through the modulation from B♭ to D major (again, over a tonic (B♭) pedal, and the finale begins, in typical Schumann fashion, on a tonic chord in second inversion), suddenly being wrong-footed by the crotchet upbeat into the finale's polonaise rhythm.

The unusual and virtually unshakeable character of the syncopated theme perhaps makes it unsurprising that when Schumann – as was his wont – recalls an earlier movement in the finale it is not the soloist's lyrical melody but the syncopated theme that resurfaces (Example 4:6). Its return seems to unnerve the soloist, who plays a bland accompanimental line out of keeping with the rest of the movement. The bass line begins to move more slowly, as if remembering the pedal notes of the previous movement, and the harmony shifts to a modally changeable F sharp. Moreover, the strong rhythmic impetus of the Polonaise is interrupted. Unlike other instances where Schumann provides a reminiscence of an earlier theme in the final movement (as in the first Violin Sonata or the Cello Concerto, to mention only two), it is difficult to interpret the recurrence of the syncopated figure as a benign revenant, something that helps guide the various strands to a conclusion. It does not occur at a critical moment, such as just prior to the recapitulation, but interrupts the flow of the development. Its effect is to disturb; it is, perhaps, the voice that cannot be silenced.

Joachim thought the 'graceful suggestions of the dreamy Adagio' in the finale to be one of the movement's more interesting details.[74] Overall, though, he criticized the finale for its repetitiveness; he thought the development became monotonous and that there was 'a certain characteristic rigidity of rhythm'. The brilliant figuration was unsuited to and ineffective on the violin. Part of the problem with the writing – as well as the awkwardness of the way it lies under the fingers – is Schumann's dependence on arpeggio figures, and of phrases that run from lower to upper registers. Because of the change in timbre and volume that naturally occurs on stringed instruments, it can become difficult for the solo line to penetrate through the orchestral texture. Along similar lines, Joachim complained that the instrumentation does not lend sufficient support to the increasing intensity of the material in the first movement, the overall effect of which he said was of 'an aesthetic obstinacy, now taking a violent onward urge, now dragging defiantly'.

Joachim's distaste for the 'obstinate' and repetitive figuration in both first and last movements of the Violin Concerto queries the emphasis on thematic connections mentioned earlier. Reinhard Kapp has gone to great lengths to prove the motivic integration of the first movement's exposition.[75] Such analytical approaches are implicitly redemptive, in their argument for a logical coherence to Schumann's late style. By the outer movements of the Violin Concerto, however, we seem to have reached tipping point: it is difficult not to listen to this music and wonder whether these repetitions could have been driven by anything other than obsession.

Take, for example, the opening of the finale (Example 4:7). As in the Cello Concerto, the final two movements are linked; here, though, the connection is not prompted by the remembrance of themes past, but by the repetition of a diminished chord over the slow movement's syncopated figure. The finale's theme is itself inherently repetitive and where new figuration is introduced, such as in bars 57–8, it is immediately treated sequentially. The same is true of most of the material in the movement; thus, even when the main theme is not being repeated, something else is.

Andrew Bowie observes, with regard to the repeated phrases of the Scherzo of Beethoven's op. 135, that repetition can easily become something 'bordering on madness': to say something too often threatens 'its very existence as meaningful articulation' in music as much as in speech.[76] Bare repetition such as that found in the outer movements of the Violin Concerto is heard as a

Example 4:7 Violin Concerto, ii, bb. 51–60

harbinger of 'madness' because, according to Deleuze, it exhibits a mechanical element 'that serves as a cover for a more profound element . . . the death instinct'.[77] While the lurching repetitions of the Violin Concerto's finale might bear comparison with the rocking motion of the depressive, however, it is worth remembering Hume's observation: that repetition changes nothing in the object repeated, but something in the mind that contemplates it. In fact, with the Violin Concerto we are so aware of the work's reception history that we cannot but listen to it as a late work. But there are other things that also mark this music – its D minor mood, the fragile beauty of the second movement's main melody, its thematic obsession. Maybe the way to explain it is in Barthesian terms: that beneath the surface of this music we can detect a body that beats. It is a body coming to its end, though: if the finale's underlying polonaise rhythm resembles a pulsing heart, we listen carefully less for a voice than for a breath.

Notes

1. Adorno, 'The autonomy of art', *The Adorno Reader*, ed. Brian O'Conner (Oxford: Blackwells, 2000), p. 251.
2. 'Robert Schumann über sich selbst (Tagebucheinträge aus dem Jahr 1830)', in Ernst Burger, *Robert Schumann: Eine Lebenschronik in Bildern und Dokumenten, Robert Schumann: Neue Ausgabe sämtlicher Werke* (Mainz: Schott, 1998), VIII:1, p. 342. The emphasis placed on individualism within Romanticism is discussed – somewhat problematically – by Bernhard Giesen's *Intellectuals and the German Nation: Collective Identity in an Axial Age*, trans. Nicholas Levis and Amos Weisz (Cambridge: Cambridge University Press, 1998), pp. 80–102.
3. On music's connection with subjectivity more generally see Andrew Bowie, *Aesthetics and Subjectivity from Kant to Nietzsche* (Manchester: Manchester University Press, 2003), pp. 227–56.
4. Franz Brendel, 'Robert Schumann with reference to Mendelssohn-Bartholdy and the development of modern music in general (1845)', trans. Jürgen Thym, *Schumann and his World*, ed. R. Larry Todd (Princeton: Princeton University Press, 1994), pp. 323–4.
5. Brendel, 'Robert Schumann', p. 328.
6. Brendel, 'Robert Schumann', p. 330.
7. Brendel, 'Robert Schumann', p. 331.
8. 'Erst vom Jr. 1845 an, von wo ich anfing alles im Kopf zu erfinden und auszuarbeiten, hat sich eine ganz andere Art zu componiren zu entwickeln begonen.' See Schumann's entry in the *Kurtztagebuch* for July 1846, *Tagebücher Band II 1836–1854*, ed. Gerd Nauhaus (Leipzig: Deutscher Verlag, 1987), p. 402.
9. Richard Taruskin, *The Oxford History of Western Music: The Nineteenth Century* (Oxford: Oxford University Press, 2005), III, p. 316.
10. Taruskin, *The Oxford History*, III, p. 318.
11. Marilyn Butler, 'Plotting the revolution: The political narrative of romantic poetry and criticism'; and David Aram Kaiser, *Romanticism, Aesthetics and Nationalism* (Cambridge: Cambridge University Press, 1999). Andrea K. Henderson discusses alternative models of subjectivity in *Romantic Identities: Varieties of Subjectivity, 1774–1830* (Cambridge: Cambridge University Press, 1996).
12. For such an exploration of earlier in the nineteenth century see Theodore Ziolkowski, *German Romanticism and its Institutions* (Princeton: Princeton University Press, 1990).

13. For discussion of these changes from a Hegelian perspective see Barbara Titus, *Conceptualizing Music: Friedrich Theodor Vischer and Hegelian currents in German music criticism, 1848–1887* (PhD University of Oxford, 2005).

14. Brian Vick, *Defining Germany*, p. 206.

15. For further discussion see Titus, *Conceptualizing Music*, pp. 32–3; and Ernst Lichtenhahn, 'Musikalisches Biedermeier und Vormärz', *Schweizer Beiträge zur Musikwissenschaft* 3 (1980), 7–35.

16. Schumann, *Tagebücher* I, p. 339.

17. On the conflicts experienced between the predominantly Roman Catholic region and its largely Protestant monarchy see Friedrich Keinemann, *Das Kölner Ereignis. Sein Widerhall in der Rheinprovinz und Westfalen*, 2 vols. (Münster: Aschendorff, 1974).

18. Thomas Nipperdey, 'Der Kölner Dom als Nationaldenkmal', *Historische Zeitschrift* 133 (1981).

19. Quoted by Jonathan Sperber, 'Festivals of national unity in the German revolution of 1848', *Past and Present* 136 (1992), 124. For further discussion see Otto Dann (ed.), *Religion, Kunst und Vaterland: Der Kölner Dom im 19. Jahrhundert* (Cologne, 1983).

20. For extended discussion of *Rheinlieder* in the 1840s see Cecelia Hopkins Porter, *The Rhine as Musical Metaphor: Cultural Identity in German Romantic Music* (Boston: Northeastern University Press, 1996).

21. Wasielewski, *Robert Schumann*, pp. 270–1.

22. Linda Correll Roesner, 'Werkgeschichte', *Robert Schumann Neue Ausgabe sämtlicher Werke: Serie I: Orchesterwerke, Werkgruppe 1: Symphonien Band 3. Symphonie op. 97* (Mainz: Schott, 1995), pp. 181–2. All translations of reviews of the Third Symphony are taken from Roesner.

23. See letters to Simrock 19 March and 15 July 1851; Erler, *Robert Schumann*, pp. 138–9.

24. Wasielewski, *Robert Schumann*, p. 456.

25. J. C. H., *Signale für die musikalische Welt* 9:8 (1851), 73–4.

26. Ludwig Bischoff, *Rheinische Musikzeitung*, I: 35 (1 March 1851), 276–7. A third performance was conducted by Schumann in Düsseldorf on 15 March 1851 at his annual benefit concert, but only given a brief notice. Early reviews are put in context by Ernst Lichtenhahn, 'Sinfonie als Dichtung: Zum geschichtlichen Ort von Schumanns "Rheinische" in *Schumanns Werke – Text und Interpretation*, ed. Akio Mayeda and Klaus Wolfgang Niemöller (Mainz: Schott, 1987), pp. 17–26.

27. *NZfM* 36 (March 1852), 117.

28. *NZfM* 36 (March 1852), 132.

29. In this regard, note should be taken of recent articles about Schumann's Second Symphony, which argue that the peculiarities of its form can be accounted for by allowing for the music's narrative content: see Anthony Newcomb, 'Once more between Absolute and Program Music: Schumann's Second Symphony', *19th-Century Music* 7:3 (1984), 233–50; and Ludwig Finscher, 'Zwischen

absoluter und Programmusik': Zur Interpretationen der deutschen romantischen Symphonie', *Festschrift Walter Wiora zum 70. Geburtstag: Über Symphonien*, ed. Christoph-Hellmut Mahling (Tutzing: Schneider, 1979).

30. Robert Schumann, 'Symphonie von H. Berlioz', *Gesammelte Schriften über Musik und Musiker*, pp. 68–100.

31. Letter to Robert Schumann, 10 December 1851 (*Corr.*, Vol 24, No. 4355), cited in Roesner, 'Kritischer Bericht', p. 195, n. 61.

32. Wasielewski, *Robert Schumann*, pp. 455 and 458.

33. Roesner, 'Kritischer Bericht', p. 180. Roesner further critiques Wasielewski's claims about the connections between the compositional process and the timing of Schumann's visits to Cologne on p. 184.

34. Daverio, *Robert Schumann*, p. 466.

35. Michael Struck, '"Am Rande der großen Form": Robert Schumanns Ouvertüren und ihr Verhältnis zur Symphonie (mit besonderer Berücksichtigung der Ouvertüre zu Shakespeare's *Julius Caesar*, op. 128', *Probleme der symphonistischen Tradition im 19. Jahrhundert* (Tutzing: Schneider, 1990), pp. 239–78.

36. Linda Correll Roesner, 'Schumann's "parallel" forms', *19th-Century Music* 14 (1991), 265–78.

37. Jensen, *Schumann*, p. 156.

38. Sperber, 'Festivals of national unity', 132.

39. Michael Struck discusses the occasional function of the *Fest-Ouvertüre* in 'Kunstwerk – Anspruch und Popularitätsstreben – Ursachen ohne Wirkung? Bemerkungen zum *Glück von Edenhall* op. 143 und zur *Fest-Ouvertüre* op. 123', *Schumann in Düsseldorf: Werke-Texte-Interpretationen* (London: Schott, 1993), pp. 265–314.

40. The Lower Rhine Music Festival began in 1818; it had not taken place from 1848–50 because of the revolutions, nor was there a festival in 1852. On the move from the Festival being a celebration of regional identity to becoming an international event, see Andreas Eichhorn, 'Vom Volkfest zur "musikalischen Prunkausstellung". Das Musikfest im 19. Jahrhundert als Forum bürgerlicher Selbstdarstellung', 5–28. For more on the history and changing constitution of the Lower Rhine Music Festival see Celia Hopkins Porter, 'The New Public and the Reordering of the Musical Establishment: the Lower Rhine Music Festivals, 1818–1867', *19th-Century Music* 3:3 (1980), 211–24.

41. Schumann's music continued to be programmed at the Festival into the 1860s. See Porter, 'The New Public', 215.

42. Schumann was involved in four concerts between 15 and 17 May. Rehearsals had begun on the 11th. The orchestra numbered 160 and the chorus 490. Kapp, 'Das Orchester Schumanns', *Musik-Konzepte Sonderband: Robert Schumann II*, ed. Heinz-Klaus Metzger and Rainer Riehn (Munich, 1982), p. 200.

43. Diary entry 30 March 1852, cited in Porter, *The Rhine*, p. 193.

44. According to Porter, Schumann conducted very little at the *Männergesangfest* in Düsseldorf, August 1852. *The Rhine*, p. 287, n. 62.

45. Cited in Porter, *The Rhine*, p. 194.

46. Deputy Mayor Wortmann, cited in Porter, *The Rhine*, p. 194.

47. As Porter points out, Schumann was not against dilettantes per se – he included several amateur-connoisseurs in his own music making – tensions arose more between their attitude and those of the professional musicians also taking part in concerts. *The Rhine*, p. 197.

48. Steinberg, *Listening to Reason*, p. 130.

49. Steinberg, *Listening to Reason*, p. 131.

50. Letter of 11 December 1839, *Briefe. Neue Folge*, p. 175. For discussion of the implications of Berlioz's approach see Edward T. Cone, *The Composer's Voice* (Berkeley: University of California Press, 1974), pp. 81–114.

51. Gilles Deleuze and Félix Guattari, *A Thousand Plateaus: Capitalism and Schizophrenia*, trans. Brian Massumi (London: Continuum, 1987), p. 386.

52. Michael Struck, '"Gewichtsverlagerungen": Robert Schumanns letzte Konzertkompositionen', *Schumann in Düsseldorf: Werke – Texte – Interpretationen. Bericht über das 3. Internationale Schumann-Symposium am 15. und 16. Juni 1988 im Rahmen des 3. Schumann-Festes, Düsseldorf* (London: Schott, 1993), pp. 43–52.

53. Berthold Litzmann, *Clara Schumann. Ein Künstlerleben. Nach Tagebüchern und Briefen* (Leipzig: Breitkopf und Härtel), II, p. 258.

54. The composition and performance history of the Cello Concerto is described at greater length by Joachim Draheim in 'Das Cellokonzert a-Moll op. 129 von Robert Schumann: Neue Quellen und Materialien', *Schumann in Düsseldorf*, pp. 249–64.

55. Joachim Draheim prepared an edition of the transcription for violin, which was published by Breitkopf und Härtel in 1987; see also his '"Dies Concert ist auch für Violine transscribt erschienen": Robert Schumanns Cellokonzert und seine neuentdeckte Fassung für Violine', *Neue Zeitschrift für Musik* 148 (1987), 4–10.

56. Litzmann, *Clara Schumann*, II, p. 297.

57. *Berliner Musikzeitung*, 17 January 1855, 9:3 (1855), 17.

58. Letter to Isac Glickman, 11 August 1963, quoted in liner notes by Alexander Ivashkin to *The Unknown Shostakovich* (Chandos Records Ltd, 2000), CHAN 9792. Shostakovich had been asked to reorchestrate the concerto by Mstislav Rostropovich. For more information see Klaus Wolfgang Niemöller, 'Robert Schumanns Cellokonzert in der Instrumentation von Dmitri Shostakowitsch: Ein Beitrag zur Schumann-Rezeption in der Sowjetunion', *Beiträge zur Geschichte des Konzerts: Festschrift Siegfried Kross zum 60. Geburtstag* (Bonn: Schröder, 1990), pp. 411–21.

59. Schumann's Cello Concerto, performed by Steven Isserlis with the Deutsche Kammerphilharmonie Bremen conducted by Christoph Eschenbach, directed by Steve Ruggi (Bullfrog Films, VHS (1–56029–714-X)).

60. Marcel Brion complained that the *Concert-Allegro mit Introduction* (op. 134) was: 'a brilliant and clever work but less poetic than preceding ones; in it we see

a certain lassitude, a poverty of invention, and even a superficiality, redeemed to some extent by masterly technique. Here the piano is no longer the confidant of the soul but a brilliant instrument somewhat heartlessly displaying its virtuosity.'
Brion, *Robert Schumann*, p. 342.

61. See letter to Joachim 8 October 1853, *Briefe. Neue Folge*, pp. 379–80.

62. *NZfM* 40 (1854), 42.

63. *NZfM* 45 (1856), 199.

64. Hanslick, 'Joseph Joachim' (1861), *Aus dem Concert-Saal: Kritiken und Schilderungen aus 20 Jahren des Wiener Musiklebens, 1848–1868* (Vienna: Braumüller, 1897).

65. Michael Struck, *Robert Schumann Violinkonzert D-Moll (WoO 23)* (Munich: Fink, 1988), pp. 17 and 72.

66. *NZfM* 49 (1860).

67. Schumann began to compose the Violin Concerto on 21 September 1853, orchestrated it on 3 October and produced a piano score a few days later. For more on the compositional process see Struck, *Robert Schumann Violinkonzert D-Moll*, pp. 7–51.

68. Letter of 5 August 1898, *Briefe von und an Joseph Joachim*, ed. Andreas Moser (Berlin: Bard, 1911), pp. 486–7.

69. For an account of the Violin Concerto that concentrates on the influence of Clara, Brahms and Joachim and their ghosts, see Hellmuth von Ulmann, *Die veruntreute Handschrift: Robert Schumanns Violinkonzert und seine Tragödie. Geschichte einer Recherche* (Heilbronn: Salzer, 1981).

70. The soloist was Georg Kulenkampff with the Berlin Philharmonic under Karl Böhm. Eugenie responded to her critics with 'Eugenie Schumann und das letzte Werk ihres Vaters Robert Schumann: Eine Antwort', *Zeitschrift für Musik* (March 1938), 241–3.

71. Sadly, the primary reason the Concerto was performed, it seems, was that even a late and untried work by Schumann was preferable to the 'Jewish' Mendelssohn's Violin Concerto; also for anti-Semitic reasons, neither of Joachim's nieces nor Yehudi Menuhin were allowed to be the soloist. See Michael Struck, *Die umstritten späten Instrumentalwerke Schumanns. Untersuchungen zur Entstehung, Struktur und Rezeption* (Hamburg, 1984), pp. 324–6. In December 1937, Menuhin premiered the Concerto with piano accompaniment at Carnegie Hall, and with full orchestra in St Louis.

72. Letter of 5 August 1898, p. 487.

73. For example, Maurice Lindsay, 'The works for solo instrument and orchestra', *Schumann: A Symposium*, ed. Gerald Abraham (Oxford: Oxford University Press, 1952), p. 258; and Gerard Heldt, 'Konzertante Element in Robert Schumanns Instrumentalwerke', *Robert Schumann: Universalgeist der Romantik*, ed. Julius Alf and Joseph A. Kruse (Düsseldorf: Droste, 1981).

74. Donald Francis Tovey described Schumann in the Violin Concerto has having 'broken through enforced night by melody'; see his 'Letter to the editor:

"Schumann's last concerto: case for production", *The Times* (24 January 1938), 18.

75. His analysis can be found in *Studien zum Spätwerk Robert Schumanns* (Tutzing: Hans Schneider, 1984), pp. 79–101.

76. Bowie, *Aesthetics and Subjectivity*, pp. 251–2.

77. Gilles Deleuze, *Difference and Repetition*, trans. Paul Patton (London and New York: Continuum, 1994), pp. 17–18.

Despite Schumann's fame as a composer of small-scale and intimate works, his chamber music in general tends to be overlooked; today only the first and third of the op. 41 Quartets and the Piano Quintet op. 44 have an important presence in the performance repertoire. Yet one of his earliest major pieces was the C minor Piano Quartet (1828–9, incomplete), and altogether he wrote almost two dozen chamber music works, over half of them between 1849 and 1853.[1] Those composed after his move to Düsseldorf in 1850, which will be the focus of this chapter, include the *Märchenbilder* for viola and piano op. 113, three violin sonatas, the Third Piano Trio in G minor, op. 110, the *Märchenerzählungen* for clarinet, viola and piano, op. 132 and *Fünf Romanzen* for cello, now lost (Schumann's accompaniments to Bach and Paganini could also be classed as chamber music but for reasons outlined elsewhere are discussed in Chapter 3). As can be seen from this list, the late chamber music falls into two groups: pieces that seem to be illustrative and naïve in tone (the fairy-tale or *Märchen* works) and others that are more abstract and complex. The reason for the divide can be credited to Schumann's circumstances and to changing aesthetics – of chamber music generally, but also of the composer's late style.

As Music Director in Düsseldorf Schumann was responsible for the musical activities and education (*Bildung*) of the community. Thus he founded a Quartettkränzchen in November 1851 to read through and discuss chamber music to complement the Singekränzchen, which specialized in singing early polyphony. He did not write any music to be played by the Quartettkränzchen, however, and despite the accessibility of some of the *Märchenmusik* Schumann's late chamber music was not geared towards amateurs.

Instead he took advantage of the professional performers around him.[2] The dedicatee of the A minor Violin Sonata, op. 105 and *Märchenbilder* was his concertmaster Wasielewski; the D minor Violin Sonata, op. 121 was dedicated to the violinist Ferdinand David, and the Piano Trio in G minor, op. 110 to the town's resident piano trio (Wasielewski, Carl Heinrich Reimers, and Schumann's deputy Julius Tausch). Two years later the arrival of Joseph Joachim in Düsseldorf encouraged not only the composition of the Violin Concerto and *Phantasie* for Violin and Orchestra (discussed in the previous chapter), but also the F. A. E. Sonata and Schumann's Third Violin Sonata. Brahms, one of Schumann's fellow contributors to the F. A. E. Sonata, has been considered an influence on the *Märchenerzählungen* and the *Fünf Romanzen* for cello. The availability of these performers meant that Schumann was able to write technically complex music, which on occasion verged on the virtuosic (and which even these musicians found challenging). These were not pieces only to be played at home but also to be performed in public, reflecting that the status of the genre more generally was changing from *Hausmusik* to art music.[3]

Crucial to the changing status of chamber music was the increased interest in and understanding of quartets by Schubert and Beethoven – particularly the latter's late quartets. Schumann's response to these composers deserves a book in itself; there is much to be said about Schubert's 'heavenly lengths' and Schumann's use of repetition, about both composers' memory processes, and about Beethoven as a model for thematic integration. The point I would like to tease out here, though, is the rather fraught relationship in these late works between classicism and experimentalism. Beethoven's late quartets might not have been fully appreciated until some time after his death – it is a commonplace to say they finally came of age in the modernist era – but long before that, their radicality was recognized, at least by a few.[4] Schumann's final chamber works have never been accorded the same weight even within the composer's oeuvre. This despite them sharing many of the same experimental features of the quartets and quintet from 1842: from beginning *in medias res*, to sustained tonal ambiguity, strong lyrical and epigrammatic impulses and interruptive gestures.[5] But they are heard differently. In the earlier quartets the innovations are thought to revitalize and critique classical paradigms. In the Third Piano Trio and three violin sonatas they are thought of as fissures, as failures in and of the form.[6]

Schumann's late chamber music lies on the fault-line between 'architectonic' and 'logical' form: the former privileging structural and phrasal balance, the latter thematic process.[7] Indeed one of the deciding factors in the re-evaluation of Beethoven's late quartets was critics' focus on form as process. In 1938, Walter Riezler used Schumann as a comparison:

> We still read that Beethoven's last works entirely lack real form, and that its place is taken by a 'succession of visions' . . . This may perhaps apply to some of Schumann's works, for with him sonata form is indeed simply a framework that holds the release of emotions within due bounds, but remains outside the actual musical substance and is thus always clearly in evidence. It is the opposite with Beethoven's last works, for in them framework and content are so entirely one that the former is not seen.[8]

Riezler's implication that Schumann's forms are like a 'succession of visions' resonates quite nicely with the *Märchenbilder*, whose imagistic qualities are discussed below; also the notion that sonata form acts primarily as scaffolding for the music is certainly borne out in the recapitulations of the violin sonatas. But there are other modernist models that allow the structural skeleton to show. For example, Adorno described convention in late Beethoven as appearing in 'a form that is bald, undisguised, untransformed'.[9] As in the late poems of Friedrich Hölderlin, Adorno argued, Beethoven eliminated the middle element that conventionally connects moments together because it was 'external and inessential'.[10] Here, it seems, there might be a more positive way to describe the fractures of Schumann's late music.

In the Introduction to this book, I mentioned that while the formal idiosyncrasies of Schumann's earlier works are often explained by recourse to literary models – most notably the novels of Jean Paul and Friedrich Schlegel's aesthetic of the Romantic fragment – no comparable poetic paradigms have been offered for the music from the 1850s. No doubt this reflects the limited amount of literature on the late works as a whole. It might, though, also be symptomatic of a different attitude towards content and form on the part of the composer and his listeners. More recent composers such as Luigi Nono, György Kurtág and Wolfgang Rihm have paired Schumann with Hölderlin, and there are some striking parallels between them that I want to explore in this chapter. Aside from the occasionally fractured quality of their late styles, composer and poet have similar biographies and, up to a (crucial) point, a similar reception, to which a brief introduction might be useful here.

Hölderlin (1770–1843) enjoyed some early success with his novel *Hyperion* (1797/9) but succumbed to mental illness and was admitted to an asylum in Tübingen in 1806. He remained institutionalized until the end of his life. Throughout most of the nineteenth century, he held a marginal position; his illness was thought by many to have affected the quality of his work and, as with late Schumann, critics noted his poetry's 'darkness'. It was not until the twentieth century that Hölderlin's poetry began to be re-evaluated and came to be held in high regard, particularly by philosophers (and more problematically by the Nazis).[11]

Schumann knew Hölderlin's poetry, his interest apparently having been piqued by the poet's 'madness'; according to Emil Flechsig, he 'spoke about it with fear and awe'.[12] He copied excerpts from the first complete edition of the poetry (published in 1826), passages that emerged later as epigraphs for the *Neue Zeitschrift für Musik*. As discussed in Chapter 6, his original title for *Gesänge der Frühe* was *An Diotima*, which might have been a reference to Hyperion's beloved. Yet despite these biographical parallels and the composer's appreciation of the poet, there has been little exploration of possible connections between their creative approaches, with the exception of Daverio, who interpreted the transition between the final two movements of the Piano Concerto as parallel to Hölderlin's 'alternation of tones' and who wrote of the opening chorus of Part III of the *Szenen aus Goethes Faust*, 'Waldung, sie schwankt heran': 'that the Jean-Paulian fantasy and humour, not to mention the Hoffmannesque grotesquerie, of much of Schumann's earlier music is giving way to a sobriety redolent of Friedrich Hölderlin's mature poetry'.[13] Daverio thus only invokes Hölderlin with regard to music composed around 1845, rather blandly explaining the comparison as exemplifying Schumann's multi-faceted Romanticism. The reason for not putting more pressure on the possible connections between poet and composer might be continuing anxiety over biography and the potential to overstress the influence of mental illness on these artists' creativity, often-ignored tensions between literary and musical models, and what for Schumann is still an unresolved relationship between a concept of late style and modernism – unlike Hölderlin his final works have not been reclaimed as modernist before their time. By comparing them we may still lack a satisfactory solution to the mysteries of Schumann's late style but we may gain some insight into what makes that style so problematic, and whether responsibility for the judgement lies within the works or within us.

Hölderlin is far from the only potential model for Schumann's late chamber music, in recognition of which the first part of this chapter is primarily concerned with a different angle to the question of form and content, conservatism and radicalism. The *Märchenbilder* and *Märchenerzählungen* seem to belong to a realm far removed from the experimentalism of late Beethoven. With their fairy-tale themes and simple, folkish tone they hark back to the Biedermeier idyll of the 1840s. In this Schumann was similar to artists such as Alfred Rethel (1816–59), Adrian Ludwig Richter (1799–1860) and the head of the Düsseldorf School, Wilhelm Schadow (1789–1862), who found post-1848 materialism distasteful and disturbing.[14] Richter (who produced the title page for the first edition of the *Album für die Jugend*) increasingly concentrated on illustrations for folk-tales and ballads, evoking Germanic heritage by using a deliberately archaic style of wood engraving that stretched back to Dürer.[15] In his satirical autobiographical novella *Der moderne Vasari* (1854), Schadow portrayed the contemporary art world as driven by the market-place and forgetful of history.[16] Although Schumann seems to have known and appreciated Richter and Schadow better, it is Rethel who most poignantly mirrors him both personally and stylistically.

In 1840 Rethel won a commission to complete a series of murals portraying scenes from the life of Charlemagne, in the Imperial Chamber in the town hall of his birthplace, Aachen. Disagreements with the civic authorities over his approach to the subject meant that painting did not begin until 1846. Before he had completed two frescoes, the revolutions of 1848 erupted. The integration of Church and State by the Holy Roman Empire no longer seemed relevant, and Rethel found the commission an increasingly heavy burden. He sought relief in a series of small-scale wood engravings on a more macabre theme than his friend Richter's fairy-tales: *Another Dance of Death*. Their format was intended to ape the broadsheets popular after the uprisings, with their simple verses and woodcuts. The theme was apparently inspired by Ferdinand Freiligrath's 1848 poem *From the Dead to the Living*, which chided survivors of the barricades for failing to continue fighting for the cause for which their comrades had died. Although Müller von Königswinter (later Schumann's friend and doctor in Düsseldorf) complained that the series was 'a caricature of the whole tendency of our time', the engravings were extremely popular among conservatives as a warning against the consequences of revolution.[17]

Rethel spent the winter of 1848 in Dresden; after the revolutions he returned to complete the Aachen frescoes and continued *Another Dance of Death*. But the engravings took on a more personal, rather than a political, tone. In *Death of a Friend* (1851), Death tolls a bell: a ghost in the tower ringing out the custodian's passing (Illustration 1). That sense of foreboding is maintained in the frescoes; in the concluding scene (Illustration 2), in which Otto III visits the crypt, the corpse of Charlemagne sits upright in his throne, as imposing as the pillars framing him. Otto and his followers, bowing in cloaks and headscarves, seem fluid and fragile – more human – in comparison. Their light barely reaches the corners of the crypt, making the forms into 'weighty angular masses' and distracting the viewer's gaze from what should be the focus of attention – Charlemagne – as does the irregular arch-shape of the fresco, which was originally fitted above a window.[18]

Schumann visited the Aachen frescoes in August 1851, describing Rethel as out of sorts and affected ('sehr verstimmt und afficirt').[19] The artist had recently married but was suffering from a nervous illness. He travelled to Rome the following year but on his return to Germany was declared insane and in May 1853 entered Richarz's asylum at Endenich, where Schumann was admitted the following year.[20] Little has been made of the parallels between their fates and their work – whether they liked each other's art or not, they

Illustration 1   Richard Julius Jungtow after Alfred Rethel, 'Der Tod als Freund'

pursued equivalent goals. There are striking parallels between their striving with large-scale forms on grand historical and nationalist themes, and their mastery of small forms.[21] Also, the gloomy colours and block-like forms of the Aachen frescoes might be compared to the dark timbres and sectional structures of Schumann's instrumental works.[22] Although *Another Dance with Death* enjoyed a success unrivalled by any late music by Schumann, the shared attitudes expressed in their last creative years underscore the extent to which the age in general was changing. The new generation had no patience with the conservative idealism that Rethel's or Schumann's artworks advocated. Increasingly, they were considered remnants from a previous age.

Schumann's persistence with chamber music in the 1850s can be construed as a retreat from the modern mainstream, where music dramas and

Illustration 2   Alfred Rethel, 'Kaiser Otto III. in der Gruft Karls des Großen'

tone poems were the order of the day. As Carl Dahlhaus explained, at this time chamber music was traditionally considered the preserve of the educated middle classes, a 'nature reserve for conservatives too dazed by the new music to do anything but cling to the old'.[23] Of course, Schumann did not only write chamber music in his final years. The characterization of him as a composer of small forms – of lieder and chamber music – served a political purpose: to put him more firmly in opposition to Wagner and Liszt. This process was most obvious in Adolf Schubring's series of 'Schumanniana' articles, the first of which appeared in 1859, the year Brendel officially pronounced the formation of the New German School.[24] Schubring declared himself a *Schumannianer* and made a case for a Schumann School, distinct from the 'conservative' Mendelssohnians and the 'progressive' *Zukunftsmusiker*. Its members included Carl Ritter, Theodor Kirchner, Woldemar Bargiel, and – most significantly – Brahms, all of whom excelled in solo piano and chamber music. Schubring's project established Schumann as a perpetrator of small forms; by the close of the 1870s he was declared 'Der musikalische Romantiker *par excellence*'.[25]

The greatest influence over Schumann's posthumous reputation was probably Brahms – directly given his role in preparing the Collected Edition, and indirectly through the reception of his own works. It was Brahms more than Schumann who embodied conservative opposition to the New German School. However, in the twentieth century his reputation was transformed by Arnold Schoenberg's essay 'Brahms the Progressive'. The technique of developing variation Schoenberg prized is another example of modernists' preference for logical over architectonic form. Recent scholars have implied that Brahms's motivic manipulation had its roots in Schumann's music, in the thematic treatment of pieces such as the *Märchenerzählungen*. There is something to be said for the comparison: not least in the way it implicitly connects Schumann – the late Schumann – to the modernist trajectory. That the *Märchenerzählungen* should be the example invoked, however, puts a question mark over attempts to explain the chamber music only within the context of Biedermeier nostalgia. Even a nature reserve might produce new species.

The lengthy introduction to this chapter has been an attempt to give some context for the following examination of the works. In order to consider the relationship between content and form in regard to Schumann's late style, which seems fundamental to understanding the achievements and historical significance of the chamber music, discussion is divided into two parts. The first is about the *Märchenmusik*, its relationship to German Romantic aesthetics and visual arts, Hölderlin and Brahms. The second is about the Third Piano Trio and violin sonatas, and again makes use of Hölderlin as a point of comparison for questions of structure and poetics. A theme that emerges is whether the fracturedness or 'brokenness' of Schumann's late style is something that should be understood as a failure of form or whether it indicates instead a failure on our part to appreciate these pieces for what they are, rather than what they might have been.

Picture stories

According to Adolf Schubring, the *Märchenmusik* belonged to Schumann's greatest genre: the modern Romantic epic.[26] Although evocative of a certain 'höchst romantisch' atmosphere, what epic stories the *Märchenbilder* and *Märchenerzählungen* tell is ambiguous: their movements have no descriptive titles as in *Waldszenen*; instead there are just suggestions for tempo and mood.[27] As fairy-tale 'pictures' (*Bilder*) and 'stories' or 'narrations' (*Erzählungen*), these are conceptual pieces in the same way that *Kinderszenen* is about childhood rather than for children: the illustrations from a fairy-tale rather than its story; the sound of the storyteller's voice rather than her words.

'Wo bin ich? Ist's Wahrheit, ist's ein Traum?' ('Where am I? Is this reality or a dream?'). The rose's question in Schumann's 'very charming and idyllic märchen' *Der Rose Pilgerfahrt* (already mentioned in Chapter 2) was fundamental to the German Romantic appreciation of the fairy-tale.[28] Aside from their sense of accessing national heritage through the folk tradition, it was the fairy-tale's connection, through the irrational and fantastical, to the subconscious that appealed to writers such as E. T. A. Hoffmann, Clemens Brentano, Ludwig Tieck and La Motte Fouqué. Novalis explained: 'All fairy-tales are no more than dreams of that native world that is everywhere and nowhere'.[29] Those dreams were the 'confessions of a true, synthetic child – of an ideal child' whose meaning (innocent or otherwise) had to be constructed by the reader.[30]

The dreaminess and interpretative openness of Romantic fairy-tales were matched by their representation in the visual arts.[31] Paintings by artists such as Moritz von Schwind and Philipp Otto Runge were full of symbolism and allegory, and tried to capture moments from fairy-tale scenes to be animated by the viewer's imagination.[32] As mentioned in Chapter 2, the vogue for illustrated ballad books and the decoration of musical scores established a close link between pictures and words that began to extend to music – particularly through fairy-tales. According to Novalis, 'A fairy-tale is truly like a dream image – without coherence – an *ensemble* of wondrous things and incidents – e.g. a *musical fantasy*'; while Tieck claimed *Märchen* need 'a quietly progressive tone, a certain innocence of representation . . . which hypnotizes the soul like quiet musical improvisations without noise and clamour'.[33]

Tieck's description fits Schumann's *Märchenbilder* remarkably well. The last movement is cast in a reflective mood, its major key lending a consoling air to its 'melancholy expression' ('Langsam, mit melancholischem Ausdruck' reads the subtitle). Piano and viola begin the theme together, one of many instances in the chamber music of Schumann's much maligned doubling of parts. From the end of bar 4 the viola pursues the melody a sixth below the piano's right hand, and frequently takes the lower voice (such as from the end of bar 12 to bar 22) (Example 5:1). The timbral effect is cloudy, particularly with the *pp* dynamics, but enriches the overall texture and very subtly draws out the main interest of the movement, namely its use of offbeat slow moving harmonies. At the end of bar 12, for example, the third phrase ends by cadencing onto E (v of VI); the next phrase begins as a repetition of the opening melody (with the viola's melody beneath

Example 5:1 op. 113, iv, bb. 1–15

the piano's) but in the flat submediant of E, underpinned by an open fifth C–G. By the end of bar 14, A has reasserted itself in the bass. These shifts make the harmonic changes seem somehow abrupt despite the languorous atmosphere, as at the retransition to the opening theme in bars 58–62 (Example 5:2) where the modulation from F major to D major is made by suddenly introducing a syncopated pedal on an open fifth, D–A.

The slow harmonic rhythm, which often moves by step, gives the music a planar quality akin to a landscape. Indeed the moment of C major in bars 12–14 could be compared to light shifting over the scene; perhaps

Example 5:2   op. 113, iv, bb. 57–64

the shadow of a cloud. This sense of time changing the way we perceive something – a landscape or a melody – might be extended to explain the effect of transitions in the *Märchenbilder*. The final bars of the last movement remember the ascending semiquaver triplet figure the piano had developed through the middle section (Example 5:3), suggesting that the theme could continue beyond its cadence (as was also implied by the continuation of the viola's demisemiquaver arabesques in the transition shown in Example 5:2). In the second movement, all transitions between sections of the miniature rondo (ABACA) use the same figure: the viola plays a repeated triplet quaver descending triad, underpinned by sustained seventh chords in the piano, all over a four-bar diminuendo and ritardando (Example 5:4). Each time it seems as if the kaleidoscope has been turned to reveal a new image.

The formal strategies of the *Märchenbilder* might thus be characterized as episodic: movements are in rondo or ternary forms. Their internal sections are framed; often one thematic or harmonic world fades to be replaced by another, much as the illustrations from a fairy-tale skip from one scene to another. All movements, with the exception of the third, end by fading away to *pianissimo*. The music suits its *Bilder* title. Yet there is also a poetic model

Example 5:3   op. 113, i, bb. 90–94

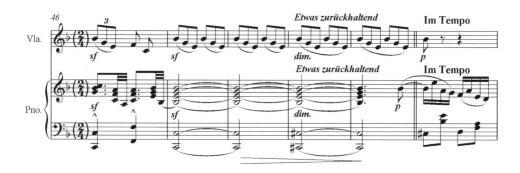

Example 5:4   op. 113, ii, bb. 46–51

that might be co-opted to describe the way the *Märchenbilder* characterize sections and make transitions between them.

Hölderlin conceived of poetry as bearing a 'basic tone' or mood (*Grundton* or *Stimmung*) that provides underlying unity. Of the infinite possibilities, he decided there were three basic tones: the ideal, the naïve and the heroic. These three correspond with different types of representation on the continuum between life and art. Thus the naïve is subjective and lyrical, describing events in a coherent and precise manner, which lends a pictorial quality to the whole. The heroic is energetic, striving, passionate and objective. The ideal is reflective, intellectual and concerned with absolute unity. Although not all music fits easily into the three types, they correspond quite well with the different moods of the *Märchenmusik*.[34] For example, the D minor outer sections of the third movement of the *Märchenbilder*, with their perpetual semiquaver triplets and occasional chordal outbursts, seem heroic, while the more lyrical B major middle section might be characterized as naïve.

The crucial problem for Hölderlin was how to move from one tone to another: in this regard music seems to have provided him with a model

Example 5:5 op. 113, iii, bb. 36–40

solution. The poet's skill, according to the doctrine 'Wechsel der Töne' (the 'alternation of tones'), lies in making deft transitions between each tone, for it is in those transitions, as each tone strives towards the next through time, that poetic meaning is found. Within a poem, the order of tones may seem random in terms of content but they are connected by spirit – a binding thread – which, in the poet's words, 'might retain its presentness not in one isolated moment and then another, but rather *in* one moment *as* another, continuously'.[35] Thus Hölderlin compares the transitions between tones to modulations in music. The last movement of the *Märchenbilder*, which blurs sections by overlapping motives and tonal regions, seems to prove his point. However, the transitions of the third movement seem more abrupt; the semiquaver triplets suddenly stop and the modulation is unprepared, sidled into by the triple repetition of a leading-note appoggiatura and out of by a circle of fifths (Example 5:5). It is those stepwise inflections – from natural to sharp and back again – that make the music 'retain its presentness', making the new harmony and thematic material seem at once foreign and familiar.

Hölderlin's 'binding thread' seems similar to the network of subtle 'witty' connections (*Witz*) heard in Schumann's earlier works, such as the *Davidsbündlertänze*.[36] But there are some important differences. The concept of *Witz* promotes fleeting and oblique points of contact but, as in the late songs, the connections made in the *Märchenmusik* are both more abstract and more consistent. For instance, in a similar manner to the Maria Stuart lieder, the *Märchenerzählungen* keep to a close harmonic circle – from B flat major to G minor, G major and back to B flat major – and the movements of the *Märchenerzählungen* within themselves are thematically focused to a degree not found in the *Märchenbilder*. Similarities between them tend to reside in their harmonic rhythm and use of texture. For example, the fairy-tale's gentle hypnosis is conveyed in the slow harmonic movement of the first and third movements, with their extended use of pedals and sharing of themes between instruments.[37] The heroic tone breaks through in the fourth movement; the outer sections' repeated angular figures are of the same ilk as the dotted rhythms of the finales to the Third Violin Sonata and Violin Concerto.[38] While the middle section in the flat submediant (G flat major) provides contrast, it is also very repetitive motivically and harmonically; the piano keeps to the same three-semiquaver figure throughout while the viola and clarinet rarely break from their parallel thirds, and the section is marked to be repeated.

The second movement of the *Märchenerzählungen*, 'Lebhaft und sehr markirt', is more varied. It opens with continuous crotchet movement around G minor until the piano and viola introduce an ascending dotted-rhythm quaver figure in bar 9. The strident opening crotchet theme returns in bar 17, incorporating the dotted rhythm. This pattern of motivic repetition over harmonic sequences continues through the remainder of the first section, as if a mutating miniature rondo, the main theme constantly being encroached upon by new elements from the episodes. Bar 60 begins an extended middle section in E flat major, the cello and viola introducing a triplet melody in parallel thirds repeated from bar 68 by the piano. Its triplet figure is incorporated by the clarinet and viola into the return of the opening theme in bar 96 (Example 5:6) before they return to their original material which is repeated verbatim, with a twelve-bar coda.

Yet while the second movement of the *Märchenerzählungen* begins as if setting out on a fairy-tale hero's journey – tramping into the forest, sword and horn strapped to the back – it soon is distracted from the path: there is no real sense of a narrative trajectory. This is perhaps inevitable given the large-scale ternary structure, which of course recapitulates material from the first section. But the piece does not end with a triumphant return or sense of closure; instead in the last bars the music fades away, as had the scenes from the *Märchenbilder*. It is as though our hero is trapped in one of those ballad book illustrations, permanently about to go deeper into the forest, but never moving forward. In this respect the *Märchenerzählungen* go against Daverio's description of Schumann as a storyteller who, like all natural raconteurs, 'loves to digress, to linger reflectively on a pertinent (and sometimes impertinent) detail, to reminisce, to dart backward and forward in time'.[39] The block-like and repetitive construction of the movements might introduce new material in some sections but seems more static than digressive, or scenic rather than temporal. Perhaps this is because of the dreamlike qualities ascribed to fairy-tales by Romantic authors such as Novalis. The visual model has something to offer, for it leaves narrative to the eye – or rather the ear – of the beholder. But the imagistic structures of

Example 5:6   op. 132, ii, bb. 90–107

the *Märchenmusik* might be a limiting factor to appreciating development on a smaller scale and in more explicitly musical terms: on the level of the motive.

As has already been mentioned, the *Märchenerzählungen* are often said to prefigure the thematic processes of Brahms.[40] Certainly the extent of the repetition and allusion is striking. However, it does not quite reach Brahms's

Example 5:7a op. 132, i, bb. 1–5

Example 5:7b op. 132, i, bb. 13–15

level of sophistication; there is some use of sequence (particularly in the third movement) but less evidence of development – the factor that most impressed Schoenberg. For example, there are three main motivic characters in the first movement: (a) the piano's arpeggiated demisemiquavers, which are almost perpetual; (b) the arching melody first played by the viola; and (c) the transitional two-bar phrase begun by the clarinet at the end of bar 13 (Example 5:7a and 5:7b). Figures (a) and (b) both stress the second beat of the bar. Figure (a) is shared between all three instruments – at first in a rising sequence. In bar 11, the viola initiates a new motive, incorporating the piano's demisemiquaver rhythm with what might be a reference to the semiquavers of figure (a), but there is no definitive intervallic connection between them (the motive continues under (c) in the example). And while as the movement progresses the motives are sometimes fragmented and sometimes extended by sequence they do not evolve in the sense of, say, a Brahms Intermezzo. It is the repetition that provides consistency rather than development of a motivic kernel.

The *Märchenerzählungen* thus seem to fall somewhere between conjuring scenes from a fairy-tale and pursuing proto-Brahmsian developing variation: the storyteller does not quite get the balance between gripping narrative and allowing his listeners' imagination freedom to roam. In the tenuous transitions between sections and the endless repetitions when they fail to mesmerize, there is a sense of brokenness – perhaps of the failure of late style. Brokenness has long been a trait associated with Schumann; from the gruesome wooden contraption (or chiroplast) with which he attempted to lengthen and strengthen his finger that instead ended his hopes for a career as a performer, to the abrupt juxtapositions of the early piano cycles. Even the infamous fragment might be conceived of as a crucial-but-missing cog for the smooth running of a musical machine – or perhaps better, as a cog (spiky as a hedgehog) to a machine we have lost. The metaphor of Schumann being 'broken' has most resonance, though, with the late chamber works. These are felt to have special access to the composer, in part because they were played first by his circle of friends in intimate settings. Small ensembles of solo instruments are also somehow connected with ideas of personal expression. Even before Roland Barthes famously heard in Schumann's *Kreisleriana* a 'body that beats' we have tended to think of piano music especially as letting us engage with the man behind the notes.[41] The problem with the late chamber works is that the composer's body is far from healthy.

Indeed, it is close to breakdown; a sense of which extends to responses to the music and that feeds into anecdotes about Schumann's last years. The strongest image is of the incarcerated composer improvising at the piano. According to Wasielewski, 'it was heartbreaking to have to see the mental and physical power of the noble, great man completely broken . . . The playing was unpleasant. It made the impression that the force from which it came was completely paralysed.'[42] In Alger's 1871 translation of Wasielewski's biography, an even more provocative image was provided for Schumann's playing: 'It seemed as if the force whence it proceeded were injured, like a machine whose springs are broken, but which still tries to work, jerking convulsively.'[43] The composer, broken at – and maybe by – his instrument is particularly evocative for the Third Piano Trio and violin sonatas, which were described in terms of creative exhaustion. The Third Violin Sonata, with its strangely vacant bars and virtuosic passagework, even suggests technical breakdown – the machine still trying to work, but going nowhere. Again, however, we might simply have misunderstood the cracks in the system; maybe they indicate not weaknesses in the foundations but new roots growing up: 'Der Morgen der erwacht ist aus den Dämmerungen' ('The morning woken out of twilight shades').[44]

Broken pieces

The momentary dreamlike images we might have expected to encounter in the *Märchenmusik* appear in some passages of the 'purely' instrumental late chamber pieces. As they do, more famously, in earlier works. The first two piano trios, op. 63 in D minor and op. 80 in F major, were composed in the summer of 1847. In an 1848 review, Alfred Dörffel described the D minor Trio as having broken the spell of what had been 'a long romantic dream'.[45] The most noteworthy aspect of its first movement was considered to be its novel thematic combinations, but against this proto-Brahmsian developing variation come moments of other-worldliness. In the development there arrives a *sul ponticello* chorale whose harmony floats from F to A♭. Dörffel heard the passage as evoking the higher spheres of the Mater Gloriosa's final exhortation to the penitent Gretchen at the end of *Faust*: 'Komm! Hebe dich zu höhern Sphären! Wenn er dich ahnet, folgt er nach' ('Come, rise to higher spheres! Sensing your presence, he will follow').

A parallel moment of 'sublime removal' occurs in the Second Piano Trio's first movement with a quotation from the second song from the Eichendorff *Liederkreis*, op. 29, 'Intermezzo' (Example 5:8).[46] The song's text, in which the poet contemplates a portrait of his lost love, can be linked to the famous distant voices of Schumann's earlier pieces:

Mein Herz still in sich singet
ein altes schönes Lied,
das in die Luft sich schwinget
und zu dir eilig zieht.

My heart sings gently
a lovely old song
which soars though the air
and flies towards you.

The lyrical melody as it appears in the Trio is at once recognizable and self-contained; it is introduced by several bars of C major quaver arpeggios in the piano, the mood relaxing from *forte* quaver climax to *piano* legato dotted

Example 5:8 Second Piano Trio, i, bb. 103–13

crotchets. Its status as a quotation is undeniable. What is noticeable about the interruptions of the later music in comparison is that the voices are unplaceable; the poet seems no longer to have a clear memory of his lover's portrait, just a sense that he has seen or heard something like it before.

For example, towards the end of the exposition in the first movement of the Third Piano Trio, a new melodic arch emerges (Example 5:9). In contrast to the preceding material, for twelve bars the instruments move together on the beat, with occasional hemiolas. The harmonic rhythm also moves more quickly, following the melody in parallel sixths. Although it sounds like inserted material, it is not as clearly framed as the song quotation in the Second Piano Trio; the rising and falling motive of the first subject continues virtually throughout and while the change to duple rhythms suggests a chorale the melody is not idiomatic. It is a fragmentary reference, rather as the Jena Romantics described the events of a fairy-tale. But the passage also serves a structural function shown, perhaps counter-intuitively, by its replacement in the development. While the development continues the

Example 5:9   Third Piano Trio, i, bb. 50–9

figuration from the first subject and includes an exact repetition of the violin's melody for the second subject, over an F pedal in the cello, the 'chorale' passage does not follow on as it had before. Instead the F pedal returns in the piano, and violin and cello begin a new pizzicato fugato along with will-o'-the-wisp flourishes. It is as if there is a space in the sonata-scheme for an alternative theme or figuration, a kind of intermezzo, whose surface attraction might be a quotation or allusion but whose deeper significance is structural. Thus the reiteration of material from the first and second subjects in the development is balanced by the new pizzicato theme. On the other hand, as if to confirm the recapitulation, the chorale passage returns in its original position, like the second subject reharmonized in the tonic major.

The difference between surface and structural form can also be explained as a displacement of theme and harmony. As often occurs in Schumann, the beginning of the recapitulation in the first movement of the Third Piano

Example 5:10 Third Piano Trio, ii, bb. 41–6

Trio is falsely broadcast five bars early by the return of the first subject over the subdominant. Generally speaking, structural points are often under-cut by not being given the strongest harmonic definition, mostly by the use of chords in inversion. The second movement obscures its tonic of E flat major at its opening by its inversions and displacement of strong cadences, intensifying the feeling that the melody has been caught in mid-phrase. It still sounds like that on its recapitulation; the more dramatic middle section suddenly deflating onto a tonic 6/4 chord with flat seventh (Example 5:10) as if the intervening material had been nothing more than a bad dream. The third movement also begins with the fifth in the bass, emphasizing the rhythmic and thematic importance the quaver upbeat will have throughout.

The final movement of the Third Piano Trio is perhaps the most distinc-tive in terms of the relationship between theme, harmony and form. Its title, 'Kräftig, mit Humor', remembers the mood of Schumann's earlier piano pieces – most obviously *Humoreske* (op. 20) and *Novelletten* (op. 21) – and it shares with them some structural features.[47] Unlike the earlier movements of the Trio, which focus on a small number of themes, after its exposition, the finale incorporates several new sections with occasional repetitions of the first subject, as if a kind of sonata-rondo. While each theme is clearly characterized there is some sharing between sections and between movements; for example, the syncopated theme of bars 38–48 is taken from the middle section of the second movement. As in many of Schumann's chamber movements, there is a fugal working of the main theme just before the recapitulation proper, and sequential development of themes, such as the triplet motive introduced in bars 102–9. This last example demonstrates Schumann's ability at thematic development, as it is essentially a development of the main theme's opening intervals, reworked as transitional material (Example 5:11).

On the other hand, other sections include new figures that seem to bear no particular relationship to the main theme. Bars 68–94 (Example 5:12), for instance, suddenly leap into G minor and a sixth theme, with an ascending melody characterized by dotted rhythms and quasi-militaristic flourishes. The theme is counteracted by a descending figure that switches emphasis away from the second and fourth beats of the bar on to the first and third beats, and swaps the jaunty dotted rhythms for sidling chromatic triplets. Despite being a melodic sequence (the figure is repeated a third higher) the harmony remains the same – it is simply presented in a different inversion – until it cadences on to the dominant in bar 84. Another new figure is now introduced, an arching quaver arpeggio that provides dominant preparation for the return of the G minor theme at the end of bar 88. The theme and the two added figures thus contrast with each other in terms of the character, contour and rhythm of their motives. There are no obvious motivic connections between them. Within a brief section such as this it seems almost superfluous to have so much new material. However, each element contributes towards the harmonic structure: from theme in the tonic, to transition via the first figure to the dominant preparation of the second figure, back to theme in the tonic. We might think back to Riezler's description of form remaining outside the actual musical substance in Schumann. But it is not quite that straightforward. The return of the G minor theme is interrupted in bar 94; the harmony is diverted to E flat major, and the violin begins the fugal section with a syncopated and chromatic version of the first theme. The G minor theme thus is forgotten almost as abruptly as it arrived. If the formal framework for this music is only external scaffolding, it has the occasional structural folly to support.

Example 5:11   Third Piano Trio, iii, bb. 101–11

Clara described the Third Piano Trio as 'truly mighty music' ('eine wahrhaft gewaltige Musik'). Others have not been convinced. Philipp Spitta heard Schumann's genius in individual features but declared that in the main, the Trio 'speaks of exhaustion'.[48] Presumably he thought it predicted the composer's eventual mental collapse. More recent musicians similarly consider the Third Piano Trio to encapsulate something of the essence of late Schumann. For example, the second of Wolfgang Rihm's three *Fremde*

Example 5:12   Third Piano Trio, iv, bb. 66–91

Example 5:12 (*cont.*)

Szenen (1982–4) is subtitled 'Charakterstück' and was described by the composer as a portrait of Schumann and his style.[49] Despite the echo of *Kinderszenen*'s 'Von fremden Ländern und Menschen' in the *Szene*'s title, Rihm's music responds most strongly to the G minor Trio, whose rhythms can be heard in the piece, along with certain sounds associated with Schumannesque topics, such as medical equipment.[50] Taking his cue from the word 'chamber', Rihm's music evokes deserted rooms in which the forbidden can take place – or in which the forbidden has taken place.[51] At the back of the composer's mind when he invoked other chambers and medical equipment might have been Schumann's incarceration and treatment in the asylum: perhaps to him broken at the piano.

Certainly it was to the chamber music that Schumann's friends and family turned once he had entered Endenich. Clara recalled one evening in April 1854 when she and Joachim – in the company of Brahms – were moved so strongly by the Second Violin Sonata they did not want to continue playing.[52] The piece had been written soon after the First Violin Sonata and the Third Piano Trio in autumn 1851. Today the First Violin Sonata is better known, praised because of its formal workings and its seeming return to the Florestan and Eusebius alternations of the earlier music.[53] Evaluation of the second sonata has proved more problematic.[54] Charles Rosen describes it as less immediately attractive and poetic than the first.[55] Yet Schumann and his contemporaries tended to rate the two sonatas the other way round.

On its first public performance on 21 March 1852 at a benefit matinée in the Leipzig Gewandhaus, the A minor Sonata, op. 105 was praised by most of the press, with the exception of the ardent Wagnerite, Theodor Uhlig (1822–53). Where others celebrated the 'rich profusion' of the sonata, with its 'interesting combinations, sophisticated elaboration of lofty motifs, nobility and profundity of feeling',[56] Uhlig accused Schumann of 'musical banality, not to say commonplaces'.[57] The music was laboured because Schumann had been over-prolific, Uhlig claimed. He had become 'a composer who exists, musically speaking, only on paper . . . Schumann is in fact so remote from life, that is to say from reality, that, as the sonata in question shows, he is capable of writing entire movements in which, for example, violin and piano alternate in passages.' Beethoven should not be used as an excuse; even he made mistakes of judgement and these should be avoided rather than copied. Schumann's followers, Uhlig claimed, were beginning to turn their backs on him: 'because there is "no further progress" to be discerned in his compositions. Schumann has indeed now passed his musical peaks and the only thing that can save him from mediocrity is to moderate his output.'

Various counter-arguments could be used against Uhlig's review: the sonata was a commercial success; as Albert Dietrich and Clara discussed after the Leipzig concert, Schumann's compositions often took a while to reveal their delights to listeners;[58] and – the editor of the *Neue Zeitschrift für Musik* subsequently explained to Schumann – Uhlig's criticism became increasingly cruel in the last year of his life ('I did not print his really harsh reviews of his work, which did go too far', Brendel admitted).[59] Yet many of Uhlig's points have been echoed by commentators on the late works, if not the A minor Violin Sonata in particular; from the repetition of motives (as predicted, Beethoven has been invoked as a model) to the notion that by this time Schumann had passed his prime. Alongside the exhaustion Spitta detected in the Third Piano Trio, the chamber music seems to have been the place where Schumann is heard to have expressed his *horror vacui* – a term coined in the mid-nineteenth century to describe the artist's attempt to fill the feared blank canvas.

As Uhlig expressed in his description of the First Violin Sonata, that sense of a vacuum is felt most strongly in the final movement. It begins with an even more extended presentation of the tonic, A minor, than the *Märchen* pieces, the piano's left hand persisting with semiquaver octaves for the first six bars. The perpetual semiquaver movement is maintained in the treble, piano and violin chasing the theme usually a bar apart. The rhythm is only broken by the second subject's emphatic crotchets and introduction of legato phrasing; but even in this section a memory of the trembling octaves remains in the bass of bar 28. Towards the end of the exposition the first theme creeps back in: with the repeat it seems as though the cycle will never end. And the development section begins with the first theme in the tonic, until the quaver-two-semiquaver rhythm of the second subject takes over in bar 65. The first theme even makes an appearance in the E major passage from bar 78, disturbing the violin's lyrical melody with triplet accompaniment by reminding them of its existence (bars 82 and 88–92) (Example 5:13). In bar 101 the theme returns over a nine-bar-long bass pedal on E; the slightly truncated recapitulation in the tonic begins in bar 117. Just before the coda there is an often cited example of Schumann's tendency to recall a theme from an earlier movement: in this case, from the opening Allegro (Example 5:14). Although this is a striking moment, it is not a complete break from the surrounding material; the pedal F is still played as octave semiquavers in the bass, and the right hand of the piano interjects with the ascending first theme. The Coda in particular proves Uhlig's point about the repetitious aspect of the thematic alternation between violin and piano: from bar 184 the violin follows

Example 5:13 First Violin Sonata, iii, bb. 88–91

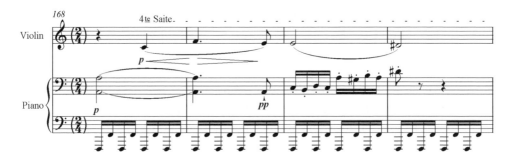

Example 5:14 First Violin Sonata, iii, bb. 168–71

the piano lead, only breaking the pattern to play in parallel octaves from bar 192.

The unremitting nature of the finale to the A minor Violin Sonata caused – and still causes – some problems in performance; Clara described it as 'more unyielding' ('mehr störrische') than the other movements, a word Wasielewski also chose as he explained Schumann had expected the violin part to have a different effect: 'I was unable to convey the unyielding, brusque tone of the piece to his satisfaction' ('Ich vermochte ihm nicht genügend den störrischen, unwirschen Ton des Stückes wiederzugeben').[60] The composer's dissatisfaction might have been one motivation for him writing another Violin Sonata soon afterwards; indeed Schumann said – presumably at least half-jokingly – that he had not liked the First Violin Sonata, so he wrote another one.[61] Like its predecessor, the Second Violin Sonata was completed within a few days (28 October–2 November 1851). Its title – *Zweite grosse Sonate für Violine und Pianoforte* (second 'great' or 'grand' sonata) – declares its different stature and by putting 'for violin and piano' rather than the conventional 'for piano and violin' (as in op. 105) acknowledges the violin's prominent role.[62] The first performance was given in Düsseldorf by Clara and Wasielewski on 15 November, alongside the G minor Piano Trio (for which Clara and Wasielewski were joined by Reimers). Clara seemed very excited by both pieces, describing the new Violin Sonata as 'another work of wonderful originality, with a profundity and grandeur such as I have scarcely ever encountered – it really is utterly overwhelming music'.[63] Wasielewski described it as a 'profoundly serious and, except for the charming slow movement, dark piece of music . . . [it] is incomparably more significant than its predecessor' and, he admitted, had taken careful rehearsal to master.[64] Ruppert Becker (Wasielewski's successor as concertmaster in Düsseldorf) and Joachim were also enthusiastic, the latter praising the D minor Sonata for its 'unity of mood and the conciseness of its themes'.[65]

The introduction of the Second Sonata is marked 'Kurz und energetisch', a very different character to the 'leidenschaftlichem Ausdruck' of the First Sonata's opening movement. Piano and violin begin with a chordal theme that provides a framework over which the violin's melody subsequently drapes itself in a cadenza-like manner, extending into dominant preparation for the arrival of the allegro in the tonic, D minor (Example 5:15). The violin's affirmation of the main theme at this point is supported by accompanimental figuration derived in part from the introduction; there is thus a satisfying amount of motivic integration between the sections, a model for which might be the first movement of Beethoven's *Kreutzer* Sonata, op. 47.[66]

Where Schumann impresses in the Second Violin Sonata is precisely in the kind of thematic development and formal integration I have claimed to be sometimes absent from the other late chamber music. Carl Debrois van Bruyck likened the Sonata to a mysterious woman's smile, singling out two passages for particular praise:

the heavenly transition to B major in the second movement, with the entire following intertwining of the two themes, where towards the end one seems so clearly to hear the sound of horns from the piano; and then the melody in the third movement which begins suddenly after the echo of the Scherzo.[67]

Both van Bruyck's examples show Schumann manipulating form and content to great effect. Presumably by the transition to B major in the second movement van Bruyck meant the transition to the coda (Example 5:16). The rondo's theme drops down to *piano* in bar 192, quickly building by sequence over an F sharp pedal through to *forte* four bars later. The ascending quavers

Example 5:15 Second Violin Sonata, i, bb. 1–6

Example 5:16 Second Violin Sonata, i, bb. 201–8

of the theme now drive an ascent towards the bigger climax on to B major. A variation of the theme's dotted crotchets rings out, the open fifths in the piano's left hand perhaps being the horns heard by van Bruyck. While nothing like this passage has been heard before it has emerged from the available thematic material and a moment of harmonic magic. It is hard not to agree with van Bruyck:

Example 5:17   Second Violin Sonata, iv, bb. 100–2

In such beautiful passages I catch sight of eternity and sink into it with a shudder of rapture, and I should like to tread underfoot any wretch who can still speak to me of chords of the fourth and the sixth, of suspensions, resolutions and all the rest!

In contrast to the finale of the First Violin Sonata, the fourth movement of the Second manipulates its thematic material to create a convincing and dynamic sonata form. Part of the reason for its vigour is that it is not so harmonically static; although the tonic is emphasized in the beginning it is by cadences, not pedals. The first theme reappears at the end of the exposition in combination with a secondary motive, making the re-emergence of the theme with the repeat much more palatable. Similarly, in the development section, thematic material is broken down and reassembled with other figures, and there is greater use of harmonic sequence, all of which makes for a more exciting journey to the recapitulation, which really feels earned. The one odd moment comes just before the recapitulation, in bar 101 (Example 5:17). For the first and only time the piano takes over the violin's diminished seventh flourishes. Meanwhile the violin, which has been preparing for the return of the main theme by frequently returning to its opening figure, gives it up to play – again, for the only time – three *forte* octave Ds. It is a strange moment for the performers, a sudden eruption before the music subsides into a *piano* rendition of the main theme and the beginning of the recapitulation. There is a feeling that at this crucial transition the composer experienced vertigo – should he resist the form and look into the void? – a sense intensified in a parallel moment in the first movement of the Third Violin Sonata, of which more shortly.

Hanslick detected 'a certain passionate urgency' in the outer movements of the Second Violin Sonata, and praised the whole for themes that were 'easy to grasp . . . and at the same time piquant'.[68] He thought the inner movements 'technically grateful (*dankbare*) and brilliant' but missed the intensity of Schumann's other works: 'It is not merely a case of Schumann's former vigour overstepping its own measure and the boundaries of art, and losing its way in a gloomy jungle. Rather, it is a conspicuous decline of all spiritual powers, a waning of the earlier energy and plenitude of ideas'. Significantly, Hanslick was writing in 1857, the year after Schumann's death, and he seems acutely aware that this was one of the composer's late works.[69] Only a very gullible ear, he writes, 'can be deceived as regards the lack of true musical power, by the artificial ardour of the Finale and suchlike'. Hanslick's focus on Schumann's illness in general disgusted Clara, who thought it only of interest to doctors.[70] We might disagree with her, but on trying to write about the late works today, how to negotiate such filtering of the music through the composer's biography remains a challenge.

As mentioned in other chapters, there are moments of relief from the dour aspects of the late music. For example, Albert Dietrich explained that the F. A. E. Sonata was written as a joke (*Scherz*) for Joachim, who had to guess the composer of each movement at a gathering in Schumann's home probably on 28 October 1853.[71] Schumann had completed the Sonata's Intermezzo and Finale, Dietrich the first movement and Brahms a Scherzo. The next day, Schumann began two more movements that along with the Intermezzo and Finale were to create his Third Violin Sonata in A minor.[72] On 13 November Clara played it through with Wasielewski at the home of Friedrich Heimsöth, Professor of Classics and rector at Bonn University and the leader of the city's Choral Society.

Although Ute Bär claims that during Schumann's lifetime the Third Violin Sonata was 'wholeheartedly accepted' by his wife and friends, its significance was not straightforward.[73] Michael Struck suggests that the sonata was a source of 'consolation in the face of Schumann's mental illness' ('ein Trost angesichts von Schumanns Geisteskrankheit'), particularly while he was at Endenich: as quoted in the Introduction, after playing through the Third Sonata with Joachim in early March 1854 Clara confided to her diary: 'It is the only thing that can ease my pain – his music!'[74] After his death, however, it was performed only occasionally in private, perhaps because of the lack of fair copies; there is neither a complete manuscript nor a copyist's copy of the Third Sonata extant. It also seems as though attempts were made to prevent the work from being made known to the public. When Albert Dietrich was approached about publishing the F. A. E. Sonata, he explained that Schumann's other movements had been added shortly before his illness and that Clara would not be able to hand them over.[75] Clara had in fact begun to prepare the work for publication not long after Schumann's death. She decided only to offer the second and third movements that, she suggested, could be presented as 'Two Fantasy pieces' or 'Andante and Scherzo from an as yet unfinished sonata'.[76] The following year, on the advice of Joachim, she withdrew the offer.[77] The movements were too closely bound up with the work to be published separately, she explained.[78] Despite the publisher's repeated requests she remained firm. Not until 1956 did the Third Violin Sonata appear in print, and it was given its first public performance by the then leader of the Bavarian Radio Symphony Orchestra, Gerhard Seitz, and Margaret Kitchin at the Wigmore Hall.[79] Almost all reviews were negative, as were those for the German premiere two years later. Schumann's mental decline could be 'clearly detected in the strangely unfocused form and contour of the work [and] its almost restless improvisatory disconnectedness'; even more positive responses admitted 'a somewhat asthmatic quality in the syncopations of the passage work'.[80]

The opening of the Third Sonata, a movement not based on the F. A. E. motto, is strikingly similar in manner to that of the Second. Both begin with a slow introduction in $\frac{3}{4}$, beginning with two pairs of descending chords on the first and second beats, their top notes forming the start of the main theme. In contrast to the Second Sonata, whose motivic procedures were explained previously, after the opening chords of the Third Sonata the piano introduces a creeping semiquaver figure whose recurrence throughout the introduction is punctuated by demisemiquaver flourishes and returns of the opening chords in various transpositions (Example 5:18). The overall effect is much more unsettled than in the Second Sonata: the Allegro continues to offer a range of melodic material aside from the motive derived from its opening chords, and seems unwilling to stay in the tonic for any length of time. More than anything, the different figurations resemble those of the Violin Concerto, with its semiquaver arabesques decorated with mordents; while such embellishment-for-its-own-sake makes sense in a virtuosic showcase piece, it is a little out of place here. The violin part also suffers from the Concerto's problem that its virtuosic writing, while not impossible to play, does not sit easily under the fingers – especially the leaps to the double stops – an awkwardness that increases in the sonata's later movements. At times the difficulty of this piece lies not so much in its vaunted virtuosity, as in its writing for the instrument, which contributes to the music's feeling of brokenness.

The Allegro is in a modified sonata form, with a development that repeats the first and second subjects in various tonal areas (C major to G major to E minor). The repetitions make the structure seem rather clumsy, particularly in comparison to Schumann's other violin sonatas. But where the

Example 5:18   Third Violin Sonata, i, bb. 1–8

third most significantly diverges from its predecessors is not so much in the repeats of the themes, but in their characters. The First Violin Sonata does not have a slow introduction but its allegro does have a very distinctive opening theme, which Schumann exploits to maximum effect as a transitional, modulatory and reminiscence motif. While the Second Sonata's themes are not so strongly characterized as those of the first, they are tightly woven into the motivic fabric of the Allegro and, as in the First Sonata, are easily recognizable when they make an unexpected appearance in a later movement. In the Third Sonata, the Allegro's themes are at once distinctive and not so well defined; whereas the other sonatas build from quite minimal material, here an assortment of possibilities is presented, among them the head motives of the first and second subjects –

Example 5:19 Third Violin Sonata, i, bb. 99–102

indeed, the first subject is little more than a head motive, lasting only two bars, while the second subject lasts only four. Continuing and joining the subjects are series of ornamental figures, usually a couple of bars long, presented in a kind of chain (of which more later). This is only broken in bar 100, where suddenly there is a whole bar's rest before the beginning of the recapitulation (Example 5:19). The empty bar is strange because it seems simply to take out the last measure of a four bar phrase. It is of course the parallel moment to bar 101 in the finale of the Second Violin Sonata discussed earlier – and here the sense of looking into the void is even greater. Whereas, in the First Sonata, Schumann pulls the tempo back to reintroduce the first theme gently, and in the Second Sonata smoothly joins the sections with a circle of fifths, here there is not even an attempt to hide the divide. The music seems stuck on the same dotted rhythm and harmony, which might be dominant preparation for the return of the tonic but which seems oddly unsophisticated.[81] The recapitulation begins on a tonic chord in second inversion, which creates a funny disjunction between harmony and voice-leading; the bass line ends in bar 99 on B and lands on E in bar 101, almost as if that were the cadence rather than a V-I onto A minor, and indeed E continues as an internal pedal for the next four bars.

The idiosyncratic treatment of theme and form in the Third Violin Sonata can easily be written off as late style at its most extreme, as demonstrated by responses to the work's premiere. However, there are alternative models for the relationship between content and form that might help explain how this music is structured, from its peculiar treatment of transitions to its presentation of motives. One suggested by Nono, Kurtág and Rihm is Hölderlin's use of parataxis: the placing of the elements of a sentence in series in which they are not bound to each other by conjunctions or subordinate clauses.[82] According to Susan Gillespie, this grammatical trope 'creates a kind of disjunction and nonspecificity that undermine logical clarity and causality, leaving room for a certain vagueness, and for interpretation'.[83] The late hymn 'Half of Life' exhibits the paratactical tendency on smaller and larger structural levels:[84]

Mit gelben Birnen hänget	With yellow pears hangs down
Und voll mit wilden Rosen	And full of wild roses
Das Land in den See,	The land into the lake,
Ihr holden Schwäne,	You loving swans,
Und trunken von Küssen	And drunk with kisses
Tunkt ihr das Haupt	You dip your heads
Ins heilignüchterne Wasser.	Into water, the holy-and-sober.
Weh mir, wo nehm' ich, wenn	But oh, where shall I find
Es Winter ist, die Blumen, und wo	When winter comes, the flowers, and where
Denn Sonnenschein,	The sunshine
Und Schatten der Erde?	And shade of the earth?
Die Mauern stehn	The walls loom
Sprachlos und kalt, im Winde	Speechless and cold, in the wind
Klirren die Fahren.	Weathercocks clatter.

There are no obvious connections between the moments of the poem; instead they are lined up in sequence. While the two stanzas balance – the first describing the summer of sensuous love, the second the winter of rejection – they also have the potential to destroy each other. Not only in terms of their contrasting content, but also through their form, they threaten to break the poem in half. Another way of putting this might be to say that there is thesis and antithesis, but no synthesis – or that the potential for synthesis is simultaneously offered and denied by the caesura in the middle.

Adorno credited the paratactical structures with lending Hölderlin's late poems their musicality. The poetry *becomes* musical as a result of the way its elements are conjoined or juxtaposed to each other within the larger structural context that creates the meaning, Adorno argued.[85] He praised Hölderlin's use of parataxis as 'an antiprinciple' of form whose 'most intimate tendency [is] dissociation'. Thus not only are the boundaries of acceptable grammar pushed, explains Gillespie; the writing strains at the bounds of conceptual thought, deploying its linguistic extremism in an attempt, ultimately, to transcend language. Adorno described the architectonic form of Hölderlin's poems as 'subcutaneous . . . a form literally composed as in music'; explaining, 'they approach the structuring of the sonata forms in the music of the same period, an articulation in terms of movements, of discrete contrasting units within a unity'.[86]

Such paratactical, 'musical', grammar has potential parallels in late Schumann. This might seem like a perverse attempt to convert a verbal musicality into a musical verbalness, but there are ways in which the peculiarities of the Third Violin Sonata, for example, can be explained by recourse to the poetic model. First, the motivic chains heard in the first movement might be paratactical on a sentence-to-sentence level. Second, there is the already mentioned crucial but problematic role assigned by Schumann to transitions, which indicates a possibility of parataxis functioning on a larger scale. Third, Adorno incorporates within his discussion of parataxis, Hölderlin's 'dissociation into names', of the poet making sudden connections between ancient and modern scenes and figures, something that might be paralleled in Schumann's predilection for quotation.

The end of the development from the first movement of the Third Violin Sonata is worth returning to as the starting point for discussion of how Schumann's treatment of motives might be thought paratactical. Simply to list each rhythmic motive as it occurs in the violin part between bars 80 to 100 shows how there is little continuity between them, although they are repetitive within themselves (for comparison: the equivalent twenty bars before the recapitulation in the first movement of the First Sonata are much more interconnected, particularly as the melodic contours of the motive are all related to the main themes).[87] In the last movement of the Third Sonata there is another example of disconnected treatment of themes; in bar 59 a fugato on an inversion of the theme is begun by the piano but soon abandoned for the main theme itself, after two bars of which the fugal material returns (Example 5:20). A variation of the main theme returns six bars later, to be disrupted by the fugue: as if in exasperation, the opening chordal motto returns. Within the context of the fugue, the main theme almost seems like a quotation – although on its final appearance, the same could be said of the fugue.

Quotations often mark and sometimes seem to make transitions happen in Schumann. The slow movement of the Second Violin Sonata is a good example. It is the thematic hub of the work, in the sense that in its middle there is a somewhat livelier section, which breaks into semiquaver triplets, summoning a return of the first movement's opening chords. Everything else in this section sounds like a quotation too, from the rising triplet figure in parallel thirds, which might refer to the second movement's rondo theme, to the more lyrical, *pianissimo* theme over a B pedal that is reminiscent of the first sonata's Allegretto (the melody van Bruyck cited as one of the Sonata's highpoints). Part of the beauty of this movement comes from the tricks it plays on your memory. There are few direct citations, but they sound like they come from elsewhere. The most obvious example of this is the main theme of the movement's outer sections, a chorale melody Christopher Reynolds connects to versions of 'Vater unser' by Cherubini, Spohr, and

Example 5:20 Third Violin Sonata, i, bb. 57–84

Example 5:20 (*cont.*)

Example 5:21   Albert Dietrich, F. A. E. Sonata, i, bb. 19–20

Mendelssohn. But the tune does not fit the Cherubini model exactly, nor do the harmonies, which Schumann blurs by the extended tonic pedal. The violin's 'singing' of the melody at first is tentative, initially pizzicato and then falteringly bowed, and I think the vagueness of the allusion is significant; to find a specific source for it rids the melody of its uncanniness.

We are used to the idea that Schumann enjoyed alluding to other music, and that he liked playing games with ciphers and extra-musical references. Many of these references are considered to give the music its meanings – they put him in a particular historical and compositional context, and often are used to link his life and works. Nowhere is this more apparent than in the collaborative composition of the F. A. E sonata. What is perhaps surprising about the sonata is how explicitly Dietrich's Allegro and Schumann's Intermezzo present the motto. Dietrich does not reveal its complete form until bars 19–20, but its arrival is well prepared by the harmonic and melodic profile of the preceding passage (Example 5:21). Schumann's inclusion of the motto in his Intermezzo is all the more striking because in contrast to the other movements it seems so simple (Example 5:22). The recurrences of the theme, together with the near constant quaver motion in the piano, lend the Intermezzo a gentle, consoling quality. But by always presenting the theme at the same pitch, as the movement progresses the theme seems increasingly to stand outside the surrounding music, declaring itself an external reference.

Something similar to this 'otherness' of the F. A. E. motto in Schumann's Intermezzo is touched on in Adorno's discussion of Hölderlin. The status of abstractions in Hölderlin's hymnic work, Adorno argues, is polarized into names and correspondences on the one hand and concepts on the other. Within the names 'there always remains an excess of what is desired but

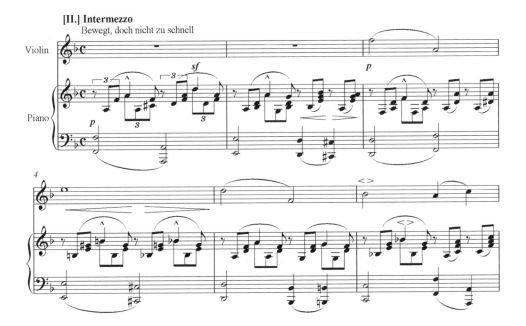

Example 5:22   Intermezzo, bb. 1–6

not attained . . . they are relics . . . of the aspect of the idea that cannot be made present: they are marks of a process'.[88] Having divested themselves of immediacy, the names have their own life. Or, as Michael Hamburger explains it, Hölderlin relies 'not on argument but on particulars charged with the most concentrated significance, on the mere naming of a person or thing or their invocation by signs, where less daring poets . . . would have presented a sequence of arguments and metaphors'.[89] There may be a sense in which Schumann's allusions to other movements and pieces in this music act in a similar way, surprising us by defamiliarizing the known – such as the fragmented chorale melody in the Second Sonata, which of course is, like Hölderlin's poems, a kind of hymn – and by making external references explicit, as in his presentation of Joachim's motto in the Third Sonata's Intermezzo. Both methods mark the process of quotation just as the quotations – in the Second Sonata, in Brahms's Scherzo, etc – mark transitions. Form and content thus become one, much as Adorno claimed happens in late Hölderlin.

The poet was another asylum patient who played the piano, but while he and Schumann suffered similarly dismal – if you will, broken – ends, the reputation of Hölderlin's late works has enjoyed a re-evaluation in recent decades that Schumann's have yet to undergo. One possible reason for this is that the parataxis and 'alienness' (to borrow Adorno's word) of Hölderlin's late hymns is not so far away from the techniques and subjects of modernist writers such as James Joyce, T. S. Eliot, and Samuel Beckett. As Theodore Ziolkowski has commented, 'the discontinuities, the acceptance of incoherence, the paratactic style, the striking images, the drastic line breaks, the depersonalization: all these characteristics of his poetry, misunderstood and ridiculed by Hölderlin's contemporaries, strike us as congenially modern' – he is irresistible to semioticians, philosophers and artists alike.[90] There is not the same sense that the late Schumann was a modernist before his time. Although Nono, Kurtág and Rihm have made a connection between Hölderlin and Schumann, the composer invariably is glimpsed through a nostalgic mist; he is a cipher for Romantic subjectivity. Robin Holloway has even described his engagement with Schumann's music in the *Fantasy-Pieces on the Heine 'Liederkreis'* as means to escape a modernist impasse.[91] The works contemporary composers engage with almost always come from the late 1830s and early 40s; unlike with Hölderlin, it is not the late works that appeal to modern sensibilities, but the earlier ones. The irony and the challenge of the late works is not that they are more 'mad' or inventive than the earlier ones, but more conventional. And comparing the music to norms almost always means we think about it in terms of success and mastery or failure. Where Adorno's description of Hölderlin's 'subcutaneous' musical structure makes it seem radical, even when the form he invokes is that of a sonata, when Schumann writes a sonata the structure can only be compared to tradition.

Of course, it is to late Beethoven that Adorno compares Hölderlin's 'musical' structures, with their elimination of the external and inessential middle element.[92] The way in which Beethoven makes visible and lays bare convention, Adorno sees as defining the late style, with its insertion of conventional formulae and phraseology, of 'decorative trills, cadences and fiorituras'.[93] Where in Beethoven these 'empty gestures' paradoxically are thought to mark the disintegration of convention, the opposite seems to be the case for late Schumann, whose use of virtuosic ornamentation according to Daverio responds to the composer having to address 'his listeners (and interpreters) in a language they could understand, while at the same time not sacrificing the claims of art'; in other words, within the conventional syntax of a 'public' style. Schumann's virtuosic violin writing in the Third Sonata (and the *Phantasie* and Concerto) is said to serve a specific musical function rather than existing for its own sake, which has of course long been an excuse for excessively ornamental passagework some might accuse of being meaningless.[94] Admittedly, there is little doubt that florid music such as the final pages of the Third Violin Sonata signals closure. But neither does it sound like good virtuoso writing, in the sense that the violinist *struggles* with all those arpeggios, rather than transcends them.

Indeed, the greatest strain between the work and the performer in the Third Violin Sonata is probably its rejection by the virtuoso for whom it was written. According to most formulations, virtuosity spotlights 'the extreme occasion' of performance.[95] While, as Jim Samson and Paul Metzner point out, the virtuoso performance is part of the nineteenth-century celebration of 'public man', somehow emphasizing the performance of Schumann's sonata seems wrong.[96] For a start, it has not been performed in public that much, and anyway sonatas for violin and piano – especially ones in part composed as a joke or game between friends – tend to be chamber music, for intimate settings. They are not the places for this kind of virtuosic display, even when they are transferred to the public stage as gradually happened to Schumann's chamber works.

Nor is the violin the obvious instrument for such writing. Its virtuoso performance seems to work differently to other instruments. The violin does not have the mechanical associations of piano playing, the automaton ancestry of wind instruments, or the ventriloquist tendencies of singing. The commentary around the most famous virtuoso violinist of the nineteenth century, Paganini, tends to credit his technical wizardry and his bewitchment of listeners to supernatural phenomena – to that infamous liaison with the devil. Even his technical daring and mastery were said to be driven by 'the demon of mechanism' ('le démon du mécanisme') rather than mechanism itself. Schumann himself referred to Paganini's '*poetic* virtuosity', the origins of which might, as Samson extrapolates, derive from the connotative value of the violin, which seems to function as an extension of the performer, of his arm and so his body; in contrast, say, to the piano, which demands the player to master an external machine.[97]

Nonetheless, even if the violin does not harbour obvious mechanical connotations, its virtuoso performer is still capable of breaking down. Earlier the awkwardness of Schumann's writing for the violin in the Third Sonata's introduction and the arpeggiation that ends the finale was mentioned; in these passages the body of the performer, her fingers and arms, are contorted and stretched into 'unnatural' positions. The distortion of the violinist's smoothly drawn curves of the bow and the curl of her left hand puts her at risk of being ripped apart by her broken chords. This breaking of the performer's body brings us back to the alleged weakness of Schumann's late music, to the master broken at, or maybe by, his instrument. We cannot easily transfer the image of the composer flailing like a malfunctioning machine at his piano to the music of the Third Violin Sonata. But I would like to suggest that the reason for thinking the piece fails is that through its awkward passages, through the fractures and repetitions of the music, we hear too much of the man beneath; we are too aware that we are listening to, and so inevitably listening for, the late Schumann. The somatization of the composer, a recurring image of recent scholarship on Schumann, is double-edged. For Barthes, it emphasizes the subjectivity of this music, somehow excusing the composer from communicative or discursive failure by stressing his human, visceral presence. In other words, we all fail when trying to play Schumann. With regard to the late works in particular, it is significant that somatization is the term now used in medical circles in place of 'psychosomatic illness'. By allowing Schumann's body into our experience of the music, we accept with it our imaginings of his illness. This only increases the potential for us to hear failure and sickness, the fissures in the structure, the breakdown of the musical machine.

Such incompleteness, even such failure, has precedents in Schumann's earlier music. It might even be said that recent scholarship on the Romantic fragment and other literary models fetishizes such states – why not then extend their sympathy to the late works? Schumann himself offered a resonant paradigm for artistic endeavour. Depressed as he accompanied Clara on a recital tour of Russia in the spring of 1844, he gave up sketching the second scene of *Faust* and diverted his creative energies to writing poetry. He completed five lengthy poems, all apart from the last inspired by the great bell tower to Ivan Velikii in St Petersburg. As Daverio comments, they 'invite interpretation as an allegory for the problem of creative artistry'.[98] Yet they take a very different path from Schiller's famous eulogy to the founding of a great bell in 'Das Lied von der Glocke'. At the end of Schumann's first poem about the making of the bell, a portion breaks off as it is lifted from the mould. One of the spectators blames the fault on the artist's hubris. In the next poem the czar forgives 'the artist's great but flawed undertaking', ordering: 'The striving of the artist who envisioned the highest / Shall be sanctified / Whether or not the deed was fulfilled.'[99]

The symbol of the bell returns in different contexts throughout Schumann's creative life; of the tolling chords in the coda of 'Ende vom Lied' in the *Fantasiestücke*, op. 12, he had told Clara: 'everything ultimately dissolves into a merry wedding – but my distress for you came back at the end, and the wedding bells sound as if commingled with a death knell'.[100] The czar's response to the cracked bell of the 1844 poems seems to continue Faust's theme of man being redeemed by striving. The cracked bell in itself might represent the irregularity of modern art in comparison to the classicism of

Schiller. Or as in Rethel's engraving, it might be Death as friend that tolls the bell, saving the artist from life's agony.

Schumann might thus have approved of Martin Heidegger's borrowing of an image from Hölderlin to compare the work of art to a bell: 'the commentator causes it to resound (*Erläuterung*: interpretation, commentary contains *lauten*, to sound, peal); he makes us hear what it holds wholly by itself, as when snow falls on the bell'.[101] On considering Schumann's late works, we might be dealing with a cracked bell, with music that aims for greatness but is somehow flawed. While it might be harder to reach a clear interpretation of such pieces, it is worth trying to 'hear what it holds wholly by itself'. As suggested of the narratives in the *Märchenmusik*, we might approach like the viewer of a fairy-tale illustration, making up a story for ourselves. That, perhaps, is the lesson to learn from comparing Schumann to Hölderlin: to listen less for how the sounds were made – through illness or inspiration – than how they sound under the snowfall of today. Some of it will appeal, some will not. But at least then we can adjust the frame, revealing those corners of the picture that, kept out of the sun for many years, have retained their original, vibrant tones.

Notes

1. For a survey of Schumann's chamber music, see Hans Kohlhase, *Die Kammermusik Robert Schumanns. Stilistische Untersuchungen* (Hamburg: Verlag der Musikalienhandlung Wagner, 1979); and John Daverio, '"Beautiful and abstruse conversations": the chamber music of Robert Schumann', *Nineteenth-Century Chamber Music*, ed. Stephen E. Hefling (New York: Schirmer, 1998), pp. 208–41.

2. The significance of chamber music for Schumann can be gauged in Linda Correll Roesner's observation that it seems to have spurred the revision of the 1841 D minor Symphony into the Fourth Symphony (op. 120) along with the preparation of the Third Symphony for publication and, we might conject, the orchestration of *Der Rose Pilgerfahrt*. See her 'Ästhetisches Ideal und sinfonische Gestalt: Die D-Moll-Sinfonie um die Jahrhundertmitte', *Schumann in Düsseldorf: Werke–Texte–Interpretationen*, ed. Bernhard Appel (London: Schott, 1993), pp. 55–72.

3. Paris was ahead of the game in this regard, with Baillot's quartet and quintet concert series (1814–40). The Hellmesberger Quartet reintroduced public chamber music concerts to Vienna in the early 1850s. See James Johnson, *Listening in Paris: A Cultural History* (Berkeley: University of California Press, 1995), pp. 204–5.

4. For an overview of modernist responses to late Beethoven, see Stephen Rumph, *Beethoven after Napoleon: Political Romanticism in the Late Works* (Berkeley: University of California Press, 2004), pp. 222–45.

5. For further discussion see Julie Hedges Brown, 'Higher echoes of the past in the finale of Schumann's 1842 piano quartet', *Journal of the American Musicological Society* 57:3 (2005), 514–15.

6. Adorno refers to Schumann's 'blind repetition of the sonata' in 'Richard Strauss at 60', trans. Susan Gillespie, *Strauss and his World*, ed. Bryan Gilliam (Princeton: Princeton University Press, 1992), p. 408.

7. The terms are Jacques Handschin's; see Carl Dahlhaus, *Nineteenth-Century Music*, trans. Bradford J. Robinson (Berkeley: University of California Press, 1989), p. 255.

8. Walter Riezler, *Beethoven*, trans. G. D. H. Pidrock (New York: E. P. Dutton, 1938), p. 234; cited in Rumph, *Beethoven After Napoleon*, p. 227.

9. Adorno, 'The late style (I)', *Beethoven: The Philosophy of Music: Fragments and Texts*, trans. Edmund Jephcott, ed. Rolf Tiedemann (Cambridge: Polity Press, 1998), p. 124.

10. Adorno, 'Parataxis: on Hölderlin's late poetry', *Notes on Literature*, trans. Sherry Weber Nicholson (New York: Columbia University Press, 1992), p. 133.

11. For an overview of Hölderlin's reception in the nineteenth and twentieth centuries see Rainer Nägele, 'Poetic revolution', *A New History of German Literature*, ed. David E. Wellbery (Cambridge, Mass.: Belknap Press of Harvard University Press, 2004), pp. 511–16.

12. Emil Flechsig, 'Erinnerungen an Robert Schumann', *Neue Zeitschrift für Musik* 67 (1956), 396; cited in Eric Frederick Jensen, *Schumann* (Oxford: Oxford University Press, 2001), pp. 11 and 47. Schumann took an interest in many artists who suffered from mental illness such as the poet Franz Anton Sonnenberg (1779–1805) and, as mentioned in Chapter 1, Nikolaus Lenau, a fascination which Jensen claims was spurred by his sister Emilie's drowning in 1825.

13. Daverio, *Robert Schumann*, pp. 314 and 305. He also applies the concept of 'alternation of tones' to Brahms in 'The *Wechsel der Töne* in Brahms's *Schicksalslied*', *Journal of the American Musicological Society* 46 (1993), 97–104. Leon Botstein cites (in 'History, rhetoric, and the self: Robert Schumann and music making in German-speaking Europe, 1800–1860', *Robert Schumann and his World*, ed. R. Larry Todd (Princeton University Press, 1994), p. 5) Wilhelm Dilthey's 1905 essay on Hölderlin ('Das Erlebnis und die Dichtung'), which comments that the unregulated feeling and fantasy of the poetry brings to mind Schumann and Nietzsche. Adorno likens Schumann's identification with woman in *Frauenliebe und Leben*, 'the declaration of war on the appropriation implicit to the male, patriarchal order', to traits of Hölderlin; see 'The late style (II)', *Beethoven: The Philosophy of Music*, p. 155.

14. For an introduction to these artists see William Vaughan, *German Romantic Painting* (New Haven: Yale University Press, 1980); for more on Schumann's relationship to them see Leon Botstein, 'History, rhetoric, and the self', pp. 37–9.

15. See Bernhard R. Appel, '"Actually, taken directly from family life": Robert Schumann's *Album für die Jugend*', *Schumann and his World*, pp. 184–8.

16. For further discussion of the state of the Düsseldorf School of Art in the 1850s see Cordula Crewe, '1826, November 30: art between muse and marketplace', *A New History of German Literature*, pp. 531–5.

17. Cited in Vaughan, *German Romantic Painting*, p. 235.

18. Vaughan, *German Romantic Painting*, p. 231.

19. Schumann, *Tagebücher, Band II: 1836–1854*, ed. Gerd Nauhaus (Leipzig: VEB Deutscher Verlag, 1987), p. 429. Rethel had completed four of the seven intended scenes; his assistant Joseph Kehren executed the rest. Schumann and Rethel did not seem to know each other very well but they had mutual friends in Eduard Bendemann, Julius Hübner and Robert Reinick (who wrote the verses for *Another Dance of Death*). On 25 December 1848 Schumann recorded exchanging gifts at Bendemann's with a Rethel present; it is not entirely clear who that was (the editors suggest a Madame Rethel). *Tagebücher, Band III*, ed. Gerd Nauhaus (Leipzig: VEB Deutscher Verlag, 1982), p. 479.

20. Richarz diagnosed Rethel with 'Dementia, general paralysis' (the latter term presumably meaning syphilis), declared him incurable and discharged him on 2 May 1854. He died under his mother's care in 1859. See Jensen, *Schumann*, p. 326.

21. According to Botstein, 'the later, more bizarre and fragmentary work of late Schumann can be related to the smaller Rethel etchings'; 'History, rhetoric, and the self', p. 39.

22. Reinhard Kapp invokes Karl Friedrich Lessing's use of shading as a model for Schumann's orchestral colours in 'Das Orchester Schumanns', *Musik-Konzepte Sonderband: Robert Schumann II*, ed. Heinz-Klaus Metzger and Rainer Riehn (Munich, 1982), pp. 191–236.

23. Dahlhaus, *Nineteenth-Century Music*, pp. 252–61; here p. 253.

24. Ironically, the ten articles appeared in Brendel's *Neue Zeitschrift für Musik* until 1863; when the *Allgemeine Musikalische Zeitung* returned to print in 1868, Schubring published two further articles about Schumann and Brahms.

25. Joseph Rubinstein, 'Über die Schumann'sche Musik', *Bayreuther Blätter* 2 (1879), 218.

26. D.A.S. [Adolf Schubring], 'Schumanniana Nr. 4', *Neue Zeitschrift für Musik* 54 (1861), 213; translated by John Michael Cooper in *Schumann and his World*, p. 371.

27. Berthold Litzmann, *Clara Schumann: Ein Künstlerleben* (Leipzig: Breitkopf und Härtel, 1905), II, p. 282.

28. The description is the composer's, from 27 December 1851; quoted in Jensen, *Schumann*, p. 342.

29. Quoted in Vaughan, *German Romantic Painting*, p. 193.

30. Novalis, quoted in Marina Warner, *From the Beast to the Blonde: On Fairy Tales and Their Tellers* (London: Vintage, 1995), p. 188. The challenge of interpretation was taken up in the twentieth century, of course, by psychoanalysis; see Sigmund Freud on Hoffmann's *Sandman* and Moritz von Schwind's painting *Dream of a Prisoner*, in his *Introductory Lectures on Psychoanalysis*, trans. Strachey (Harmondsworth: Penguin, 1978), p. 167; and Bruno Bettelheim *The Uses of Enchantment: The Meaning and Importance of Fairy Tales* (New York: Knopf, 1976).

31. Dreams themselves were thought of primarily as visual phenomena: for further discussion with regard to Schumann's *Genoveva* see Laura Tunbridge, 'Weber's Ghost: *Euryanthe, Genoveva, Lohengrin*', *Music, Theatre and Politics: 1848 to the Third Reich*, ed. Nikolaus Bacht (Aldershot: Ashgate, 2006), pp. 9–29.

32. For further discussion see Vaughan, *German Romantic Painting*, pp. 193–213.

33. 'Ein Märchen ist eigentlich wie ein Traumbild – ohne Zusammenhang – Ein *Ensemble* wunderbarer Dinge und Begebenheiten – z.B. eine *musikalische Phantasie*.' Quoted in Beate Julia Perrey, *Schumann's 'Dichterliebe' and Early Romantic Poets: Fragmentation of Desire* (Cambridge: Cambridge University Press, 2002), p. 27; the Tieck is from Marianne Thalmann, *The Romantic Fairy Tale* (Ann Arbor: University of Michigan Press, 1964), p. 34.

34. David Constantine complains that it is difficult to be sure that an arrangement of words is the equivalent of a tone; he gives music as the better analogy. *Hölderlin* (Oxford: Clarendon Press, 1988), p. 127. Hölderlin's tones might be understood under the more general nineteenth-century rubric of *Seelenzustände*.

35. Hölderlin, 'Über die Verfahrungsweise', quoted in Daverio, '*Wechsel der Töne*', 102–3.

36. On the idea of *Witz* in Schumann's earlier works see John Daverio, 'Schumann's "Im Legendenton" and Friedrich Schlegel's *Arabeske*', *19th-Century Music* 11:2 (1987), 150–63; Nicholas Marston, '"Im Legendenton": Schumann's "unsung voice"', *19th-Century Music* 16:3 (1993), 227–41; and Anthony Newcomb, 'Schumann and Late Eighteenth-Century Narrative Strategies', *19th-Century Music* 11:2 (1987), 164–74.

37. Daverio comments on the 'suspended quality of the music'; a product of the phrase structure, blurred harmonic progressions, and ambiguous form; see 'Beautiful and Abstruse Conversations', pp. 233–4.

38. On their '"eckige" und schwere Gestik' see Reinhard Kapp, *Studien zum Spätwerk Robert Schumanns* (Tutzing: Hans Schneider, 1984), p. 177.

39. Daverio, *Crossing Paths: Schubert, Schumann, and Brahms* (Oxford and New York: Oxford University Press, 2002), p. 245.

40. Brahms's storytelling practices are also thought to have been influenced by Schumann; see Jonathan Bellman, '*Aus alten Märchen*: the chivalric style of Schumann and Brahms', *Journal of Musicology* 13 (1995), 117–35.

41. For a discussion of Barthes's theory of the body and Schumann's Second Violin Sonata see Thomas Kabisch, 'Robert Schumann und Roland Barthes: Überlegungen zur Violin-Sonate d-Moll op. 121', *"Denn in jenen Tönen lebt es" Wolfgang Marggraf zum 65. Geburtstag*, ed. Helene Geyer, Michael Berg and Matthias Tischer (Weimar: Hochschule für Musik Franz Liszt, 1999), pp. 207–27.

42. Wilhelm Joseph von Wasielewski, *Robert Schumann: Eine Biographie* (Leipzig: Breitkopf und Härtel, 1906), p. 497.

43. Wilhelm Joseph von Wasielewski, *Robert Schumann: A Biography*, trans. A. L. Alger (Boston: O. Ditson, 1871), p. 186.

44. From one of Hölderlin's last Scardanelli poems, 'Der Frühling'; in *Poems and Fragments*, trans. Michael Hamburger (London: Anvill, 2004), pp. 768–9.

45. Review in *Neue Zeitschrift für Musik* 29 (1848), 113; cited by Daverio, *Robert Schumann*, p. 322.

46. Daverio, *Robert Schumann*, p. 326.

47. On 'Humor' in Schumann's piano music see Heinz J. Dill, 'Romantic Irony in the Works of Robert Schumann', *Musical Quarterly* 73 (1989), 188; and Ulrich Tadday, 'Life and Literature, Poetry and Philosophy: Robert Schumann's Aesthetics of Music', *Cambridge Companion to Schumann*, ed. Beate Perrey (Cambridge: Cambridge University Press, 2007). Daverio likens the form of the finale to the mosaic-like construction of many of the *Novelletten*; see *Robert Schumann*, p. 479.

48. Philipp Spitta, *Ein Lebensbild Robert Schumanns* (Leipzig: Breitkopf und Härtel, 1882), p. 85.

49. Alastair Williams, 'Swaying with Schumann: Subjectivity and tradition in Wolfgang Rihm's *Fremde Szenen* I–III and related scores', *Music and Letters* 87 (2006), 379–97.

50. Wolfgang Rihm, '*Fremde Szenen I–III*', *Ausgesprochen. Schriften und Gespräche*, ed. Ulrich Mosch (Mainz: Schott, 1997), II, p. 333.

51. A similar focus on forbidden chambers features in Francis Dhomont's acousmatic melodrama *Forêt profonde* (1994–6), based in part on Schumann's *Kinderszenen*, op. 15.

52. Berthold Litzmann, *Clara Schumann: ein Künstlerleben nach Tagebüchern und Briefen* (Leipzig: Breitkopf und Härtel, 1903–8), II, p. 312.

53. On the Florestanian and Eusebian elements of the first sonata, see Daverio, *Robert Schumann*, p. 479.

54. However, in 1928 Henry McMaster concluded that only the D minor Violin Sonata was worthy of mention from the music Schumann composed between 1850–3: 'The remaining works consist of nothing more than automatism.' Quoted in Jensen, *Schumann*, p. 283.

55. Charles Rosen, *The Romantic Generation* (London: HarperCollins, 1996), p. 689.

56. *Signale*, vol. 10, 2 April 1852, 161–3; for further reviews including Uhlig's see Ute Bär's 'Kritischer Bericht' to *Robert Schumann. Neue Ausgabe sämtlicher Werke Series II: Kammermusik, Band 3: Violinsonaten* (Mainz: Schott, 2004), pp. 199–202.

57. Uhlig, *Neue Zeitschrift für Musik* 37:12 (17 September 1852), 117–20.

58. See Dietrich's diary for 17 May 1852, cited in Bär, 'Kritischer Bericht', p. 201.

59. Letter from Franz Brendel to Schumann, 22 January 1854, cited in Bär, 'Kritischer Bericht', p. 202.

60. Litzmann, *Clara Schumann*, II, p. 264; Wasielewski, *Aus siebzig Jahre* (Leipzig: Breitkopf und Härtel, 1897), p. 125. Clara and Joachim continued to play the Sonata together in the 1850s and 1860s.

61. Wasielewski, *Robert Schumann*, p. 469.

62. Daverio explains the Second Sonata's difference in character as being 'the large dimensions, seriousness of tone, and thematic integration characteristic of the public style'; see *Robert Schumann*, p. 463.

63. Litzmann, *Clara Schumann*, II, p. 265; and letter of 19 November 1851 to her mother; Bär, 'Kritischer Bericht', pp. 244–5.

64. Wasielewski, *Robert Schumann*, p. 469.

65. Letter to Arnold Wehner, 10 September 1853, *Briefe von und an Joseph Joachim*, ed. Johannes Joachim and Andreas Moser I, (Berlin: Bard, 1911), p. 74.

66. In a letter of 18 January 1850 Ferdinand David had urged Schumann to write a piece for violin and piano similar to his op. 73 *Fantasiestücke* (originally for clarinet and piano but also arranged for violin – a version David played with Clara in Leipzig on 9 March 1852) explaining: 'playing Beethoven's A major Sonata over and over again begins to get on one's nerves' – a comment Schumann may have remembered as he began the Second Violin Sonata. Clara described Schumann's Second Sonata as 'the most magnificent after Beethoven's in A'; 6 January 1853 to Avé Lallemant; Bär, 'Kritische Bericht', p. 245. On the *Kreutzer* Sonata's use of material from its Introduction in its Presto, see Rudolph Réti's *Thematic Patterns in Sonatas of Beethoven*, ed. Deryck Cooke (New York: Da Capo Press, 1992), pp. 145–65.

67. Letter to Schumann, 25 November to 1 December 1853, reprinted Renate Federhofer-Königs, *Ein Schumann-Verehrer aus Wien*, 296. Translated in Bär, 'Kritischer Bericht', p. 269.

68. Eduard Hanslick, *Geschichte des Konzertwesens in Wien*, part 2: *Aus dem Concertsaal. Kritiken und Schilderungen aus den letzten 20 Jahren des Wiener Musiklebens* (Vienna, 1870: reprint Hildesheim/New York, 1979), p. 168.

69. According to Renate Federhofer-Königs, the first public performance of the Second Violin Sonata in Vienna took place on 11 January 1857. In contrast to Hanslick's judgement, Clara had included the Sonata as part of the *Hausmusik*

organized after the 33rd Lower Rhine Music Festival in late May 1855, and after Schumann's death she and Joachim continued to perform the work, which was taken up by other ensembles such as Henri Vieuxtemps and Alfred Jaëll, and Brahms and Ferdinand Laub.

70. Letter to Brahms, 6 February 1877, *Clara Schumann – Johannes Brahms*, II, p. 3. Hanslick's essay 'Robert Schumann in Endenich' is in *Am Ende des Jahrhunderts* (Berlin, 1899), pp. 317–42. A recent translation by Susan Gillespie is included in *Schumann and his World*, pp. 268–87.

71. Letter to Hermann Erler, 17 July 1884; Bär, 'Kritischer Bericht', p. 384, n. 5. There is some disagreement about whether the Sonata was performed on 28 October and speculation over the meaning of Joachim's motto, heard in the opening violin line of Dietrich's movement and the middle section of Brahms's. A month after the Sonata's performance, Joachim explained that the letters stood for 'frei aber einsam' or 'free but lonely', expressing his disappointment at the breaking of his engagement to Gisela von Arnim, who had been present with her mother Bettina at the gathering on 28 October. Gisela was the pretty garden-girl who presented Joachim with the anonymous manuscript in a basket of flowers. See Joachim's letter to Schumann, 29 November 1853; *Briefe von und an Joseph Joachim*, ed. Johannes Joachim and Andreas Moser, Vol. 1, *Die Jahre 1842–1857* (Berlin: Bard, 1911), p. 109.

72. See Bär, 'Kritischer Bericht', p. 386; and Michael Struck, *Die umstrittenen späten Instrumentalwerke Schumanns* (Hamburg: Wagner, 1984), p. 518.

73. Bär, 'Kritischer Bericht', p. 387.

74. Michael Struck, *Die umstrittenen späten Instrumentalwerke Schumann*, p. 524; Litzmann, *Clara Schumann*, II, p. 304.

75. Letter to H. Erler; Bär, 'Kritischer Bericht', p. 390.

76. Letter to J. Schuberth, 26 December 1859; Bär, 'Kritischer Bericht', p. 392. Clara also explains that she is not willing to publish the Violin Concerto, 'beautiful though individual parts of it are' ('so schön es auch in Einzelheiten ist') or the Five Romances for Cello.

77. See Joachim's letter to Clara 5 July 1860; Clara replied on 9 July. *Briefe von und an Joseph Joachim*, I, pp. 105 and 106.

78. Letter to Brahms, 13 July 1860, *Clara Schumann – Johannes Brahms*, I, p. 315.

79. Robert Schumann, *Sonata No. 3 in A minor*, ed. Oliver W. Neighbour (London: Schott, 1956).

80. *Münchner Merkur*, vol. 10, Munich, 11 February 1958; and *Münchner Abendzeitung*, vol. 11, no. 35, 10 February 1958; cited in Bär, 'Kritischer Bericht', p. 396.

81. According to the *Neue Ausgabe*, p. 428, the bar was marked to be left empty ('ein Tact leer zu lassen'); Reinhard Kapp has suggested an alternative that fills in the blank.

82. See Carola Nielinger-Vakil, 'Quiet revolutions: Hölderlin fragments by Luigi Nono and Wolfgang Rihm', *Music and Letters* 81 (2000), 245–74; David Gabriel Blumberg, '*Singen möcht ich . . .*': *Hölderlin's echo in new music* (PhD diss., University of California at Berkeley, 1996); Nicola Gess, 'Dichtung und Musik: Luigi Nonos Fragments – *Stille, An Diotima*', *MusicTexte: Zeitschrift für Neue Musik* 65 (1996), 18–30; and Friedrich Spongemacher, 'Hommage: György Kurtág und die Musik Robert Schumanns', *Robert Schumann: Philologische, analytische, sozial- und rezeptionsgeschichte Aspekte* (Saarbrücken: Saarbrücker Druckerei, 1998), pp. 219–27.

83. Susan Gillespie, 'Translating Adorno: language, music, and performance', *Musical Quarterly* 79 (1995), 57.

84. *Friedrich Hölderlin: Poems and Fragments*, trans. Michael Hamburger (London: Anvil Press, 2004), pp. 460–1.

85. Adorno, *Philosophie der neuen Musik*; cited in Gillespie, 'Translating Adorno', 57.

86. Adorno, 'Parataxis: on Hölderlin's late poetry', p. 130.

87. Incidentally, a possible musical model for this kind of motivic presentation can be found in the works of Niels Gade, to whom Schumann dedicated the Piano Trio, op. 110 that, as mentioned, was written in 1851, between the first and second violin sonatas. Gade's variation-like use of small cells has been seen as a kind of paratactic formal procedure preserved from the Danish tradition that counters Classical phrase structures – something that is supposed to have left its mark on Grieg's cyclic works, but which might well have influenced Schumann before that. See Kjell Styllstad, 'Thematic structure in relation to form in Edvard Grieg's cyclic work', *Studia musicologica norvegica* III (1977), 75–94.

88. 'Parataxis: On Hölderlin's late poetry', p. 123.

89. Michael Hamburger, Introduction to *Friedrich Hölderlin: Poems and Fragments*, pp. 41–2.

90. Theodore Ziolkowski, 'Breathing in verse', *London Review of Books* 26:18 (23 September 2004), 21.

91. Cited in Williams, 'Swaying with Schumann', 385.

92. 'Parataxis: on Hölderlin's late poetry', p. 133.

93. 'The late style (I)', *Beethoven: The Philosophy of Music*, p. 124.

94. For further discussion see Jim Samson, *Virtuosity and the Musical Work: The 'Transcendental Studies' of Liszt* (Cambridge: Cambridge University Press, 2003), p. 85.

95. Edward Said, *Musical Elaborations* (London, 1991); cited in Samson, *Virtuosity and the Musical Work*, p. 4.

96. Paul Metzner, *Crescendo of the Virtuoso* (Berkeley: University of California Press, 1998).

97. Samson, *Virtuosity and the Musical Work*, p. 82.

98. Daverio, *Robert Schumann*, p. 292.

99. Daverio, *Robert Schumann*, p. 293.

100. Letter 19 March 1838, *Clara und Robert Schumann Briefwechsel: Kritische Gesamtausgabe*, ed. Eva Weissweiler (Stroemfeld: Roter Stern, 1984), I, p. 121.

101. Quoted by Paul de Man in *Blindness and Insight: Essays in the Rhetoric of Contemporary Criticism* (Minneapolis: University of Minnesota Press, 2nd edn. 1983), p. 253.

6 | In search of Diotima

Diotima is dead,
Where are the heroes
And my pulsing song?[1]

Renew thyself completely each day;
do it again, and again, and forever again[2]

Back to Schumann at the piano. There are two important images: first, Henri Fantin-Latour's lithograph 'Le dernier thème de Robert Schumann', in which the composer sits at the keyboard, above him swirling angels dictating his 'last theme', completed just before his 1854 suicide attempt (Illustration 3).[3] Second, Wasielewski's report of the composer improvising in the asylum, a machine whose springs are broken but which still tries to work, jerking convulsively. From divine inspiration to a malfunctioning machine – captured here is the problem of late Schumann. Were those really the spirits of Schubert and Mendelssohn or just his psychosis, poeticized? Did the collapse of the man mean the collapse of his music?

Perhaps because Schumann's fame rests mostly on the early piano cycles *Papillons*, *Carnaval*, and *Kreisleriana*, it is in this genre that the question of the failure of his late style is most urgent. Solo piano music seems directly connected with the composer: Roland Barthes heard in it 'the body that beats'; Gerhard Dietel thought it 'esoteric' – invoking the realm of secrecy, security and terror, the *heimlich* or 'homely' and thus also the *unheimlich*, the 'unhomely' or uncanny.[4] As Michael Steinberg glosses it, 'Musical inwardness travels with the sonic language of the piano. The piano moves on ambiguous terrain between privacy, domesticity and performance.'[5] Schumann's final illness traverses the same ground, raising questions about how the private circumstances of the composer became public knowledge; or, in other words, the extent to and manner in which his music can 'perform' his illness.

Schumann returned to piano cycles with *Waldszenen*, op. 82, begun on Christmas Eve 1848 and published in October 1850. The three *Fantasiestücke*, op. 111 were finished in August 1851 and *Gesänge der Frühe* in October 1853. It was followed four months later by the hallucinated theme,

Illustration 3   Henri Fantin-Latour, 'Le dernier thème de Robert Schumann'

on which Schumann wrote a set of variations (WoO 24, published in 1939). Apart from *Bunte Blätter* and *Albumblätter* – discussed in Chapter 3 – Schumann also composed *Ball-Szenen* and *Kinderball* for piano duet (op. 109, June 1851, and op. 130, September 1853), *Drei Clavier-Sonaten für die Jugend* (op. 118, June 1853), and *Sieben Clavierstücke in Fughettenform* (op. 126, May-June 1853). He would continue writing fugues in the asylum.

Given the familiarity of the earlier piano cycles, it is probably inevitable that the later works are viewed through their filter. According to Erika Reiman, the piano cycles from the 1850s 'do not depart significantly from the precedents he had established for himself in the 1830s'.[6] John Daverio argues that op. 111 reintroduces the Davidsbündler characters of the *Fantasiestücke* (op. 12), composed in 1837, while *Gesänge der Frühe* is said to return to the previous cycles' tendency to make networks of subtle 'witty' connections, with motivic links being found between movements 1 and 2, and 2 and 4.[7] In contrast, and I think rightly, Anthony Newcomb divides the piano works into three phases, each representing 'fundamental aesthetic changes of course rather than gradual stylistic development': 'one can scarcely speak of a single Schumann', he reminds us.[8] This is not to say that the strict division of the composer's oeuvre is to be advocated or that the late piano cycles do not bear any relationship to the earlier pieces – far from it. But in order to understand their marginal position, we need to think about the cracks between earlier and later works, rather than papering them over in order to argue for some kind of redeeming ancestry.

Waldszenen exemplifies the differences between Schumann of the 1830s and the 1850s. As was often the case, the nine pieces were composed quickly.[9] Unusually, though, eighteenth months were spent revising them.[10] This seems to contradict Master Raro's often cited declaration that 'the first concept is always the most natural and the best' ('Die erste Konzeption ist immer die natürliche und best'), but fits with Schumann's turn to revising his earlier piano works at around the same time (discussed in Chapter 3).[11] As described by Eric Frederick Jensen, the alterations made were minimal; they included double-dotting some rhythms in 'Verrufene Stelle' and a few harmonic revisions, but primarily involved changes in texture.[12] The most significant revisions had to do with the conclusions of movements. Often Schumann decided to return to his opening theme, which might not seem so unusual except that, in 'Herberge' and 'Vogel als Prophet', he returned to the original material without significantly adapting it to create a stronger sense of an ending. For example, while 'Eintritt' returns to its opening figure in bar 40 but extends it into a final cadential arpeggiation, 'Herberge' simply repeats its first two bars at the end, with only minimal acknowledgement that the context is different (a grace note tonic is provided by the bass and the final two chords are converted into a perfect cadence) (Example 6:1, bars 55–6). As in the last movement of the *Märchenbilder*, it is as if the theme could continue, endlessly. A similarly 'open' ending is found in 'Vogel als Prophet' (Example 6:2). In his first version, Schumann had ended prosaically, with two bars of a new cadential dotted figure.[13] On revision, these bars were replaced by the opening theme. The effect, again, is one of departure rather than conclusion; we leave the bird fluttering around the branches, and then we simply move on to the next scene.

Schumann had concluded movements in a similar manner back in the 1830s, as is apparent from 'Romanze' (1835), published in *Albumblätter*, and 'Abendmusik' (1841) in *Bunte Blätter*. There is also a connection with the famous 'open' endings associated with the aesthetics of the Romantic fragment, as manifest in *Dichterliebe*, the Eichendorff *Liederkreis* and the earlier piano cycles. As David Ferris points out, the potential conclusiveness of movements or songs in these 'fragmentary' works is called into question through a number of means: harmonic, rhythmic, textural and registral.[14] For example, the fragmentary status of *Dichterliebe*'s 'Im wunderschönen Monat Mai' is famously created primarily by its final tonal ambiguity; the piano accompaniment continues with the same figuration throughout, and peters out on a dominant seventh. Closure is questioned in *Arabeske* (op. 18), the seventh movement of *Kreisleriana*, and the final three movements of *Davidsbündlertänze* by harmonic vagary and the introduction, at the very end of movements, of new figuration.[15] The kind of musical openness put forward in *Waldszenen*, though, is conceived differently: not by obscuring a movement's sense of resolution, but by making it plain. Thus the final tonics of 'Herberge' and 'Vogel als Prophet' are not in doubt and, unlike the previous song and piano pieces, the material they end with is not a kind of evocative, cycling accompanimental figure, a voice from afar, or a self-declared conclusion (*Arabeske* ends with 'Zum Schluss'); on the contrary, they close by clearly restating their opening themes. Such straightforward repetition queries the movements' sense of an ending. Somehow it is too bald and perfunctory. The recurrence of the opening material in the movements from *Waldszenen* act in a similar manner to the perfect cadence Schumann substituted for the original sustained dominant chord at the end of the fifth movement of *Kreisleriana* when he revised it in 1850. What was once transparent – or, perhaps better, diaphanous – becomes opaque.

Yet this does not make the endings of the movements from *Waldszenen* more straightforward to interpret. In many ways, their peremptoriness forecloses the hermeneutic openness prized by the aesthetics of the fragment, replacing it with a much tighter knot to unpick. An alternative formal aesthetic is at work, one to do with repetition and restoration: with the said, rather than the unsaid. This is music that tells us it is saying something – but it is unclear precisely what (an ambiguity that often causes listeners to accuse it of emptiness, as discussed later). In this regard, a comparison might

Example 6:1 'Herberge'

Example 6:1 (*cont.*)

Example 6:2　'Vogel als Prophet', bb. 40–42

be made to the fairy-tale chamber music, with its use of frames and ternary forms. There is a similar sense in some of the *Waldszenen* movements of the music falling into sections, without the complicated narrative schemes detected in *Humoreske*, op. 20 or *Novelletten*, op. 21.[16] And, as indicated in the endings of 'Herberge' and 'Vogel als Prophet', repetition is key. For example, in 'Vogel als Prophet', the only interruption to the birdlike figuration comes in bars 18–24, where there suddenly emerges a muscular, chorale-like theme in G major. On its repetition, the melody ascends to E flat major and, just as surprisingly, disappears, to be replaced by the opening figuration, which continues as if nothing has happened – and, as already mentioned, continues to the end of the movement as if nothing ever will disturb its peace (Example 6:3).

The chorale-like melody has several possible sources, the significance of which may be derived from the movement's original motto, from Eichendorff's 'Zwielicht' ('Twilight'): 'Hüte dich, sei wach und munter!' ('Be on your guard, be awake and alert!'). Christopher Reynolds suggests the melody's source might be a line from the boys' chorus in Part III of Schumann's *Szenen aus Goethes Faust* that similarly warns innocents.[17] Other references postdate *Waldszenen*, suggesting that this was a theme that in some ways haunted the composer: the soloist's theme in the second movement of the Violin Concerto, and the *Letzter Gedanke* are both prophesied by the bird's chorale in *Waldszenen*. Whichever way it is read, the central melody of 'Vogel als Prophet' seems a message of danger – rather like the birds of Pfarrius's 'Warnung', Lenau's 'Einsamkeit' and the Kulmann lieder discussed in Chapter 1.[18]

Yet while this may be the case, the melody's fleeting appearance and the way in which the 'bird' music continues, as unimpressed as the fishes listening to St Anthony's sermon in *Des Knaben Wunderhorn*, implies that it could not have been too sinister. The disturbing event is framed to prevent everyday equilibrium from being upset, much as Schumann's friend and

Example 6:3 'Vogel als Prophet', bb. 17–25

contemporary Adalbert Stifter used *Rahmenerzählung* or framing narratives in many of the short stories in his collection *Bunte Steine* (1853). Stifter's narrative techniques have been described in Chapter 3, but are worth returning to here as they seem pertinent to the understanding of Schumann's use of ternary form in his late piano pieces. For example, in 'Granit', a boy is tricked into anointing his feet with pitch. He runs into the house, where his mother – upset at his having left a trail of pitch over her freshly scrubbed floor – beats him. The boy's grandfather cleans his feet and takes him for a walk, during which he tells him the story of a plague the area had suffered many generations before. A pitch-burner's family had fled to the woods to escape infection but all die except for their young son, who survives on berries and wild fruit. He finds a very ill girl, and without thinking of the risk, tends her back to health. The magic song of a bird reveals an antidote for the plague, and life returns to normal. Later the boy and girl marry and become prosperous and well respected members of the community. By the end of the grandfather's tale, he and the boy have returned home; familial order is restored and the boy is blessed by his mother as he falls asleep.

The crucial point in relaying such tales, for Stifter, was their maintaining of the status quo: of the return to 'normal' bourgeois family life despite periodic disappearances and unusual goings on. In other words, the bird that announces the plague cure (or the flute-playing girl with the abnormally big head in 'Tourmaline') is of less consequence than the fact that the everyday continues. These tales fantasize about 'normality' rather than dwell on the fantastic. As such, they reverse the preoccupations of earlier Romantic writers such as Schumann's beloved Jean Paul (to whom Stifter's earlier stories are often compared). That change in attitude might again reflect the different situation in which the composer found himself by the 1850s: the 'paralysing quietude' of Stifter's *Bunte Steine* has been interpreted as a dissociative response to the upheavals of 1848, an attitude Schumann seems partly to have shared.[19] Might, then, the composer's approach to thematic consistency and the 'framing narratives' of ternary forms bear some relationship to the writer's *Rahmenerzählung* and yearning for stability? 'What ends the day tired / rises new-born tomorrow' ('Was heut gehet müde unter, / hebt sich morgen neu geboren') claims the last stanza of Eichendorff's 'Zwielicht'. 'Yet much is lost in the night – take care, be wakeful and alert!' ('Manches geht in Nacht verloren – hüte dich, sei wach und munter!'). The optimism of day being threatened by the ominous gloom of twilight in Eichendorff's poem resonates with commentaries about the onset of Schumann's late style, and will reappear on considering the composer's final, dusky alba: *Gesänge der Frühe*. In preparation for that, though, we might think again about the composer's use of thematic and formal structures in the other late piano cycles.

The ternary design of movements is a larger-scale manifestation of Schumann's repetitive treatment of thematic material. Melodic figuration tends to be repeated in different harmonic areas, as if they were objects being viewed from various angles. 'Vogel als Prophet', for example, shifts its opening four bars from G minor to D minor; the same melody is then repeated with some embellishment in F major (bar 8) and cadences on to C major in bar 12. There is then a two-bar melodic sequence based on the head motive that cadences again on to C before circling back to G minor. The first two bars are repeated and the middle section begins. As already explained, the chorale melody moves from G major to E flat major before returning to the music of the first section, which is repeated verbatim.

'Herberge' (see Example 6:1) uses sequences and repetitions in a less closed circle than 'Vogel als Prophet', but nonetheless they remain fundamental to the movement's overall form. Its opening four bars are repeated, bringing the harmony around to V. The dotted rhythm of bar 3 is then used as a motive for development in bars 10–18, bars 15–18 following a stepwards rising sequence. Bars 19–20 are repeated before their semiquaver final flourish is extended by sequence in bars 23–4 and leads into a return of the opening melody in the bass line in bar 24. Bars 33–48 match bars 9–24, in the sense that they use similar motives in a repetitive and sequential manner. The melody of bars 19–20 provides material for bars 48–55 and the movement ends, as already mentioned, with a return of the melody from the opening two bars. There is undeniably an extensive amount of motivic interconnectedness, but what this observation does not convey is that the effect is not one of satisfying cohesion but of a strange disjointedness. Perhaps this is because the music falls clearly into sections of two or four bars, eschewing for the most part the kind of metrical displacement associated with Schumann's earlier piano music. But it also has to do with the repetitiveness of its small-scale sequences and overall structure. Had the returning melody at the end been continued, it would feel like a miniature rondo. As it stands, it resembles more the paratactical structures described in the Third Violin Sonata (see Chapter 5): a broken chain.

In many ways Schumann's treatment of motives and themes in 'Vogel als Prophet' and 'Herberge' is an extension of his 'partiality for sequences'; one of the traits Robert Haven Schauffler lists as quintessentially Schumannian.[20] Arguably, that partiality is motivated here by this being illustrative music. The bird has to keep fluttering, just as a hunter's song such as *Waldszenen*'s 'Jagdlied' has to be quasi-strophic – in other words, repetitive. The fairy-tale and childish aspect of the pictorial piano music also seems to encourage sequence and repetition over development, in keeping with its deliberate surface simplicity. Although they oil modulations and transitions, sequences tend not to be used to fragment and reassemble themes according to some kind of proto-Brahmsian 'developing variation', as they had been in Schumann's earlier works and sonata forms. Instead, they are expanded almost to a structural principle; as is evident by the number of ternary forms and by the way in which movements such as 'Herberge' are structured.

A precedent for Schumann's structural use of sequences in *Waldszenen* and the other late piano cycles can be found in many of the movements from *Kinderszenen* and the *Album für die Jugend* (op. 68), which are built by the sequential repetition of phrases. *Kinderszenen*'s 'Bittendes Kind' repeats each two-bar phrase as an echo, the only deviation being the strange high G natural that appears over the final chord; 'Glückes genug' repeats its first eight bars before presenting them again a tone higher; and, of course, there are the many somnolent melodic repetitions of 'Träumerei'. As in much of the *Album für die Jugend*, *Waldszenen*'s 'Einsame Blumen', 'Verrufene Stelle', and 'Freundliche Landschaft' all focus on a particular motive or rhythmic figure.

Indeed, the use of ternary forms, the building of themes and formal units from a small amount of material, four-square phrase structures, and the use of repetition as a structural device and in thematic construction, are all characteristics of nineteenth-century children's works.[21] 'Puppenwiegen-liedchen', the movement Schumann added to the first of the *Drei Clavier-Sonaten für die Jugend* at the request of the publisher Julius Schuberth, according to Roe-Min Kok is crammed with non-musical and musical signifiers of children and childhood.[22] In part these associations derive from its diminutive title; it is a lullaby (*Wiegenliedchen*) for a child's toy. But it also has to do with the movement's ternary form and concentration on a few motivic cells.[23] Kok concludes that 'the movement has a mechanical feel to it', perhaps reflecting Schumann's exaggeration of the conventions of children's music for the sake of Schuberth's commercial requirements: it is the 'the image of a (mute and lifeless) doll'.

Yet all these characteristics (including the metaphors of mechanical puppetry) could be applied as well to the 'artful' piano cycles from the 1850s.[24] The overlap between Schumann's children's music and his late style more generally has been one cause for critical uncertainty over the latter's aesthetic status. Although the music for children might have had some commercial success, reviewers and professional performers overlooked the *Drei Clavier-Sonaten für die Jugend*, *Ball-Szenen* and *Kinderball*, probably because they were intended for instructional purposes and domestic settings.[25] There is also the larger issue of the music's deliberate simplicity, which tends to defy extended analytical or critical examination. How much of interest can be said about a piece in ternary form, which focuses on a small amount of motivic material in a repetitive rather than developmental manner, and which falls into regular phrases? Is Schumann's late style not a progression or maturation of his compositional techniques, but in fact a regression?

The problem perhaps lies not with Schumann as such, but with our notions of what a late style should consist of. According to Adorno's now classic formulation:

The maturity of the late works of important artists is not like the ripeness of fruit. As a rule, these works are not well rounded, but wrinkled, even fissured. They are apt to lack sweetness, fending off with prickly tartness those interested merely in sampling them. They lack all that harmony which the classicist aesthetic is accustomed to demand from works of art, showing more traces of history than of growth. The accepted explanation is that they are products of a subjectivity or, still better, of a 'personality' ruthlessly proclaiming itself, which breaks through the roundedness of form for the sake of expression, exchanging harmony for the dissonance of its sorrow and spurning sensuous charm under the dictates of the imperiously emancipated mind. The late work is thereby relegated to the margins of art and brought closer to documentation.[26]

Adorno is referring, of course, to Beethoven, but certain aspects of his commentary can be related to Schumann's late style. For instance, his acknowledgement that 'references to Beethoven's biography and fate are seldom absent from discussions of his last works. It is as if, in face of the dignity of human death, art theory wanted to forfeit its rights and abdicate before reality.' But the reality that Schumann and Beethoven are thought to have faced, and the margins of art to which their late works are relegated, is very different. As demonstrated by *Waldszenen*, the children's music and the *Fantasiestücke* (of which more in a moment), Schumann's last piano pieces are well rounded and harmonious. As such they do not fit into the Adornian, Beethovenian model of musical progress; they are not part of the modernist trajectory according to which music advances historically through increasing complexity and harmonic emancipation. Yet Schumann's last works are still considered to proclaim a personality. Herein lies the problem, for the personality proclaimed – or the reality before which considerations of Schumann's late style abdicate – is sick. According to most accounts, this is not subjectivity breaking forth, but the subject broken, suffering from mental illness and creative failure. The composer is no longer puppet master but the mechanical puppet itself, empty of autonomous expression.

There is, what is more, a sense of controlled containment in the later piano pieces, something that again contradicts Adorno's image of fissured and wrinkled fruit. If anything, Schumann's produce becomes smoother with age, overripe and sweet – more classicist and regular. Often the late piano music is described as being abstract and detached.[27] This sense is perhaps encouraged in the *Fantasiestücke*, op. 111, by the fact that, unlike Schumann's earlier *Fantasie* pieces – opp. 12 and 17 for solo piano, op. 73 for clarinet and piano, and op. 88 for piano trio – the movements have no poetic titles.[28] In this respect, op. 111 might be similar to the *Märchenbilder* and *Märchenerzählungen*, which give no clue to the poetic content of individual movements despite their global titles relating to fairy-tales.

Franz Brendel described movements of the op. 12 *Fantasiestücke* as containing 'certain, clear primary sections and others that do not protrude clearly at all but rather serve merely as backgrounds. Some passages are

Example 6:4 *Fantasiestücke*, op. 111, ii, bb. 57–62

like points made prominent by the rays of the sun, whereas others vanish in blurry contours.'[29] Light shines more consistently on the op. 111 *Fantasiestücke*, which are made up entirely of 'clear primary sections'. Where the op. 12 *Fantasiestücke* digress, the op. 111 *Fantasiestücke* distil. There are only three movements, which move from C minor to A flat major (with a middle section in C minor), and back to C minor. Such limited harmonic movement between movements is typical of late Schumann, as seen in *Märchenerzählungen* and the Maria Stuart lieder. The second and third movements are in ternary form. While the latter returns to material from its middle section as a kind of coda, no such structural-thematic embellishment is offered in the former. Instead, it repeats its opening section virtually verbatim, as if an expansion of the repeated melodies in *Waldszenen*'s 'Herberge' and 'Vogel als Prophet'. The gentle opening melody revolves around a descending third (5-4-3); its rhythm lingers on the first beat of almost every bar, and its bass line and inner voices move mostly by step. The melody of the central C minor section ascends rather than descends, and is accompanied by constant quaver triplets. Its *fortissimo* climax, however, is somehow diminished on being repeated, hemmed in by the first- and second-time barlines. Only a quaver rest (with pause) is needed before the opening melody resumes (Example 6:4). At the very end, the melody begins once more with the simplest of decoration: rising octaves in the treble that frame the descending melodic third and the slightly awkward repeated bass E flat of the original second bar is lifted to F.[30] The melody's eternal returns are both natural and deeply disturbing; a refrain that renews itself completely each day, as Thoreau might say – or the half-buried memory of a fairy-tale you were once told and now are trying to tell again.

The contrast between sections of the second *Fantasiestück* is comparable to the segmented forms of some of Schubert's Impromptus. With both composers there is a sense of enclosure; the outer sections of the second movement from the *Fantasiestücke* could even be characterized as 'late Schumann', while the long slurs over the more tempestuous middle section seem more in keeping with his earlier style.[31] I will return to the question of metaphorical language in commentary on the late works of both composers later, but here a brief digression about how Schumann perceived Schubert's last piano sonatas might cast an interesting light on his own late style. Schubert's last three piano sonatas were famously 'found' by Schumann in Vienna in the winter of 1838–9. His essay about them in the *Neue Zeitschrift für Musik* wondered if their worth would have been judged differently were the date of their composition not known:

Whether they were written on the deathbed or not, I cannot say. From the music itself one might dare to conclude that they were; and yet it is also possible . . . that through the melancholy word 'Allerletzte' [the publisher Diabelli's description of the Sonatas] the imagination is impregnated with thoughts of impending death.[32]

Schumann describes four aspects of Schubert's late style: a greater simplicity of invention; the spontaneous renunciation of glittering novelty; the spinning out of certain common musical ideas where he would otherwise have combined new threads from one period to the next; and that although it is 'always musically rich with song, it ripples along from page to page as though it might never end, never obstructed for the sake of effect, here and there interrupted by isolated impulses of greater vigour which, however, are quickly [assuaged]'. Schumann, it could be said, is describing his own late style before its time.

Perhaps he was *telling the tale* of late style. Gilles Deleuze and Félix Guattari describe three aspects of the refrain.[33] One: 'a child in the dark, gripped with fear, comforts himself by singing under his breath . . . The song is like a rough sketch of a calming and stabilizing, calm and stable, centre in the heart of chaos.' Two: the wall of sound that delimits the territory of home; a child humming while he completes homework, the housewife listening to the radio 'as she marshals the antichaos forces of her work'. Three: 'Finally, one opens the circle a crack, opens it all the way, lets someone in, calls someone, or else goes out oneself, launches forth . . . One ventures from home on the thread of a tune. Along sonorous, gestural, motor lines that mark the customary path of a child and graft themselves onto or begin to bud "lines of drift" with different loops, knots, speeds, movements, gestures and sonorities.'

Such aspects of the refrain are found in horror stories, fairy-tales and lieder, Deleuze and Guattari continue. The notion of the refrain somehow marking territory – from a sense of home (*Heimat*) or distance from it (the *unheimlich*, perhaps) – casts an interesting light on the strophic, ritornello-like and ternary forms of Schumann's late piano music. 'The refrain is rhythm and melody that have been territorialised because they have become expressive – and have become expressive because they are territorialising.'[34] In this context empty repetitions are filled with or acquire meaning; they *contain* the composer. Who might then seek escape: 'a musician requires a *first type* of refrain, a territorial or assemblage refrain, in order to transform it from within, deterritorialise it, producing a refrain of the *second type* as the final end of music: the cosmic refrain of a sound machine'.[35] That slightly altered repetition at the end of the second of the *Fantasiestücke* might be a refrain of the second type, the final end of music: transformed from within and deterritorialized, making strange subsequent hearings of its earlier versions. Moving from the sweet refrain of childhood scenes to that of the cosmos:

In the passage from one to the other, from the assemblage of sound to the Machine that renders it sonorous, from the becoming-child of the musician to the becoming-cosmic of the child, many dangers crop up: black holes, closures, paralysis of the finger and auditory hallucinations, Schumann's madness, cosmic force gone *bad*, a note that pursues you, a sound that transfixes you. Yet one was already present in the other; the cosmic force was already present in the material, the great refrain in the little refrain, the great maneuver in the little maneuver. Except we can never be sure we will be strong enough, for we have no system, only lines and movements. Schumann.[36]

Schumann. The refrain that is stronger than us, more compelling than any description of ternary forms and repeated sequences. Deleuze and Guattari's conflation of the composer's use of repetition and his mental state encapsulates how Schumann is invoked in our own fairy-tales and horror stories, haunting dreams of lost genius.[37] It is a powerful image, never more so than in his two final piano cycles, each of which have their own, ambiguous revenants: the Schubert-dictated theme of the *Letzter Gedanke* and the mythical beauty after which *Gesänge der Frühe* was originally named, Diotima.

From the A-S-C-H motto representing the home town of Ernestine von Fricken in *Carnaval* to the multiple references to Clara, absent women recur as ciphers throughout Schumann's music – particularly in the intimate genre of solo piano works. His initial title for *Gesänge der Frühe*, *An Diotima*, is more oblique than most, however. Plato's figure of ideal beauty might still be a reference to Clara. Bettina von Arnim – who visited Schumann in the asylum – is another candidate. Or perhaps Diotima is Hölderlin's spectre, the unknown beloved to whom many of the late poems are dedicated.[38] Whoever she might have been, the mysterious spirit that hovers over interpretations of *Gesänge der Frühe* serves as a symbol for our own quest to understand the refrains of late Schumann.

Aside from the shadowy figure of Diotima, there is a further cipher to confront: the placing of these pieces as songs (*Gesänge*), which seems an odd choice given that they are not for voice or, with the exception of the chorale-like texture of the first and the opening of the last piece, particularly lyrical; the part-writing is unsuitable for a chorus, depending more on the resonances of the piano.[39] Markus Waldura has claimed that the collection's title comes from the first piece, which borrows a melodic contour from Schumann's 'Zwielicht'.[40] This suggestion is alluring in that – as already mentioned with regard to 'Vogel als Prophet' from *Waldszenen* – the lied's lyrics refer to the ominous gloom of twilight, implying that the morning or dawn (*der Frühe*) of the later work's title might actually herald a darkening of the composer's outlook. But, as will be discussed, the reference is oblique even for Schumann, embedded within the inner voices of the accompaniment.

The opening *Gesang der Frühe* is deceptively simple (Example 6:5). It has a chorale-like texture and falls into four verses. This seemingly straightforward structure is constantly undercut, however. For instance, the first verse (bars 1–8) subverts an antecedent-consequent design: considering the melodic line, the close on V in bar 4 is answered by the implicit V-I of C sharp-E-D in bar 8. Cadential closure, though, is denied by the cycle of fifths motion in the bass (from bars 5–9: E-A-D-G-C sharp-F sharp-B). A similar sense of friction is felt on considering the relationship of motives to phrase structure. The piece opens with treble and bass in unison, beginning with a bare fifth leap from D to A, rising a tone and then falling a fifth to introduce a crotchet turn figure. Almost all the remaining melodic material, and much of the accompaniment, is derived from these three motives, with the exception of the final cadential figure. Yet in many ways they disrupt the underlying harmonic, metric and textural structure rather than reinforce it. Schumann's slurring of the falling fifth motive across the barline is maintained almost throughout. The four-note unit thus conflicts with the notated metre and – as the motive is treated sequentially – harmonic progressions and different densities of scoring.

The second verse follows the same harmonic pattern as the first, starting in B minor and ending on D as chord V of G. The third iteration begins by slightly thickening the first phrase's unison line, adding a further lower voice, but seems to be following the established pattern of harmonic progress. In its second half, however, changes occur. In bar 21 the expected falling third in the bass (first heard in bar 3) is replaced by a falling fifth. Above the A

Example 6:5 *Gesänge der Frühe*, i

pedal in bars 23–5 the turn figure is repeated as expected, but suddenly departs from the sequence, jumping up to E in bar 25. We are not given the final cadential figure: instead the next verse (number 4) unexpectedly breaks in, *forte*, a third harmonic reworking of that opening bare fifth D-A, presented as a V 6/4 that resolves locally onto I in bar 28 (third beat). Daverio describes the passage between bars 26–30 as the climax or, in terms that follow Adorno on Mahler, the 'breakthrough' of the piece.[41] To me, the disruption sounds more like a memory lapse on Schumann's part; as the previous two bars drifted up to a higher register and became gradually softer it seems as if he had started to daydream, then suddenly remembered the next verse. And start he hurriedly does; but too hurriedly, not waiting for the expected cadence figure. After four bars of *forte*, in the second half of bar 30 the music subsides back on to the pedal on A, manipulations of the turn figure, and a quickly dissolving fugal working of the main theme.

What the breakthrough or interruption of bars 26–30 calls into question is how much a motivic analysis of this piece can tell us about its sonic effect. The one prominent moment that seems to break from the motivic web is the falling third in the upper voice of bar 29, but we might argue that it is an ancestor of the falling third first heard in the bass line of bar 3. Of course a large amount of motivic interconnectedness is inevitable when a piece such as this is so dependent on repetitions. In other words, revealing its motivic integrity does not tell us much about what is so striking on hearing the music performed: its element of surprise.

Underneath the sequential repetitions of the turn figure in bars 6–8, the inner and bass voices seem to dissociate themselves from the melody, or the melody from them: there are consecutive seconds between the upper voices (E-D, D-C♯, C♯-B), as if they are out-of-sync with each other. Perhaps significantly, it is here that Waldura finds the melodic contour of 'Zwielicht' mentioned earlier: the alto line moves from G to C♯, D, C♯, B. Although the quotation might explain the clashing seconds, the reference seems unsatisfactory; it is incomplete, lacking the song's final note. Its next recurrence at pitch occurs in the inner voice of bars 23–6. Now we might object that the line contains a lower E not present in the vocal line, although it is in the piano introduction of 'Zwielicht' based on the same theme. The final A might be provided by the climactic 6/4 chord of bar 27. While the notion that this passage is the result of Schumann remembering his earlier song fits nicely with my somewhat whimsical suggestion that he seems during these bars to be daydreaming, the reminiscence is too weak in characterization and harmony to be of consequence to the whole.

The notion of strophic repetition and variation that might be taken from the potential association with the lied might be helpful, however. Ferris describes Schumann's setting of 'Zwielicht' as combining two opposing constructive principles – one episodic, the other continuous.[42] In other words, it combines strophic variation with the kind of weak opening (in which the tonic is not clearly defined) usually associated with end-accented, through-composed forms. It is through this combination, Ferris proposes, 'that Schumann evokes in musical terms the deceptive quality of the half-light of dusk: The song is based on a musical phrase that is not clearly defined when we first hear it, gradually comes into focus as it is varied in each succeeding strophe, and ultimately turns out to be something quite different than what we had first imagined.' Although some of the devices used in 'Zwielicht' reappear in the first of the *Gesänge der Frühe* – such as sequential patterning – the later piece seems to reverse the lied's trajectory. Perhaps this simply means Schumann is evoking the half-light of dawn, rather than dusk, but it seems indicative more of a stylistic shift. Unlike 'Zwielicht', which according to Ferris implies a closed form but never actually presents it, the theme or strophe of the first *Frühgesang* is complete in itself – it does not really grow, beyond being heard from different harmonic angles.[43] There is no contrasting middle section such as Schumann uses in other 'chorale' pieces – for example, 'Der Dichter spricht' from *Kinderszenen*, or even the last movement of the *Gesänge der Frühe*. With each reiteration of the refrain it becomes more rather than less strange – deterritorialized, Deleuze and Guattari might say.

The harmonic structure of the first *Gesänge der Frühe* contributes to the feeling of 'venturing from home on the thread of a tune'. The first 26 bars are guided by chromatic mediant relationships: we move from D major to B minor to G major. The accented A-F♯-D of bars 1, 10 and 19 trace another triad, that of the tonic, D major. One might at this point be reminded of Moritz Hauptmann's diatonic key scheme, a chain of major and minor thirds, described in *Die Natur der Harmonik und der Metrik* published in Leipzig the same year that the *Gesänge der Frühe* were composed.[44] According to Hauptmann, the major triad contained within it the dynamics for reconciling the opposing forces of each pitch: the root embodying unity, the fifth opposition, and the third resolution. Schumann's piece enacts these dynamic relationships on two harmonic levels, the local and the global. It seems at first as though the second section of the piece breaks the chain of thirds with the return of the tonic in bar 27, but the real highpoint of the piece – the G-E of bar 29 – is in fact a continuation of the mediant relationships begun in the first section: D major to B minor to G major now

Example 6:6 Johannes Brahms, 'Dem dunkeln Schoss', bb. 1–8

taken to E minor. The arrival on E minor is resolved melodically by means of Hauptmann's conciliatory third, the upper-line G slipping down to the tonic's F sharp-E-D over the V pedal, as the music restarts its sequential treatment of the turn figure, as if picking up from just before the outburst of bar 26.

Being able to theorize the harmonic relationships of Schumann's move-ment does not make them less strange. The extent to which they are unortho-dox is apparent on their being compared to Brahms's use of a version of the theme in his choral setting of Schiller's *Lied von der Glocke* (*Dem dunkeln Schoß der heilgen Erde*).[45] Although Brahms begins with all voices in uni-son, as in the Schumann, the theme itself is normalized, perhaps reterri-torialized (Example 6:6). The rhythm of the opening bar is stabilized from dotted minim-crotchet to two minims, and the characteristic falling fifth is replaced by a fourth. The theme is freed from its endless sequences, instead being extended into an eight-bar melody; while the remainder returns to its opening material throughout, each time it is varied and developed. In a way, Brahms idealizes Schumann's theme, supplying Diotima where she was only imagined before.[46] Perhaps this is only fitting, given that the piece was intended to accompany the dedication of Adolf Donndorf's new tombstone for Schumann in a ceremony held at Bonn's Old Cemetery on 2 May 1880. Memorialization tends towards a smoothing over of a composer's imperfections, if not an aggrandizement of his achievements.

While Brahms might have idealized Schumann's late music in *Dem dunkeln Schoß der heilgen Erde* the source nonetheless remains recognizable, the composer's spirit hovering over the ending, as the soprano finally supplies the original's falling fifth. The significance of memory and recognition in the first of the *Gesänge der Frühe* was sensed by Barthes, who used the piece to attempt to explain the profound effect on him of discovering a photograph of his deceased mother as a child, described in his collection of thoughts on photography, *Camera Lucida* (incidentally, another 'last' work).[47] Schumann's music embodied for Barthes his mother's 'being', and his 'grief at her death'. More generally, Barthes tells us, the photograph symbolizes the fragility of human relationships, making us aware of our own mortality alongside those we have loved. Schumann's late music might be thought the sonic equivalent of that testimony of death in the future, at once consoling and disturbing in its fractured beauty. Barthes did not include the 'Winter Garden Photograph' of his mother in *Camera Lucida*, saying it would mean nothing to anyone apart from him. But recent research has suggested that it probably did not exist.[48] This does not particularly matter: the photograph's 'fictional truth', in the words of one commentator, is 'powerful enough to survive its possible nonexistence'.[49] In contrast, the piece from *Gesänge der Frühe*, whose effect Barthes compares to the Winter Garden Photograph, almost did not come into existence: Schumann removed it from the collection, only deciding to return it just before publication.

Had the first movement of the *Gesänge der Frühe* not been included, the cycle would stand as music in search of a thematic source. No doubt, as with Hölderlin's Diotima or Barthes's Winter Photograph, one would have been invented. As it is, a few thematic connections have been found between movements. For instance, the opening melody of the first movement returns in the second movement's bass line (bars 7–8). Such links provide musical meaning and content, seeming to prove that Schumann was as invested in notions of cyclicity and clever motivic associations as he had been twenty years earlier.[50] There are certainly links between the *Gesänge der Frühe* and the earlier piano cycles. Not all the movements are as oddly structured as the first; towards its end the second movement even features two interpolations that might be characterized as arabesques (bars 23–4 and 27–8), in the manner of the *Davidsbündlertänze*.[51] Yet more often than not, critics reach for psycho-biographical explanations for the way this music works before and in preference to considering it in analytical terms, the perils of which are apparent from the epilogue to Harald Krebs's monograph *Fantasy Pieces*.[52]

As Krebs acknowledges, most of Schumann's very late music is quite sparing and conservative in its use of metrical dissonance. However, using the third of the *Gesänge der Frühe*, he attempts to recreate 'an effect of metrical dissonance' in words by superimposing 'noncongruent layers of discourse'. His aim, apparently, 'is to suggest by such superimposition the mental and emotional state of Robert Schumann in the asylum at Endenich in June of 1856'. Three strands or trains of thought are assigned to the metrical layers of the movement: 'Robert' reminisces about his recent past; 'Eusebius' longs for Clara; 'Florestan' for death.[53] There are three brief utterances by the caretaker, which 'make no impression on the main interlocutors: Schumann has withdrawn so completely into himself that no words from outside are able to reach him'. On one level, Krebs's epilogue is a remarkable experiment, bringing together words and music analysis in a fascinating way. On another, it reifies assumptions about the connection between the composer's life and works to an almost absurd extent. And there is the danger that the verbalization may stick; that Schumann's music forever will be heard as giving voice to his thoughts in the most literal sense.

Krebs's impulse to chase after the meaning of *Gesänge der Frühe* with words might be driven by the sense that, as he puts it, the composer had 'withdrawn so completely into himself'. Throughout this chapter mention has been made of the distance felt by listeners from Schumann's late piano music. The 'ambiguous terrain between privacy, domesticity and performance' inhabited by piano music, that sense of 'musical inwardness' no longer draws listeners and performers in to connect with the composer's 'beating' body.[54] No doubt this has to do with the relative unfamiliarity of the music. It might also be the result of its formal structures and aesthetic stance.

In this regard, it is intriguing that a similar metaphorical vocabulary is found in writings on Schubert's piano music, particularly the Impromptus. For example, the opening unaccompanied melody of the Impromptu in C minor (op. 90, no. 1) has been described in terms of 'confinement'.[55] 'Impenetrable' and 'inscrutable' are the terms chosen by Charles Fisk for the theme of the first of the op. 142 Impromptus; as in the second of Schumann's op. 111 *Fantasiestücke*, the recapitulatory drama is suppressed in favour of 'a simple return, almost without warning, of the opening theme'.[56] The Impromptu's treatment of the theme, Fisk concludes, signifies a closed past. Indeed, the 'sound of memory' in Schubert has been the topic of much discussion by recent scholars; there is not space here to engage fully in the parallels with

Schumann's music, but it is worth noting the qualities of 'inwardness' and 'removal from the world' heard in passages such as the A flat major section of the F minor Impromptu, or the 'withdrawal' of the opening theme from the 'action' of the C minor Piano Sonata's adagio.[57] There is a qualitative difference, though, in how Schubert's 'withdrawal' or 'inwardness' is perceived in comparison with Schumann's 'distance' (incidentally, the same is true for their treatment of repetition). The idea of Schumann's incarceration – the image of the composer viewed through the bars on the door to his asylum cell, improvising incomprehensibly at the piano – is more persistent than any we might have with Schubert.

Our greater awareness of Schumann's fate is also because the stories surrounding his illness are more striking. For example, there is the 'strange history' (Hanslick's words) of the variations on a theme in E♭ major, one of the best-known and most influential anecdotes. During a night of hallucinations in 1854, Schumann wrote down a theme apparently dictated by the spirit of Schubert:

On the unfortunate 27 February he suddenly leapt up in the midst of writing down the fifth, turbulently emotional variation, ran hatless from the house, and threw himself into the Rhine. Rescued from the waters and brought back home, he immediately sat down at his desk without a word and continued to write the variation exactly where he had left off.[58]

Music and illness are inextricably combined in Hanslick's account. The idea that Schumann could have recovered sufficiently from plunging into the fast moving currents of the Rhine to return immediately to his 'turbulent' fifth variation – without the intervention of doctors or family members – verges on the surreal. But it is a striking image: one that recurs throughout accounts of Schumann's final years, further romanticizing the last of the Romantic generation. 'Even Schumann's hallucinations', the music historian Ambros wryly commented, 'placed him in the musical pantheon' – alongside the spirit of Schubert and, in some versions of events, Mendelssohn. Although the E♭ theme (the *Geisterthema* or *Letzter Gedanke*) was published by Brahms in a supplementary volume to the Collected Works, the variations were not made public until 1939.[59]

The theme itself (Example 6:7), as has already been mentioned, is haunted by past melodies: the central chorale of 'Vogel als Prophet', the opening of 'Frühlings Ankunft', and the slow movement of the Violin Concerto. The first two-bar melody is repeated a tone lower, in both versions underpinned by a tonic pedal. It is an oddly static beginning, at least in harmonic terms; smudged only by the implied iv 6/4 chord in bar two. The next two bars

Example 6:7   Theme in E♭ major, bb. 1–8

use the same melodic contour of a falling step, followed by a rising fourth
and falling step, but continue the descent with a touch of syncopation. The
bassline finally moves, descending by step from iv to I, before cadencing on
to v. The first four bars return, now extended by a contrary-motion crotchet
two-quaver figure. Both melody and bass end by playing in unison the F-B
flat drop of the 6/4 cadence on to V. Bars 21–4 repeat a descending four-bar
phrase, treble and bass moving in parallel tenths. As is often the case, Schumann includes a few snatched grace notes in the bass, as if there is supposed
to be a pedal part – the music reaching further than the piano's keyboard
(the part-writing also suggests there could be more than two hands). The
grace notes make the dominant permeate the section, blurring the harmonic
progressions above. The descending figure heard in bar 13 returns in the
final four bars to bring the theme to a close.

The use of parallel motion between melody and bass and the minimal
melodic interest of the theme make Schumann's treatment of it in the variations all the more strange. These are melody-based variations of the kind
dismissed by Brahms.[60] In variations I and II, the melody appears complete
in the right hand; in the first variation it is embellished by triplet quavers in
the inner voices; in the second variation it is pursued in canon by the bass.
The tenor voice takes the theme in Variation III, the bass in parallel motion
with more of those gracenote basslines, which also feature in the semiquaver triplet decoration. Variation IV also places the theme in an inner voice
(in the last eight bars it returns to the treble). This is the only movement
not in the tonic E flat major, choosing instead the relative minor. The final
variation – the one Schumann was supposed to have returned to after his
suicide attempt – is certainly the most tumultuous, the inner demisemiquavers picking out the contour of the theme. Harmonically it is the most
unconventional, repeatedly placing clashes of a second (minor and major)
on the first beat of the bar. As with the parallel seconds of what may have
been a reference to 'Zwielicht' in *Gesänge der Frühe*, voices (or themes, or
hands) seem to be dislocated from one another.

Once more to Schumann at the piano: 'that instrument that had been the friend of his boyhood, the confidant of his riper years, witness of his joys and sufferings, his exaltations and depressions, an instrument that was no mere mechanical thing but a part of himself, a part he could speak to and which in turn could answer the cry of his heart'.[61] Marcel Brion's flowery description of the composer's close relationship with the keyboard – and with his music for it – fails on confronting the late piano pieces. The pages of *Gesänge der Frühe*, according to Brion, breathe a melancholy 'fraught with a terrible, uncanny presentiment'. That sense of foreboding seems to be felt by listeners most acutely as a kind of emotional distance; the piano no longer expresses 'the cry of Schumann's heart' but drains it. The instrument becomes a mechanical thing once more, as encapsulated by Wasielewski's description of the composer flailing at the keyboard like a malfunctioning machine, or Joachim's report that towards the end he had visibly deteriorated both physically and mentally: 'In feverish excitement he leafed through his earlier compositions, reproducing them in truncated form with trembling hands on the keyboard – heart- and ear-rending!'[62]

And yet: in a letter to Clara dated 19 October 1854, Schumann wrote 'Sometimes I wish you could hear me playing fantasies at the piano; those are my loveliest hours'.[63] He would occasionally play four-hand piano music with Brahms when he visited Endenich, and asked for scores to be sent him, including Brahms's op. 9 Variations (on a theme from *Bunte Blätter*) and the manuscripts of *Gesänge der Frühe* and the E flat major theme and variations. Later in the nineteenth century, another famous asylum patient, Daniel Paul Schreber, described the palliative effect of playing the piano:

During piano-playing the nonsensical twaddle of the voices which talk to me is drowned. Next to physical exercises it is one of the most efficient forms of the so-called not-thinking-of-anything-thought . . . Every attempt at 'representing' me by the 'creation of a false feeling' and suchlike is doomed to end in failure because of the real feeling one can put into piano playing.[64]

We have no idea if Schumann felt the same way; from anecdotes such as those surrounding the genesis of the *Letzter Gedanke* and his carers' unwillingness to overexcite him with musical stimuli it seems more likely that music amplified his hallucinations rather than drowned them.[65] Dr Richarz's log for 8 May 1855, for example, describes Schumann as having spent almost two hours at the piano, playing wildly and confusedly ('sehr wild und wirre'), talking loudly throughout.[66] After the evening meal he struggled against the attendant's attempts to take him to his room, threatening him with a chair. On 19 May he could only stay a short time at the piano: his whole body was trembling and vibrating.[67] His night was disturbed; sleeplessness and piano playing seem to have gone hand in hand. A particularly restless night on 10 October – with Schumann apparently shouting and screaming – led to the temporary confiscation of all his papers, books and writing materials.

The next year, Schumann is recorded as having composed some fugues. On 17 January 1856 he wanted to play something on the piano, and to revisit the fugue he had composed two days earlier. That night he was sleepless but not loudly disruptive.[68] Schumann's turn to counterpoint is often assumed to have been a means for him to 'keep demons at bay'.[69] Fugue's technical challenges might have allowed him to focus his musical thoughts.[70] He had studied counterpoint with Heinrich Dorn in the early 1830s, and later that decade devoted much time to the music of J. S. Bach (especially the Art of Fugue and the Well-Tempered Clavier), describing it as his daily bread and Bible.[71] While these studies had some influence over his composition, he did not write any substantial original fugues until 1845, when he was recovering from a major nervous breakdown. He then returned to his study of Bach (in April also delving into Cherubini's 1835 treatise *Cours de contrepoint et de fugue*), and produced *Sechs Studien* for pedal piano (op. 56), *Vier Fugen* (op. 72), and *Sechs Fugen* for organ on the name of Bach (op. 60).[72] Eric Jensen explains:

In no way do these works give an indication of Schumann's mental turmoil. But in a fragile mental state, he must have thought it helpful as a composer to be obliged to follow the numerous rules of counterpoint required by the style he had selected; in that sense, it was as if self-imposed boundaries had been erected, and some of the freedom of thought that appeared to frighten him at the time had been removed.[73]

Aside from being a means to achieve some kind of psychological and emotional equilibrium and – probably more important – to find a way back into composition, Schumann's fugal works from 1845 also indicate his 'new manner' of 'inventing and working out everything in [his] head', already discussed in previous chapters.[74] The chromatic complexity of the *Vier Fugen* required deliberation rather than the improvisation he had relied on for his earlier piano works, something acknowledged in Schumann's description of them as 'character pieces, only in strict form'.[75] Although the op. 72 fugues were completed within a month, suggesting that he had rediscovered his usual intense rate of production, the op. 60 fugues took much longer, in part because their composition was interrupted by illness and other projects (the Piano Concerto and arranging concerts), but also because he spent much longer revising them.

Schumann claimed that the op. 60 fugues would 'long outlive my other works'.[76] Posterity has not proved him right. Many commentators have heard them as forecasting the onset of his late style, with its disintegrative tendencies.[77] They are described as monotonous and impersonal, characteristics detected more often as symptoms of late style. The notion that Schumann's deterioration might have begun as early as 1845 probably results from factors already touched on in this book, such as an awareness that he had suffered a nervous breakdown not long before the fugues were composed. But it might also have to do with received ideas about the nature of counterpoint itself.

David Yearsley claims modern writers typically describe Bach's strict contrapuntal music as 'abstract, recherché, arcane, speculative'.[78] He gives the example of canon: considered 'a closed musical system without reference beyond itself'; the more complex the canon the more self-contained it is thought to be, Yearsley points out, while saying that such music is 'abstract' becomes another way of saying that it is 'devoid of broader meaning'. Yearsley's project is to prove that counterpoint was in fact 'saturated with meaning' in Bach's day. Perhaps surprisingly, a similar intention lies behind recent writings on counterpoint in Beethoven, with Stephen Rumph reading the use of 'archaic counterpoint' in op. 131 as 'an alternative to the heroic style and [its] disruptive social forces', claiming:

A stylistic and ideological fissure runs down the center of the late style that no analysis can normalize or integrate out of existence. Nor will it do to take Adorno's line and allegorize the contrapuntal obstructions as scars of disillusionment with the Restoration, as 'objective' intrusions into the subjective bourgeois consciousness . . . By 1826 counterpoint had become as fully 'integrated' or 'normalized' within Beethoven's subjective style as sonata form or motivic development.[79]

A comparable disavowal of aesthetic autonomy is found in Robert Hatten's theory of musical gesture, which proposes that fugues can embody 'plenitude as blissful expressive fulfillment'.[80] Thus Beethoven's interest in fugue as demonstrated in op. 131, 'Pleni sunt coeli' from the *Missa solemnis*, the *Hammerklavier* finale and the culmination of the *Diabelli* Variations may 'have been stimulated in part by its potential for thematic saturation', harbouring 'plenitude as its ultimate goal'.[81] The seemingly formal procedures of these fugues, 'far from being abstractly conceived, have arguable expressive or dramatic motivations', a '"poetic content" Beethoven sought to infuse into his appropriation of Baroque imitative textures and formal processes . . . This aspect of creativity in Beethoven's late style may be understood as a further dramatization and elaboration of what was already present in Bach's own dramatic and rhetorical invention – the move toward plenitude as textural, rhythmic, registral, thematic, and ultimately expressive fulfillment'.[82]

'Most of Bach's fugues are character pieces of the highest kind', Schumann wrote in a famous review of 1838.[83] In light of Yearsley's, Rumph's and Hatten's advocacy of subjectivity and 'poetic content' in fugues by Bach and Beethoven, it seems reasonable to assume that a similar case might be made for Schumann. Certainly Daverio bases his argument in favour of the fugues on their synthesis of dissimilar elements: 'unabashed lyricism, romantic wistfulness, Jean-Paulian rhapsodizing, Baroque effect, and Bachian counterpoint'.[84] Criticism of them, he points out, relies on Brendel's division of Schumann's output into subjective and objective phases, a divide of particular relevance because they were written at the inception of the composer's 'new manner of composing'. The 'objective' aspect of counterpoint indicated, to some, an ultra-rational, impersonal quality in the music, thought to result from a dimming of Schumann's imaginative impulses.

As mentioned with regard to the Third Symphony, the use of counterpoint was considered a symptom of the composer's late style: an excessive intellectualism that signalled Schumann's detachment from the world. With the final published fugues, the *Sieben Clavierstücke in Fughettenform* (op. 126), composed in late May 1853, the association between counterpoint and some kind of aphasia becomes still more pronounced. If these are character pieces they are, as Schumann explained to the publisher Arnold, mostly melancholy.[85] In keeping with the motivic repetition of other late works, the fugal subject is focused on to an unusual degree. For example, the descending chromatic subject of the second fughetta, in D minor, appears in each of its twenty-six bars with the exception of bars 9–10, which implies an inversion of the subject as a brief episode. The phrases are consistently two bars long, apart from the version of the subject presented in bars 19–20 which is stretched by half a bar, on the heels of which commences a brief stretto. The longer fughettas (especially no. 3) include a little more episodic material but not as much as might be expected. With the exception of no. 4, whose subject features a spiky falling seventh, and the perpetual semiquaver triplets of no. 6, the subjects of the fugue are gentle and meandering. For example, no. 1 only breaks from its lilting compound rhythm in bars 39–40, and rather than pursuing the climactic potential of the hemiola, draws back into a *piano* presentation of the subject; while this may be in the tonic, as in Schumann's bathetic treatment of recapitulations in sonata forms, its sense of arrival is softened by being harmonized by a 6/4 chord. The fugue seems to drift away at the end, rather than attaining the 'blissful expressive fulfillment' Hatten describes, as do nos. 3 and 7.

Example 6:8   Fugue, op. 126, no. 5, bb. 29–33

The fifth fughetta, in A minor, is considered by Reinhard Kapp to be the most intimate ('der innigsten Stücke'). Tellingly, the only real dynamic marking is *diminuendo*, with the exception of a few swells marked on the crotchet-two-quaver figure of the countersubject. The subject's languorous quality is partly achieved by its use of rests; a feature picked up on by the countersubject, based only on its descending head motif. The voices move primarily in parallel sixths and thirds, further cushioning the texture. There is as much concentration on the subject as in no. 2, but the phrases here are overlapped and fragmented a little more, in part because of the close relationship with the countersubject. In bar 29, however, a new idea emerges: the left hand's presentation of the subject in parallel thirds is embellished in the treble by descending quaver triplets (again marked *diminuendo*), followed by a brief ascending semiquaver figure (Example 6:8). These four bars are repeated in the dominant and then in varied form over a tonic pedal. Particularly in the context of these fugues, with their intense focus on the subject, the introduction of the triplets feels almost improvisatory. It is a moment when we seem to catch a glimpse of the composer at the keyboard, rather than working out the fugue in his head.

Little survives of the music Schumann wrote in the asylum, beyond a harmonization of the chorale *Wenn mein Stündlein vorhanden ist*. Much of it may have been burned by the composer along with various letters (as Richarz reports), or destroyed by family or friends. There is little point trying to guess what it may have been like: indeed, to do so seems comparable to Schumann's attempt to raise the spirit of Beethoven through his experiments at the séance. From the examples discussed in this and the preceding chapters, though, we might draw a few conclusions about the constitution of Schumann's late style. Such a list would include a tendency to focus on particular motives, which are often defined by rhythm, and a continuing predilection for sequences. The more extreme intervallic leaps and declamatory style of the vocal and chamber music (criticized as mannerism by some contemporaries) should be included, as might the clearer delineation of form. Were this latter point to be characterized as a kind of 'objectivism' or 'classicism' we might point to its contrary; to the continued use of 6/4 chords to undercut moments of recapitulation and to those occasional, surprising dissonant passages, moments of chromatic vertigo amidst the undulating landscape of mediant relationships between sections and movements.

On referring to 'late Schumann', however, we rarely have such a list in mind; instead we think of more intangible aspects, such as a sense of emotional and expressive detachment, of creative failure. The extent to which this is an immediate response to the music or whether it is informed by awareness of his biography is, as I hope this book has shown, debatable. We will probably never extricate our understanding of Schumann's music from the various images associated with his illness and incarceration – and I refer here to all his works, not simply those dating from his final years. In part this is because he was a Romantic artist, who often deliberately connected art to life. However strongly we argue for Schumann's engagement with mid-century society, culture and politics, there remains a sense that he outlived his time; that his incarceration might represent not so much his withdrawal from the world as the world's desire to distance itself from him, and his generation's concerns.

In his poem imagining Hölderlin's state of mind in the asylum, Michael Hamburger suggests he knew the world around him had changed: 'Diotima is dead. Where are the heroes / And my pulsing song?' Bereft of past glories, he is left to the world of his imagination:

No caged old panther I,
Pacing my madness.
These muttered words
Are gates, not bars,
Where only I can pass.

We would do well to take Hamburger's poem as a model for conceiving the relationship between Schumann's late music and his illness. By making too close a connection, we risk incarcerating the composer a second time, by putting words around his music, making themes and motives bars rather than gates. Perhaps the obsession with repetition and so on is ours, rather than his. We look to his music to try to find the man within, frustrated that we cannot sense the presence of Diotima, heroes or sometimes even pulsing song. Maybe that is to pace our madness.

Notes

1. Michael Hamburger, 'Hölderlin. Tübingen, December 1842', *Collected Poems 1941–94* (London: Anvil Press, 1995).
2. Thoreau, *Walden* (Boston, Mass.: Ticnor and Fields, 1854).
3. On Fantin-Latour's liking for Schumann see Frank Gibson, *The Art of Henri Fantin-Latour: His Life and Work* (London: Drane's, 1924), pp. 184–5.
4. See Roland Barthes, 'Rasch', *The Responsibility of Forms*, trans. Richard Howard (Berkeley: University of California Press); and Gerhard Dietel, *'Eine neue poetischer Zeit': Musikanschauung und stilistische Tendenzen im Klavierwerk Robert Schumanns* (Kassel, 1989), pp. 296–390.
5. Michael P. Steinberg, 'Schumann's Homelessness', *Schumann and his World*, ed. R. Larry Todd (Princeton, 1994), p. 67; and *Listening to Reason*, p. 124.
6. Erika Reiman, *Robert Schumann and the Novels of Jean Paul*, p. 8.
7. Daverio, *Robert Schumann*, p. 479.
8. Anthony Newcomb, 'Schumann and the marketplace: from butterflies to *Hausmusik*', *Nineteenth-Century Piano Music*, ed. R. Larry Todd (New York: Schirmer, 1990), pp. 258–9.
9. According to his project-book, eight pieces were drafted by 3 January 1849; 'Vogel als Prophet' was added on 6 January. See Eric Frederick Jensen, 'A new manuscript of Robert Schumann's *Waldszenen*, op. 82', *The Journal of Musicology* 7 (1989), 73.
10. Schumann seems to have given a manuscript of *Waldszenen* to its dedicatee, Annette Preusser, on 1 September 1850; the final version was not ready until 25 September, however. It was sent for engraving on 8 October and published in December.
11. Robert Schumann, *Gesammelte Schriften über Musik und Musiker* I (Leipzig: Breitkopf und Härtel, 1854), p. 40.
12. Eric Frederick Jensen, 'A New Manuscript', 77–8.
13. Jensen, 'A New Manuscript', 80.
14. David Ferris, *Schumann's Eichendorff Liederkreis and the Genre of the Romantic Cycle* (Oxford: Oxford University Press, 2000), pp. 106–7 and 139–40.
15. For more on the open-endedness of the earlier piano cycles see Laura Tunbridge, 'Schumann's piano music II: afterimages', *The Cambridge Companion to Schumann*, ed. Beate Perrey (Cambridge: Cambridge University Press, 2007).
16. For more on which see Daverio, *Crossing Paths*, pp. 125–54.
17. Christopher Alan Reynolds, *Motives for Allusion: Context and Content in Nineteenth-Century Music* (Cambridge, Mass.: Harvard University Press, 2003), pp. 77–82.
18. Eichendorff's motto, of course, is sung repeatedly as a warning signal by the titular bird of Rimsky-Korsakov's opera *The Golden Cockerel*.

19. Eva Geulen, '1848, October 11: tales of a collector', *A New History of German Literature*, ed. David E. Wellbery (Cambridge, Mass.: The Belknap Press, 2004), pp. 587–92.

20. Robert Haven Schauffler, *Florestan: The Life and Works of Robert Schumann* (New York: Henry Holt and Co., 1945), p. 479.

21. For more on which see Isabel Eicker, *Kinderstücke: an Kinder adressierte und über das Thema der Kindheit komponierte Alben in der Klavierliteratur des 19. Jahrhunderts* (Kassel: Gustav Bosse, 1995).

22. Roe-Min Kok, 'Negotiating children's music: new evidence for Schumann's "charming" late style'. I am grateful to Professor Kok for sharing this paper with me before publication.

23. On the movement's motivic treatment see Kok, 'Negotiating children's music', and Michael Struck, *Die umstrittenden späten Instrumentalwerke Schumanns*, pp. 126–7.

24. The sense that the late music was somehow independent of its creator is suggested by Marcel Brion, who asks: 'Who composed it then? Some diabolic projection of himself, some chimerical Doppelgänger, at any rate a stranger. This was his true alienation – that his music, which had hitherto been one with himself, now belonged to another.' *Schumann and the Romantic Age*, p. 352.

25. *Kinderball* was even published for solo piano by Breitkopf und Härtel in 1863 without identifying the composer. See Joachim Draheim, 'Kritischer Bericht', *Robert Schumann: Neue Ausgabe sämtlicher Werke*, Serie III:2, *Werke für Klavier zu vier Händen*, ed. Joachim Draheim (Schott: Mainz, 2001), p. 448. Schauffler comments of *Kinderball* that after the opening piece it is all 'gay and pleasant; but who would ever dream that Schumann had written them?'; *Florestan*, p. 368.

26. Theodor W. Adorno, 'Beethoven's late style', *Beethoven: The Philosophy of Music: Fragments and Texts*, ed. Rolf Tiedemann, trans. Edmund Jephcott (Cambridge: Polity Press, 1998), p. 123.

27. The last of the op. 126 fugues, for instance, is noted by Daverio for its 'quiet lyricism and for a detached, almost abstract quality'. In *Robert Schumann*, p. 478.

28. Op. 73's titles are more descriptive, like op. 111 (Zart und mit Ausdruck; Lebhaft, leicht; Rasch und mit Feuer), while op. 88 includes Romanze, Humoreske, Duett, Finale (im Marschtempo). On the significance of op. 17's movement titles see Nicholas Marston, *Schumann's Fantasie, op. 17* (Cambridge: Cambridge University Press, 1992).

29. Franz Brendel, *Schumann and his World*, p. 323.

30. Schumann's repetition of E flat in the opening two bars of the movement pre-echoes the strangely static harmony at the beginning of the *Letzter Gedanke*. Despite there not being an A flat in the first chord of bar 2, we hear it as being held over from the upbeat.

31. My thanks to Stephen Hinton and Carlo Caballero for suggesting both the similarity to the Schubert Impromptus, and the different characters in the sections of the *Fantasiestücke*.

32. Robert Schumann, 'Aus Franz Schuberts Nachlaß', *Neue Zeitschrift für Musik* (5 June 1838), reprinted in *Gesammelte Schriften* I, pp. 330–1. The translation is by Richard Kramer, *19th-Century Music* (1980), p. 198.

33. Gilles Deleuze and Félix Guattari, *A Thousand Plateaus: Capitalism and Schizophrenia*, trans. Brian Massumi (London, New York: Continuum, 1987), '1837: Of the Refrain', pp. 342–86; here pp. 343–4.

34. Deleuze and Guattari, *A Thousand Plateaus*, p. 349.

35. Deleuze and Guattari, *A Thousand Plateaus*, p. 385.

36. Deleuze and Guattari, *A Thousand Plateaus*, p. 386.

37. For more on images of Schumann in films and fiction, see Laura Tunbridge, 'Schumann as Manfred', *Musical Quarterly* 87:3 (2004), 546–69.

38. Another contemporary incarcerated poet in search of a lost imaginary love was John Clare, who believed he had two wives; the first, Patty, was real, the second – Mary Joyce – was not, having died unmarried in 1838. See Jonathan Bate, *John Clare: A Biography* (London: Picador, 2003), pp. 435–6 and 456–8.

39. The choral sonority of the first piece is emphasized by Daverio in 'Madness or Prophecy? Schumann's *Gesänge der Frühe*, op. 133', *Nineteenth-Century Piano Music: Essays in Performance and Analysis*, ed. David Witten (New York: Garland, 1997), pp. 187–204.

40. Markus Waldura, 'Zitate vokaler Frühgesänge in Schumanns *Gesänge der Frühe*, op. 133: Überlegungen zur Deutung eines irritierenden Titels', *Schumann in Düsseldorf: Werke – Texte – Interpretationen*, ed. Bernhard R. Appel (Mainz: Schott, 1993), pp. 37–54; here 41.

41. John Daverio, 'Madness or Prophecy?', p. 200; and Theodor W. Adorno, *Mahler: A Musical Physiognomy*, trans. Edmund Jephcott (Chicago: Chicago University Press, 1991).

42. David Ferris, '"Was will dieses Grau'n bedeuten?": Schumann's "Zwielicht" and Daverio's "Incomprehensibility Topos"', *Journal of Musicology* 22:1 (2005), 131–53; here 140.

43. Ferris, 'Schumann's "Zwielicht"', 153.

44. *Die Natur der Harmonik und der Metrik* (Leipzig: Breitkopf und Härtel, 1853).

45. On Brahms's piece see Michael Struck, 'Beziehungs-Probleme: Zum Verhältnis der Komponisten Schumann und Brahms, dargestellt am Beispiel von Violinsonaten', *Schumann Forschungen, Band 7: 'Neue Bahnen'. Robert Schumann und seine musikalischen Zeitgenossen. Bericht über das 6. Internationale Schumann-Symposion am 5. und 6. Juni 1997 im Rahmen des 6. Schumann-Festes, Düsseldorf*, ed. Bernhard R. Appel (Mainz: Schott, 2002), pp. 294–327, here pp. 297–301.

46. Of course Schiller's poem is the famous eulogy to the founding of a great bell mentioned in the previous chapter, a model of classicism with which Schumann's poems about the great bell tower to Ivan Velikii in St Petersburg seem to have been at odds.

47. Roland Barthes, *Camera Lucida: Reflections on Photography*, trans. Richard Howard (London: Vintage, 1981), p. 70.

48. As Diana Knight and Margaret Olin have recently demonstrated, the described photograph resembles that included in Walter Benjamin's 'A short history of photography' of Franz Kafka aged six. Diana Knight, *Barthes and Utopia: Space, Travel, Writing* (Oxford: Oxford University Press, 1997), pp. 265–6; and Margaret Olin, 'Touching photographs: Roland Barthes's "mistaken identification"', *Representations* 80 (2002), 99–118.

49. Olin, 'Touching photographs', 112.

50. Sometimes arguments for the sharing of material between movements become too broad to be meaningful; for example, Daverio considers the extended plagal cadences at the end of movements 4 and 5 to be unifying forces.

51. On arabesques in Schumann's earlier music see John Daverio, '"Im Legendenton" and Friedrich Schlegel's *Arabeske*', *19th-Century Music* 11 (1987), 150–63; and Anthony Newcomb 'Schumann and eighteenth-century narrative strategies', *19th-Century Music* 11 (1987), 164–74.

52. Harald Krebs, *Fantasy Pieces: Metrical Dissonance in the Music of Robert Schumann* (Oxford, 1997), pp. 249–52. The notion that Schumann's use of metrical displacement was connected to his mental illness was put forward by Dieter Schnebel, 'Rückungen – Ver-rückungen', *Musik-Konzepte, Sonderband Robert Schumann I* (1981), pp. 4–89.

53. Krebs draws the utterances of Florestan and Eusebius from texts Schumann set in a metrically dissonant manner.

54. See Steinberg, note 5 and Barthes, note 4.

55. Susan McClary, 'Pitches, expression, ideology: an exercise in mediation', *Enclitic* 7 (1983), 76–86.

56. Charles Fisk, *Returning Cycles: Contexts for the Interpretation of Schubert's Impromptus and Last Sonatas* (Berkeley: University of California Press, 2001), pp. 145 and 159. On Schumann's response to the op. 142 Impromptus see John Daverio, 'The Gestus of Remembering: Schumann's Critique of Schubert's Impromptus, D. 935', *Crossing Paths: Schubert, Schumann, and Brahms* (Oxford: Oxford University Press, 2002), pp. 47–62.

57. See Scott Burnham, 'Schubert and the sound of memory', *Musical Quarterly* 84 (2000), 655–63.

58. Eduard Hanslick, 'Robert Schumann in Endenich (1899)', trans. Susan Gillespie, *Schumann and his World*, ed. R. Larry Todd (Princeton: Princeton University Press, 1994), p. 271.

59. The theme appears in series 14, no. 9 of *Robert Schumann's Werke*, ed. Clara Schumann (Leipzig, 1893); the first edition of the complete set of variations was issued by Karl Geiringer.

60. See Oliver Neighbour, 'Brahms and Schumann: two opus nines and beyond', *19th-Century Music* 7:3 (1984), 266–70; and Elaine Sisman, 'Brahms and the Variation Canon', *19th-Century Music* 14:2 (1990), 132–53. Daverio compares

the treatment of the melody as 'a migrating cantus firmus' to the Impromptus, op. 5; *Robert Schumann*, p. 479.

61. Marcel Brion, *Schumann and the Romantic Age*, trans. Geoffrey Sainsbury (London: Collins, 1956), p. 344.

62. Quoted in Hanslick, 'Schumann at Endenich', p. 278.

63. Quoted in Hanslick, 'Schumann at Endenich', p. 275.

64. Daniel Paul Schreber, *Memoirs of a Nervous Illness*, trans. and ed. Ida Macalpine and Richard A. Hunter (New York: New York Review of Books, 2000), pp. xxii and 158.

65. The perils of musical interpretation with regard to psychological diagnosis are encapsulated by Hanslick, who explains that Schumann's description of Brahms's third Ballade (op.10) in B minor as 'demonic' in a letter of 6 January 1855 made those around him anxious, 'and the plan to have Schumann released from the sanatorium was abandoned'. After all, Clara saw in the music 'angels drifting through the blue sky'. No matter that Brahms, according to Hanslick, 'was more inclined toward Schumann's point of view concerning the nature of the piece'! 'Robert Schumann in Endenich', pp. 272 and 277.

66. 'Auszüge aus Dr Richarz Krankentagbuch 1856', Ernst Burger, *Robert Schumann: Eine Lebenschronik in Bildern und Dokumenten, Robert Schumann: Neue Ausgabe sämtlicher Werke* (Mainz: Schott, 1998), VIII:1, p. 331.

67. *Schumann in Endenich (1854–1856): Krankenakten, Briefzeugnisse und zeitgenössische Berichte*, ed. Bernhard R. Appel (Mainz: Schott, 2006), p. 282.

68. Ernst Burger, *Robert Schumann: Eine Lebenschronik*, p. 332.

69. Brion, *Schumann and the Romantic Age*, p. 303.

70. A comparable argument has been made to explain Schubert's counterpoint studies with Simon Sechter in the last year of his life; according to Edward T. Cone this was an attempt on Schubert's part to allay his technical insecurities as a composer. See 'Schubert's Beethoven', *Musical Quarterly* 56 (1970), 787.

71. Letter from Clara Schumann and Robert Schumann, *Briefwechsel: Kritische Gesamtausgabe*, ed. Eva Weissweiler (Frankfurt am Main, 1984), I, p. 126; and Dorn, 5 september 1839, *Briefe. Neue Folge*, p. 171.

72. Schumann's edition of Cherubini's 1835 treatise *Cours de contrepoint et de fugue* is reprinted in the *Neue Ausgabe sämtlicher Werke, Serie 7: Gruppe 3, Band 5: Studien zur Kontrapunktlehre* (Mainz: Schott, 2003).

73. Jensen, *Schumann*, p. 222.

74. See entry 1846 *TB* II, p. 402.

75. Letter 19 November 1849, *Briefe. Neue Folge*, pp. 274–5.

76. Letter to Friedrich Whistling, March 1846, *Briefe. Neue Folge*, p. 446.

77. Georg Dadelsen, 'Schumann und die Musik Bachs', *Archiv für Musikwissenschaft* 14 (1957), 58–9; Stephen Walsh, 'Schumann and the Organ', pp. 724–43; and Schnebel, 'Rückungen – Ver-rückungen', pp. 71–2.

78. David Yearsley, *Bach and the Meanings of Counterpoint* (Cambridge: Cambridge University Press, 2002), p. xiii.

79. Stephen Rumph, *Beethoven after Napoleon*, pp. 154–5.

80. Robert Hatten, *Interpreting Musical Gestures, Topics, and Tropes* (Bloomington: Indiana University Press, 2004), p. 249.

81. Robert Hatten, *Interpreting Musical Gestures*, pp. 250 and 255.

82. Hatten, *Interpreting Musical Gestures*, p. 266.

83. Schumann, *Gesammelte Schriften*, I, p. 354.

84. Daverio, *Robert Schumann*, p. 310.

85. Letter of 24 February 1853; in Wolfgang Boetticher, 'Robert Schumann und seine Verleger', *Musik und Verlag: Karl Vötterie zum 65. Geburtstag*, ed. R. Baum and W. Rehm (Kassel: Bärenreiter, 1968), p. 174.

Appendix:[1] Chronology of Schumann's compositions 1850–1856

Date of composition		Date of publication	First performance
1850			
August	Lieder und Gesänge, op. 127 no. 4	1.1854, Paul, Dresden	
	Sechs Gedichte von N. Lenau und Requiem, op. 90	12.1850, Kistner, Leipzig	
October	Neujahrslied, op. 144 (orchestration completed)	8.1854, Breitkopf und Härtel, Leipzig	11.1.1851, Düsseldorf
	Cello Concerto, op. 129	1851, Simrock, Bonn	9.6.1860, Leipzig
November	Third Symphony, op. 97 (completed December)		
December	Spreu published as Bunte Blätter, op. 99 and Albumblätter, op. 124 (see also August 1853)		
	Overture to Schiller's Braut von Messina, op. 100 (sketched)	1851, Arnold, Elberfeld	
1851			
January	Overture to Schiller's Braut von Messina, op. 100 (orchestrated)		13.3.1851, Düsseldorf
	Sechs Gesänge, op. 107, nos. 1–3, 6	6.1851, no. 3, Arnz and Co., Düsseldorf; Complete set 8.1852, Luckhardt, Kassel	
	Fünf heitere Gesänge, op. 125, no. 3	3.1853, Verlag der Heinrichshofen'schen Musikalien-Handlung, Magdeburg	
March	Overture to Shakespeare's Julius Caesar, op. 128	11.1854, Meyer/Litolff, Braunschweig	3.8.1852, Düsseldorf
	Märchenbilder, op. 113	7.1852, Luckhardt	19.3.1852, Leipzig (private)
April	Vier Husarenlieder von Nikolaus Lenau, op. 117	10.1852, Senff, Leipzig	
	Der Rose Pilgerfahrt, op. 112, version with piano	10.1852, Kistner	6.7.1851, Düsseldorf
	Der Königssohn, op. 116 (completed June)	7.1853, Whistling, Leipzig (piano)	6.5.1852, Düsseldorf

[1] Information taken from Margit McCorkle, 'Thematisch-Bibliographisches Werkverzeichnis, *Robert Schumann: Neue Ausgabe sämtlicher Werke* VIII:6 (Mainz: Schott, 2003).

May	*Romanzen und Balladen für Chorgesang*, op. 145, no. 3	2.1860, Arnold	
	Mädchenlieder von Elisabeth Kulmann für zwei Frauenstimmen, op. 103 (completed June)	10.1851, Kistner	
	Sieben Lieder von Elisabeth Kulmann, op. 104 (completed June)	10.1851, Kistner	
June	*Ball-Szenen*, op. 109 (piano, four hands)	11.1853, Schuberth, Hamburg, Leipzig, New York	
August	*Drei Fantasiestücke*, op. 111	7.1852, Peters, Leipzig	
September	*Drei Gedichte aus den Waldliedern von Pfarrius*, op. 119	5.1853, Nagel, Hanover	
	Sonata for Piano and Violin, op. 105	1.1852, Hofmeister, Leipzig	21.3.1852, Leipzig
October	Piano Trio no. 3, op. 110	10.1852, Breitkopf und Härtel, Leipzig	15.11.1851, Düsseldorf, private
November	Second Grand Sonata for violin and piano, op. 121 (completed November)	10.1853, Breitkopf und Härtel	15.11.1851, Düsseldorf, private
December	*Der Rose Pilgerfahrt*, op. 112, version with orchestra	12.1861, Kistner	
	Fourth Symphony, op. 120 (revision of 1841 D-minor Symphony)	1853, Breitkopf und Härtel	3.3.1853, Düsseldorf
	Overture to Goethe's *Hermann und Dorothea*, op. 136	3/5.1857, Rieter-Biedemann, Winterthur	
1852			
January	*Des Sängers Fluch*, op. 139 (polished October 1852)	12.1857, Arnold	30.10.1852, Düsseldorf, private
February	*Messe [Missa sacra]*, op. 147 (completed March; see also March 1853)	10.1862, Rieter-Biedemann (piano)	3.3.1853, Düsseldorf (Kyrie and Gloria)
April	*Requiem*, op. 148 (completed May)	3.1864, Rieter-Biedemann	
May	*Verzweifle nicht im Schmerzensthal*, op. 93, motet for double chorus and orchestra	1887, Breitkopf und Härtel	

(*cont.*)

Date of composition		Date of publication	First performance
June	*Die Flüchtlinge*, op. 122, no. 2 (declamation and piano)	11.1853, Senff, Leipzig	
	Vom Pagen und der Königstochter, op. 140 (completed September)	10.1857, Rieter-Biedemann, Winterthur	2.12.1852, Düsseldorf
July			
August			
September	*Gern macht' ich dir heute, Liedchen von Marie und Papa*		
October			
November			
December	*Gedichte der Königin Maria Stuart*, op. 135	7?1855, Siegel, Leipzig	
	Piano accompaniments to Bach, Sonatas and Partitas for unaccompanied violin (completed February 1853), WoO 8	12.1853, Breitkopf und Härtel	
1853			
January			
February	*Das Glück von Edenhall*, op. 143 (completed March)	2.1860, Rieter-Biedemann	23.10.1854, Leipzig
March	Piano accompaniments to Bach, Suites for unaccompanied cello (completed April)	1985 (Only Suite 3, BWV 1009)	
April	*Fest-Ouvertüre* on the *Rheinweinlied*, op. 123	4 hand piano 53, Simrock	17.5.1853, Düsseldorf
May	*Sieben Clavierstücke in Fughettenform*, op. 126 (completed June)	5.1854, Arnold	
June	*Drei Clavier-Sonaten für die Jugend*, op. 118	12?1853, Schuberth	

	Work	Publication	Premiere
August	*Faust* Overture	11.1858, Friedlaender, Berlin	13 January 1862 (complete)
	Die Orange und Myrthe hier (vocal quartet and piano)	1942, *The Musical Quarterly*	
	Albumblätter, op. 124 (put 'in order')	12.1853, Arnold	
	Concert-Allegro mit Introduction, op. 134 (piano and orchestra)	7.1855, Senff	26 November 1853, Utrecht
September	*Phantasie*, op. 131 (violin and orchestra)	6.1854, Kistner	
	'Ballade vom Haideknaben', op. 122, no. 1 (declamation and piano)	11.1853, Senff	27.10.1853, Düsseldorf
	Kinderball. Sechs leichte Tanzstücke, op. 130 (piano duet)	3.1854, Breitkopf und Härtel	
	Violin Concerto, WoO 23 (completed October)	1937, Schott, Mainz	
October	*Märchenerzählungen*, op. 132	3.1854, Breitkopf und Härtel	28/30.10.1853, Düsseldorf (private)
	Gesänge der Frühe, op. 133	11.1855, Arnold	
	Piano accompaniments to Paganini's 24 Caprices for solo violin (continued 1855)	1941, Peters, Leipzig (accompaniment to no. 24 not extant)	
	Intermezzo and *Finale* of *F. A. E. Sonata* for Violin and Piano, WoO 22	1935, Schott, Mainz	
	Third Sonata for Violin and Piano (WoO 27)	1956, Schott, Mainz	
	Fünf Romanzen for cello and piano (lost)		
November			
December			
1854			
January			
February	*Thema mit Variationen für das Pianoforte* (WoO 24)	2001, Schott, Mainz	

Bibliography

Abbate, Carolyn, *Unsung Voices: Opera and Musical Narrative in the Nineteenth Century* (Princeton: Princeton University Press, 1991).

—*In Search of Opera* (Princeton: Princeton University Press, 2001).

Adorno, Theodor Wiesengrund, *Beethoven: The Philosophy of Music: Fragments and Texts*, trans. Edmund Jephcott, ed. Rolf Tiedemann (Cambridge: Polity Press, 1998).

—*Notes on Literature*, trans. Sherry Weber Nicholson (New York: Columbia University Press, 1992).

—*The Adorno Reader*, ed. Brian O'Conner (Oxford: Blackwells, 2000).

—'Richard Strauss at 60', trans. Susan Gillespie, *Strauss and his World*, ed. Bryan Gilliam (Princeton: Princeton University Press, 1992), pp. 406–16.

Appel, Bernhard R., ed. *Schumann in Düsseldorf: Werke-Texte-Interpretationen* (Mainz: Schott, 1993).

—*Robert Schumann in Endenich (1854–1856): Krankenakten, Briefzeugnisse und Zeitgenössische Berichte* (Mainz: Schott, 2006).

—'"Actually, taken directly from family life": Robert Schumann's *Album für die Jugend*', trans. John Michael Cooper, *Schumann and his World*, ed. R. Larry Todd (Princeton: Princeton University Press, 1994).

—'"Mehr Malerei als Ausdruck der Empfindung" – Illustrierende uns illustrierte Musik im Düsseldorf des 19. Jahrhunderts', *Akademie und Musik: Erscheinungen und Wirkungen des Akademiegedankens in Kultur-und Musikgeschichte-Institutionen, Veranstaltungen, Schriften. Festschrift für Werner Braun zum 65. Geburtstag*, ed. Wolf Frobenius, Nicole Schwindt-Gross and Thomas Sick (Saarbrücken: Saarbrücken Druckerei, 1993), pp. 255–68.

Applegate, Celia, *Bach in Berlin: Nation and Culture in Mendelssohn's Revival of the St Matthew Passion* (Ithaca: Cornell University Press, 2005).

Barthes, Roland, *Camera lucida: Reflections on Photography*, trans. Richard Howard (London: Vintage, 1981).

Baudrillard, Jean, *The System of Objects*, trans. James Benedict (London: Verso, 1996).

—'The system of collecting', trans. Roger Cardinal, *The Cultures of Collecting*, ed. John Elsner and Roger Cardinal (London: Reaktion Books, 1994), pp. 7–24.

Beller-McKenna, Daniel, *Brahms and the German Spirit* (Cambridge, Mass.: Harvard University Press, 2004).

—'Distance and disembodiment: harps, horns, and the requiem idea in Schumann and Brahms', *Journal of Musicology* 22:1 (2005), 47–89.

Bellman, Jonathan, '*Aus alten Märchen:* the chivalric style of Schumann and Brahms', *Journal of Musicology* 13 (1995), 117–35.

Benjamin, Walter, *Charles Baudelaire: A Lyric Poet in the Era of High Capitalism*, trans. Harry Zohn (London: Verso, 1983).

Bettelheim, Bruno, *The Uses of Enchantment: The Meaning and Importance of Fairy Tales* (New York: Knopf, 1976).

Botstein, Leon, 'History, rhetoric, and the self: Robert Schumann and music making in German-speaking Europe, 1800–1860', *Schumann and his World*, ed. R. Larry Todd (Princeton: Princeton University Press, 1994), pp. 3–47.

Bowie, Andrew, *Aesthetics and Subjectivity from Kant to Nietzsche* (Manchester: Manchester University Press, 2003).

Johannes Brahms im Briefwechsel mit J. O. Grimm, ed. Richard Barth (Tutzing: Schneider, 1974).

Brion, Marcel, *Schumann and the Romantic Age*, trans. Geoffrey Sainsbury (London: Collins, 1956).

Brodbeck, David, 'The Joachim-Brahms Counterpoint Exchange; or Robert, Clara, and "The Best Harmony Between Jos. and Joh."', *Brahms Studies* vol. 1, ed. David Brodbeck (Lincoln and London: University of Nebraska Press, 1994), pp. 30–88.

Burger, Ernst, *Robert Schumann: Eine Lebenschronik in Bildern und Dokumenten, Robert Schumann: Neue Ausgabe sämtlicher Werke* (Mainz: Schott, 1998).

—'Schubert and the Sound of Memory', *Musical Quarterly* 84 (2000), 655–63.

Burnham, Scott, 'Landscape as Music, Landscape as Truth: Schubert and the Burden of Repetition', *19th-Century Music* 29 (2005).

Cavell, Stanley, *Philosophy the Day after Tomorrow* (Cambridge, Mass.: Belknap Press, Harvard University Press, 2005).

Clare, John, *Selected Poems*, ed. Jonathan Bate (London: Faber and Faber, 2003).

Cone, Edward T., *The Composer's Voice* (Berkeley: University of California Press, 1974).

Constantine, David, *Hölderlin* (Oxford: Clarendon Press, 1988).

Crane, Susan M., *Collecting and Historical Consciousness in Early Nineteenth-Century Germany* (Ithaca: Cornell University Press, 2000).

Dadelsen, Georg, 'Schumann und die Musik Bachs', *Archiv für Musikwissenschaft* 14 (1957), 46–59.

Dahlhaus, Carl, *Nineteenth-Century Music*, trans. Bradford J. Robinson (Berkeley: University of California Press, 1989).

—'Bach und der romantische Kontrapunkt', *Musica* 43 (1989), 10–22.

Daverio, John, *Robert Schumann: Herald of a 'New Poetic Age'* (Oxford: Oxford University Press, 1997).

—*Crossing Paths: Schubert, Schumann, and Brahms* (Oxford and New York: Oxford University Press, 2002).

—'The *Wechsel der Töne* in Brahms's *Schicksalslied*', *Journal of the American Musicological Society* 46 (1993), 97–104.

—'Schumann's "new genre for the concert hall"', *Schumann and his World*, ed. R. Larry Todd (Princeton: Princeton University Press, 1994), pp. 129–55.

—'Sounds without the gate: Schumann and the Dresden revolution', *Il saggiatore musicale* 4 (1997), 87–112.

—'Schumann's Ossianic Manner', *19th-Century Music* 21 (Spring 1998), 247–73.

—'"Beautiful and abstruse conversations": the chamber music of Robert Schumann', *Nineteenth-Century Chamber Music*, ed. Stephen E. Hefling (New York: Schirmer, 1998), pp. 208–41.

—'"One more beautiful memory of Schubert": Schumann's critique of the Impromptus, D. 935', *Musical Quarterly* 84 (2000), 604–18.

—*Einheit-Freiheit-Vaterland:* intimations of Utopia in Robert Schumann's late choral music', *Music and German national identity*, ed. Celia Applegate and Pamela Potter (Chicago: University of Chicago Press, 2002), pp. 59–77.

Davies, James Q., 'Julia's Gift: The Social Life of Scores, c. 1830', *Journal of the Royal Musical Association*, 131 (2006), 287–309.

Deleuze, Gilles, *Difference and Repetition*, trans. Paul Patton (London: Continuum, 1994).

—with Félix Guattari, *A Thousand Plateaus: Capitalism and Schizophrenia*, trans. Brian Massumi (London: Continuum, 1987).

de Man, Paul, *Blindness and Insight: Essays in the Rhetoric of Contemporary Criticism* (Minneapolis: University of Minnesota Press, 2nd edn. 1983).

Derrida, Jacques, *Archive Fever: A Freudian Impression*, ed. Eric Prenowitz (Chicago: University of Chicago Press, 1996).

Dietel, Gerhard, *'Eine neue poetischer Zeit': Musikanschauung und stilistische Tendenzen im Klavierwerk Robert Schumanns* (Kassel: Bärenreiter, 1989).

Donakowski, Conrad L., *A Muse for the Masses: Ritual and Music in an Age of Democratic Revolution* (Chicago: University of Chicago Press, 1972).

—'Bedeutung und Eigenwart der Maria Stuart Lieder', *Archiv für das Studium der neueren Sprachen und Literaturen* 214 (1977), 325–7.

Draheim, Joachim, 'Schumann und Shakespeare', *Neue Zeitschrift für Musik* 142 (1981), 237–47.

—'Robert Franz und Robert Schumann – Aspekte einer schwierigen Beziehung', *Robert Franz (1815–1892). Bericht über die wissenschaftliche Konferenz anläßlich seines 100. Todestages am 23 und 24 Oktober in Halle (Salle)* (Halle: HändelHaus, 1993), pp. 163–87.

Dunsby, Jonathan, *Making Words Sing* (Cambridge: Cambridge University Press, 2004).

Edler, Arnfried, *Robert Schumann und seine Zeit* (Laaber: Laaber Verlag, 1982).

—'Anmerkungen zu Struktur und Funktion von Schumanns Konzert-Allegro op. 134', *Schumann in Düsseldorf: Werke-Texte-Interpretationen* (Mainz: Schott, 1993), pp. 417–36.

Eicker, Isabel, *Kinderstücke: an Kinder adressierte und über das Thema der Kindheit komponierte Alben in der Klavierliteratur des 19. Jahrhunderts* (Kassel: Gustav Bosse, 1995).

Elkins, James, *Pictures and Tears: A History of People who have Cried in Front of Paintings* (New York: Routledge, 2004).

Ferris, David, *Schumann's Eichendorff 'Liederkreis' and the Genre of the Romantic Cycle* (Oxford: Oxford University Press, 2000).

—'Public performance and private understanding: Clara Wieck's concerts in Berlin', *Journal of the American Musicological Society* 56 (2003), 351–408.

—'Was will dieses Grau'n bedeuten?: Schumann's "Zwielicht" and Daverio's "incomprehensibility topos"', *Journal of Musicology*, 22 (2005), 131–53.

Finson, Jon W., 'Schumann and Shakespeare', *Mendelssohn and Schumann*, ed. Finson and Todd (Durham: Duke University Press, 1984).

—'Schumann's mature style and the *Album of Songs for the Young'*, *Journal of Musicology* 8 (1990), 22–75.

Fisk, Charles, *Returning Cycles: Contexts for the Interpretation of Schubert's Impromptus and Last Sonatas* (Berkeley: University of California Press, 2001).

Föhrenbach, Elisabeth, *Die Gattung Konzertstück in der Rezeption Robert Schumann* (Kassel: Merseburger, 2003).

Frisch, Walter, *Brahms and the Principle of Developing Variation* (Berkeley: University of California Press, 1984).

—'Brahms and Schubring: musical criticism and politics at mid century', *19th-Century Music* 7:3 (1984), 271–81.

Garratt, James, *Palestrina and the German Romantic Imagination* (Cambridge: Cambridge University Press, 2002).

Geissler, William, 'Robert Schumanns Klavierbegleitungen zu Johann Sebastian Bachs und Niccolo Paganinis Werken für Violine solo – eine problematische Hinterlassenschaft', *Schumann-Tage des Bezirkes Karl-Marx-Stadt* (1985), 24–42.

—'F-A-E, oder: Dritte Violinsonate von Robert Schumann, Düsseldorf, 1853', *Traditionsbeziehungen bei Schumann* (KarlMarxStadt: n.p., 1987), 36–47.

Ernest Gellner, *Nationalism* (New York: New York University Press, 1997).

Gillespie, Susan, 'Translating Adorno: Language, music, and performance', *Musical Quarterly* 79 (1995), 55–65.

Green, Abigail, *Fatherlands: State building and Nationhood in Nineteenth-Century Germany* (Cambridge: Cambridge University Press, 2001).

Greenfeld, Liah, *Nationalism: Five Roads to Modernity* (Cambridge, Mass.: Harvard University Press, 1992).

Grolik, Yvonne, *Musikalische-rhetorische Figuren in Liedern Robert Schumann* (Frankfurt am Main: Haag und Herchen, 2002).

Guy, John, *'My heart is my own': The Life of Mary Queen of Scots* (London: Harper Perennial 2004).

Hadlock, Heather, 'Berlioz, Ophelia, and feminist hermeneutics', *Berlioz: Past, Present, Future – Bicentenary Essays*, ed. Peter Bloom (Rochester, NY: University of Rochester Press, 2003), 123–34.

Hamilton, Kenneth, 'Liszt's early and Weimar piano works', *The Cambridge Companion to Liszt*, ed. Kenneth Hamilton (Cambridge: Cambridge University Press, 2005), pp. 57–86.

Hanslick, Eduard, *Aus dem Concertsaal. Kritiken und Schilderungen aus den letzten 20 Jahren des Wiener Musiklebens* (Vienna, 1870; reprint New York: Hildesheim, 1979).

Harrison, Robert Pogue, *Forests: The Shadow of Civilisation* (Chicago: University of Chicago Press, 1992).

Hastings, Adrian, *The Construction of Nationhood: ethnicity, religion, and nationalism* (Cambridge: Cambridge University Press, 1997).

Hatten, Robert, *Interpreting Musical Gestures, Topics and Tropes* (Bloomington: Indiana University Press, 2004).

Hauptmann, Moritz, *Briefe von Moritz Hauptmann . . . an Ludwig Spohr und Andere*, ed. Ferdinand Hiller (Leipzig: Breitkopf und Härtel, 1876).

Head, Matthew, 'Cultural meaning for women composers: Charlotte "Minna" Brandes and the beautiful dead in the German enlightenment', *Journal of the American Musicological Society* 57 (2004), 231–84.

Hedges-Brown, Julie, 'Higher Echoes of the Past in the Finale of Schumann's 1842 Piano Quartet', *Journal of the American Musicological Society* 57 (2005), 511–65.

Heimerdinger, Timo, *Tischlein rück' dich. Das Tischrücken in Deutschland um 1850. Eine Mode zwischen Spiritualismus, Wissenschaft und Geselligkeit* (Münster: Waxmann, 2001).

Hochheim, Rainer, *Nikolaus Lenau: Geschichte seiner Wirkung, 1850–1918* (Frankfurt: Lang, 1982).

Hoeckner, Berthold, 'Paths through Dichterliebe', *19th-Century Music* 30 (2006), 65–80.

Hoffmann-Axthelm, Dagmar, *Robert Schumann: 'Glücklichsein und tiefe Einsamkeit'* (Stuttgart: Reclam, 1994).

Hölderlin, Friedrich, *Poems and Fragments*, trans. Michael Hamburger (London: Anvill, 2004).

Hopf, Helmuth, 'Fehlinterpretation eine Spätstils am Beispiel Robert Schumann', *Robert Schumann: Universalgeist der Romantik*, ed. Alf and Kruse (Düsseldorf: Droste Verlag, 1981), 238–49.

Jamison, Kay Redfield, *Touched by Fire: Manic-Depressive Illness and the Artistic Temperament* (New York: Free Press, 1993).

Jarczyk, Michael, *Die Chorballade im 19. Jahrhundert* (Munich and Salzburg: Musikverlag Emil Katzbichler, 1978).

Jensen, Eric Frederick, *Schumann* (Oxford: Oxford University Press, 2001).

Joachim, Joseph, and Andreas Moser, *Briefe von und an Joseph Joachim*, 2 vols. (Berlin: Bard, 1911).

Johnson, James, *Listening in Paris: A Cultural History* (Berkeley: University of California Press, 1995).

Just, Martin, *Robert Schumann: Symphonie Nr. 4 D-moll* (Munich: Wilhelm Fink Verlag, 1982).

—'Das Orchester Schumanns', *Musik-Konzepte Sonderband: Robert Schumann II* Heinz-Klaus Metzger and Rainer Riehn (Munich, 1982), 191–236.

—'Robert Schumann: Sinfonie Nr. 4 d-moll op. 120', *Neue Zeitschrift für Musik* 143 (June/July 1982), 54–6.

Kabisch, Thomas, 'Robert Schumann und Roland Barthes: Überlegungen zur Violin-Sonate d-Moll op. 121', *"Denn in jenen Tönen lebt es" Wolfgang Marggraf zum 65. Geburtstag*, ed. Helene Geyer, Michael Berg and Matthias Tischer (Weimar: Hochschule für Musik Franz Liszt, 1999), pp. 207–27.

Kaiser, David Aram, *Romanticism, Aesthetics and Nationalism* (Cambridge: Cambridge University Press, 1999).

Kalisch, Volker, 'Schumann, Schubert, und das "Nachdenken an Vergangenes": Ein Beitrag zum Schumannschen Sonatenverständnis', *Mitteilungen der Arbeitsgemeinschaft für mittelrheinische Musikgeschichte* 60 (1993), 430–8.

Kapp, Reinhard, *Studien zum Spätwerk Robert Schumanns* (Tutzing: Schneider, 1984).

—'Schumann nach der Revolution: Vorüberlegungen, Statements, Hinweise, Materialien, Fragen', *Schumann Forschungen*, vol. 3, ed. Bernhard Appel (Mainz and London: Schott, 1993), 315–416.

Keil, Sigmar, *Untersuchungen zur Fugentechnik in Robert Schumanns Instrumentalschaffen. Hamburger Beiträge zur Musikwissenschaft* 11 (Hamburg: Wagner, 1973).

Kerman, Joseph, 'How we got into analysis and how to get out', *Critical Inquiry* 7 (1980), 311–31.

Killmayer, Wilhelm, 'Schumann und seine Dichter', *Neue Zeitschrift für Musik* (1981), 231–6.

Kirchmeyer, Helmut, *Robert Schumanns Düsseldorfer Brahms-Aufsatz Neue Bahnen und die Ausbreitung der Wagnerschen Opern bis 1856* (Berlin: Akademie Verlag, 1993).

Knechtges, Irmgard, *Robert Schumann im Spiegel seiner späten Klavierwerken* (Regensburg: Bosse, 1985).

Knight, Diana, *Barthes and Utopia: Space, Travel, Writing* (Oxford: Oxford University Press, 1997).

Knittel, K. M., '"Late", Last, and Least: On being Beethoven's Quartet in F major, op. 135', *Music & Letters* 87:1 (2006), 16–51.

Kohlhase, Hans, *Die Kammermusik Robert Schumanns: Stilistische Untersuchungen* (Hamburg: Wagner, 1979).

—'*Carnaval*, Cross-dressing, and the Woman in the Mirror', *Musicology and Difference*, ed. Ruth A. Solie (Berkeley: University of California Press, 1993), pp. 305–25.

Kramer, Lawrence, '"Little pearl teardrops": Schubert, Schumann, and the Tremulous Body of Romantic Song', *Music, Sensation and Sensuality*, ed. Linda Phyllis Austern (New York: Routledge, 2002), pp. 57–74.

Kramer, Richard, *Distant Cycles: Schubert and the Conceiving of Song* (Chicago: University of Chicago Press, 1994).

Kranefeld, Ulrike, *Der nachschaffende Hörer: rezeptionsästhetische Studien zur Musik Robert Schumanns* (Stuttgart: Metzler, 2000).

Krebs, Harald, *Fantasy Pieces: Metrical Dissonance in the Music of Robert Schumann* (Oxford: Oxford University Press, 1999).

Kross, Siegfried, 'Brahms und Schumann', *Brahms-Studien*, vol. 4 (Hamburg: Wagner, 1981), pp. 7–44.

Leader, Zachary, *Revision and Romantic Authorship* (Oxford: Clarendon Press, 1996).

Lessem, Alan, 'Schumann's Arrangements of Bach as Reception History', *Journal of Musicological Research* 7 (1986), 29–46.

Lester, Joel, 'Reading and Misreading: Schumann's accompaniments to Bach's Sonatas and Partitas for Solo Violin', *Current Musicology* 56 (1994), 24–53.

—'Robert Schumann and Sonata Forms', *19th-Century Music* 18:3 (1995), 189–210.

Litzmann, Berthold, *Clara Schumann: Ein Künstlerleben* (Leipzig: Breitkopf und Härtel, 1905), 2 vols.

Loseva, Olga, 'Neues über Elisabeth Kulmann', *Schumann und seine Dichter*, ed. Matthias Wendt (Mainz: Schott, 1993), 77–86.

Lutz, Thomas, *Crying: The Natural and Cultural History of Tears* (London: Norton, 1999).

Mahlert, Ulrich, *Fortschritt und Kunstlied: Späte Lieder Robert Schumanns in Licht der liedästhetischen Diskussion ab 1848* (Munich and Salzburg: Taschenbuch, 1983).

—'"die Spuren einer himmlischen Erscheinung zurücklassend": Zu Schumanns Liedern nach Gedichten von Elisabeth Kulmann op. 104' *Schumann in Düsseldorf: Werke–Texte–Interpretationen*, 119–40.

Maintz, Marie Luise, *Franz Schubert in der Rezeption Robert Schumanns: Studien zur Ästhetik und Instrumentalmusik* (Kassel: Bärenreiter, 1995).

—*Schumann: Fantasie, op. 17* (Cambridge: Cambridge University Press, 1992).

Marston, Nicholas, '"Im Legendenton": Schumann's "Unsung Voice"', *19th-Century Music* 16 (1993), 227–41.

Metzner, Paul, *Crescendo of the Virtuoso* (Berkeley: University of California Press, 1998).

Minor, Ryan, 'Occasions and nations in Brahms's Fest- und Gedenksprüche, *19th-Century Music* 29 (2006), 261–88.

Moser, Andreas, *Joseph Joachim: Ein Lebensbild*, 2 vols. (Berlin: Deutsche Brahms-Gesellschaft, 1908).

Müller, Annette, 'Schumann und die Kopisten der Düsseldorfer Zeit', *Robert Schumann: Philosophische, analytische, sozial- und rezeptionsgeschichtliche*

Aspekte, ed. Wolf Frobenius (Saarbrücken: Saarbrücker Druckerei, 1998), pp. 9–25.

Muxfeldt, Kristina, '*Frauenliebe* now and then', *19th-Century Music* 25 (2001), 27–48.

Nagler, Norbert, 'Gedanken zur Rehabilitierung des späten Werks', *Musik-Konzepte Sonderband: Robert Schumann I*, ed. Heinz-Klaus Metzger and Rainer Riehn (Munich, 1981).

Nauhaus, Gerd, *Robert Schumann: Szenen aus Goethes 'Faust'* (Zwickau: Kulturhaus, 1981).

—'Schumanns *Lektürebüchlein*', *Robert Schumann und die Dichter*, ed. Bernhard R. Appel and Inge Hermstrüwer (Düsseldorf: Droste, 1991), pp. 50–87.

—'*Der Rose Pilgerfahrt*, op. 112: Schumanns Abschied vom Oratorium', *Schumann Forschungen*, vol. 3, ed. Appel (Mainz and London: Schott, 1993), pp. 179–200.

Neighbour, Oliver, 'Brahms and Schumann: two opus nines and beyond', *19th-Century Music* 7 (1984), 266–70.

—'"Once more between Absolute and Program Music": Schumann's Second Symphony', *19th-Century Music* 7 (1984), 233–50.

—'Schumann and late eighteenth-century narrative strategies', *19th-Century Music* 11 (1987), 164–74.

Newcomb, Anthony, 'Schumann and the marketplace: from butterflies to *Hausmusik*', *Nineteenth-Century Piano Music*, ed. R. Larry Todd (New York: Schirmer, 1990), pp. 258–315.

Olin, Margaret, 'Touching photographs: Roland Barthes's "mistaken identification"', *Representations* 80 (2002), 99–118.

Ostwald, Peter, *Schumann: The Inner Voices of a Musical Genius* (Boston: Northeastern University Press, 1985).

Parker, Roger, *Remaking the Song: Operatic Visions and Revisions from Handel to Berio* (Berkeley: University of California Press, 2006).

Pascoe, Judith, *The Hummingbird Cabinet: A Rare and Curious History of Romantic Collectors* (Ithaca: Cornell University Press, 2006).

Pearce, Susan, *On Collecting: An Investigation into Collecting in the European Tradition* (London: Routledge, 1995).

Pederson, Sanna, 'Romantic music under siege in 1848', *Music Theory in the Age of Romanticism*, ed. Ian Bent (Cambridge: Cambridge University Press, 1996), pp. 57–75.

Pelikan, Jaroslav, *Faust the Theologian* (New Haven: Yale University Press, 1995).

Penzhorn, Silvia, 'Analytische Betrachtungen zu Robert Schumanns Mädchenlieder op. 103', *Schumann Tage* (1983), 66–71.

Perrey, Beate Julia, *Schumann's 'Dichterliebe' and Early Romantic Poetics: Fragmentation of Desire* (Cambridge: Cambridge University Press, 2002).

Perry, Jeffrey, 'Paganini's quest: the twenty-four *Capricci per violino solo*, op. 1', *19th-Century Music* 27 (2004), 208–30.

Phillips, Adam, *Darwin's Worms* (London: Faber and Faber, 1999).

Porter, Celia Hopkins, *The Rhine as Musical Metaphor: Cultural Identity in German Romantic Music* (Boston: Northeastern University Press, 1996).

—'The new public and the reordering of the musical establishment: the Lower Rhine music festivals, 1818–1867', *19th-Century Music* 3 (1980), 211–24.

Probst, Gisela, *Robert Schumanns Oratorien* (Wiesbaden: Breitkopf und Härtel, 1975).

Ramroth, Peter, *Robert Schumann und Richard Wagner im geschichtphilosophischen Urteil von Franz Brendel* (Frankfurt: Lang, 1991).

Rauchfleisch, Udo, *Robert Schumann: Leben und Werk. Eine Psychobiographie* (Stuttgart: Kohlhammer, 1990).

Reiman, Erika, *Schumann's Piano Cycles and the Novels of Jean Paul* (Rochester, NY: University of Rochester Press, 2004).

Reissmann, August, *Robert Schumann: Sein Leben und seine Werke* (Berlin: J. Guttentag, 1865).

Reynolds, Christopher, *Motives for Allusion: Context and Content in Nineteenth-Century Music* (Cambridge: Harvard University Press, 2003).

Riethmüller, Albrecht, 'Lenaus Husarenlieder als Klavierlieder Schumanns (op. 117)', *Schumann und seine Dichter: Bericht über das 4. International Schumann Symposium* (Mainz: Schott, 1993), pp. 43–54.

Rihm, Wolfgang, *Ausgesprochen, Schriften und Gespräche*, ed. Ulrich Mosch (Mainz: Schott, 1997).

Roesner, Linda Correll, 'Brahms's editions of Schumann', *Brahms Studies: Analytical and Historical Perspectives*, ed. George Bozarth (Oxford: Clarendon Press, 1990), pp. 251–82.

—'Schumann's "parallel forms"', *19th-Century Music* 14 (1991), 268–72.

—'Ästhetisches Ideal und sinfonische Gestalt: Die D-Moll-Sinfonie um die Jahrhundertmitte', *Schumann in Düsseldorf: Werke-Texte-Interpretationen* (London: Schott, 1993), 55–72.

Rooker Philips, Edward, 'The Mary Stuart Songs of Robert Schumann: key as an aspect of cycle', *Canadian Association of University Schools of Music Journal* 9 (1979), 91–7.

Rosen, Charles, *The Romantic Generation* (London: HarperCollins, 1996).

Rubinstein, Joseph, 'Über die Schumann'sche Musik', *Bayreuther Blätter* 2 (1879).

Rumph, Stephen, *Beethoven after Napoleon: Political Romanticism in the Late Works* (Berkeley: University of California Press, 2004).

Said, Edward, *On Late Style* (London: Bloomsbury, 2006).

Samson, Jim, *Virtuosity and the Musical Work: The 'Transcendental Studies' of Liszt* (Cambridge: Cambridge University Press, 2003).

Schauffler, Robert Haven, *Florestan: The Life and Works of Robert Schumann* (New York: Henry Holt, 1945).

Schnebel, Dieter, 'RückungenVer-rückungen: Psychoanalytische Betrachtungen zu Schumanns Leben und Werk', *Musik-Konzepte Sonderband: Robert Schumann I*, ed. Heinz-Klaus Metzger and Rainer Riehn (Munich, 1981), pp. 4–89.

Schneider, Michel, *La tombée du jour: Schumann* (Paris: Seuil, 1989).

Schoppe, Martin, 'Schumann und Brahms – Begegnung in Düsseldorf', *Brahms-Studien*, vol. 7 (Hamburg: Johannes Brahms-Gesellschaft, 1987), pp. 77–90.

Schreber, Daniel Paul, *Memoirs of a Nervous Illness*, trans. and ed. Ida Macalpine and Richard A. Hunter (New York: New York Review of Books, 2000).

Schubring, Adolf, 'Schumanniana no. 4: The Present Musical Epoch and Robert Schumann's Position in Musical History (1861)', trans. John Michael Cooper, *Schumann and his World*, ed. R. Larry Todd (Princeton: Princeton University Press, 1994), pp. 362–74.

Schumann, Clara, and Johannes Brahms, *Briefe aus den Jahren 1853–1896*, ed. Berthold Litzmann (Wiesbaden: Breitkopf und Härtel, 1989), 2 vols.

Schumann, Clara and Robert Schumann, *Briefwechsel: Kritische Gesamtausgabe*, ed. Eva Weissweiler (Stroemfeld: Roter Stern, 1984).

Schumann, Robert, *Briefe. Neue Folge*, ed. F. Gustav Jansen (Leipzig: Breitkopf und Härtel, 1904).

—*Gesammelte Schriften über Musik und Musiker*, ed. Martin Kreisig (Leipzig: Breitkopf und Härtel, 1914).

—*Tagebücher, Band I: 1827–1838*, ed. Georg Eisman (Leipzig: VEB Deutscher Verlag, 1971).

—*Tagebücher, Band II: 1838–1854*, ed. Gerd Nauhaus (Leipzig: VEB Deutscher Verlag, 1987).

—*Tagebücher, Band III: Haushaltbücher*, Pts. 1 (1837–1847) and 2 (1847–1856), ed. Gerd Nauhaus (Leipzig: VEB Deutscher Verlag, 1982).

—*Robert Schumann: Neue Ausgabe sämtlicher Werke*, ed. Robert-Schumann-Gesellschaft, by Akio Mayeda and Klaus Wolfgang Niemöller, in collaboration with the Robert-Schumann-Haus-Zwickau (Mainz: Schott, 1991).

Sheehan, James J., *Museums in the German Art World: From the End of the Old Regime to the Rise of Modernism* (Oxford: Oxford University Press, 2000).

Sisman, Elaine, 'Brahms and the variation canon', *19th-Century Music* 9 (1990), 132–53.

Skyllstad, Kjell, 'Thematic structure in relation to form in Edvard Grieg's cyclic work', *Studia musicologica norvegica* 3 (1977), 75–94.

Solie, Ruth A., 'Whose life? the gendered self in Schumann's *Frauenliebe* songs', *Music and Text: Critical Inquiries*, ed. Steven Scher (Cambridge: Cambridge University Press, 1992), pp. 247–69.

Spitta, Philipp, *Ein Lebensbild Robert Schumanns* (Leipzig: Breitkopf und Härtel, 1882).

Spitzer, Michael, *Music as Philosophy: Adorno and Beethoven's Late Style* (Bloomington: Indiana University Press, 2006).

Steinberg, Michael, *Listening to Reason: Culture, Subjectivity, and Nineteenth-Century Music* (Princeton: Princeton University Press, 2004).

Stekel, Hans Christian, *Sehnsucht und Distanz: Theologische Aspekte in den wort-gebundenen religiösen Kompositionen von Johannes Brahms* (Frankfurt: Peter Lang, 1997).

Sternberger, Dolf, *Panorama of the Nineteenth Century,* trans. Joachim Neugroschel (New York: Urizen Books, 1977).

Stewart, Susan, *On Longing: Narratives of the Miniature, the Gigantic, the Souvenir, the Collection* (Durham, NC: Duke University Press).

Struck, Michael, *Die umstrittenden späten Instrumentalwerke Schumanns. Hamburger Beiträge zur Musikwissenschaft 29* (Hamburg: Wagner, 1984).

—*Robert Schumann: Violinkonzert D-moll (WoO 23)* (Munich: Wilhelm Fink, 1988).

—'Gerüchte um den "späten" Schumann', *Neue Zeitschrift für Musik* 143 (1982), 52–6.

—'"Gewichtsverlagerungen": Robert Schumanns letzte Konzertcompositionen', *Schumanns Werke,* ed. Mayeda and Niemöller (Mainz: Schott, 1987), pp. 43–52.

—'Zur Relation von Quellenbefunden und analytischem Erkenntnisgewinn im Spätwerk Robert Schumanns', *Musikforschung* 44 (1991), 236–54.

—'Kunstwerk Anspruch und Popularitätsstrebungen Ursachen ohne Wirkung? Bemerkungen zum *Glück von Edenhall,* op. 143 und zur *Fest-Ouvertüre* op. 123', *Schumann Forschungen* vol. 3, *Schumann in Düsseldorf: Werke-Texte-Interpretationen,* ed. Bernhard R. Appel (Mainz: Schott, 1993), pp. 265–311.

Taruskin, Richard, *The Oxford History of Western Music: The Nineteenth Century* (Oxford: Oxford University Press, 2005).

Thalmann, Marianne, *The Romantic Fairy Tale* (Ann Arbor: University of Michigan Press, 1964).

Titus, Barbara, *Conceptualizing music: Friedrich Theodor Vischer and Hegelian currents in German music criticism, 1848–1887* (PhD University of Oxford, 2005).

Tunbridge, Laura, *Euphorion falls: Schumann, Manfred and Faust* (PhD. Diss., Princeton, 2002).

—'Schumann as Manfred', *Musical Quarterly* 87 (2004), 546–69.

—'Afterimages: Schumann's piano music II' *Cambridge Companion to Schumann,* ed. Beate Perrey (Cambridge: Cambridge University Press, 2007).

—'Weber's ghost: *Euryanthe, Genoveva, Lohengrin', Music, Theatre and Politics: 1848 to the Third Reich,* ed. Nikolaus Bacht (London: Ashgate, 2006), pp. 9–29.

Vaughan, William, *German Romantic Painting* (New Haven: Yale University Press, 1980).

Velten, Klaus, 'Robert Schumanns Lenau-Vertonungen op. 90', *Robert Schumann: Philologische, analytische, sozial- und rezeptionsgeschichte Aspekte* (Saarbrücken: Saarbrücker Druckerei, 1998), pp. 90–6.

—*Monomotivik, Sequenz und Sonatenform im Werk Robert Schumanns* (Saarbrücker Studien zur Musikwissenschaft, 4: 1990).

—'Zitate vokaler Frühgesänge in Schumanns *Gesänge der Frühe:* Überlegungen zur Deutung eines irritierenden Titels', *Schumann in Düsseldorf: Werke-Texte-Interpretationen. Bericht über das 3. Internationalen Schumann-Symposium am 15. und 16. Juni 1988* (Mainz: Schott, 1993), pp. 37–54.

Waldura, Markus, 'Strukturelle Diversifizierung – Strukturelle Vereinheitlichung: Gedanken zum Unterschied zwischen "klassischer" und "romantischer" Sonatenform am Beispiel von Schumanns 3. Klaviertrio op. 110', *Robert Schumann: Philologische, analytische, sozial- und rezeptionsgeschichte Aspekte* (Saarbrücken: Saabrücken Druckerei, 1998), pp. 42–59.

Warner, Marina, *From the Beast to the Blonde: On Fairy Tales and their Tellers* (London: Vintage, 1995).

Wasielewski, Wilhelm Joseph von, *Aus siebzig Jahren* (Leipzig: Breitkopf und Härtel, 1897).

—*Robert Schumann: Eine Biographie* (Leipzig: Breitkopf und Härtel, 1906).

Waterman, Sue, 'Collecting the nineteenth century', *Representations* 90 (2005), 98–128.

Wellberry, David E. (ed.), *A New History of German Literature* (Cambridge, Mass.: Belknap Press of Harvard University Press, 2004).

Yearsley, David, *Bach and the Meanings of Counterpoint* (Cambridge: Cambridge University Press, 2002).

Zimmermann, Hans Joachim, 'Die Gedichte der Königin Maria Stuart. Gisbert Vincke, Robert Schumann, und eine sentimentale Tradition', *Archiv für das Studium der neueren Sprachen und Literaturen* CCXIV (1977), 294–324.

Ziolkowski, Theodore, *German Romanticism and its Institutions* (Princeton: Princeton University Press, 1990).

Žižek, Slavoj, *Plague of Fantasies* (London: Verso, 1997).

—*The Parallax View* (Cambridge, Mass.: MIT Press, 2006).

Index